AUSTRALIAN ARMY CAMPAIGNS SERIES - 12

CW01390460

THE LANDING
AT ANZAC

1915

SECOND EDITION
REVISED AND EXPANDED

CHRIS ROBERTS

ARMY·HISTORY·UNIT

PROTECTING ARMY HERITAGE
PROMOTING ARMY HISTORY

National Library of Australia Cataloguing-in-Publication entry

Author: Roberts, Chris, 1945-

Title: The landing at Anzac : 1915 / Chris Roberts.

ISBN: 978-1-925275-02-5 (pbk.)

Series: Australian army campaign series ; 12.

Notes: Includes bibliographical references and index.

Subjects: Australia. Army. Australian and New Zealand Army Corps--History.
World War, 1914-1918--Campaigns--Turkey--Gallipoli Peninsula.
Gallipoli Peninsula (Turkey)--History, Military--20th century.

Dewey Number: 940.426

Published by Big Sky Publishing, Sydney

Cover and typesetting by Think Productions, Melbourne

Printed in China through Asia Pacific Offset Limited

Front cover and title page: Men of the 2nd Field Company landing in the centre of Anzac Cove around 7.20 am 25 April 1915 (AWM P02226_014_2).

Back cover background: Men of the 1st Australian Brigade landing in Anzac Cove between 7.00 and 8.00 am 25 April (AWM P00035-001).

Back cover top right: Members of the 3rd Battalion in Wire Gully between 10.30 and 11.00 am 25 April (AWM AO3226).

Back cover bottom right: Men of the 11th Battalion on the stern of HMS London around 1.00 pm 24 April (AWM AO1828).

Back cover badge 1: The New Zealand Expeditionary Force Badge was worn by reinforcements in 1917 and 1918.

Back cover badge 2: The Australian 'General Service Badge' 1904 –1948.

CONTENTS

Acknowledgements To The First Edition 1

Acknowledgements To The Second Edition 2

Introduction 4

Chapter 1   The Instruments Of Battle 8

Chapter 2   Genesis Of The Campaign 23

Chapter 3   The Opposing Armies 35

Chapter 4   Defending The Dardanelles 55

Chapter 5   An Amphibious Operation 71

Chapter 6   A Misplaced Landing 87

Chapter 7   The Plan Unravels 105

Chapter 8   Seizing Third Ridge 119

Chapter 9   Squaring Off 131

Chapter 10   Counter-Attack 147

Chapter 11   Stalemate 170

Conclusion 187

Postscript 195

Appendix 1 197

Appendix 2 201

Appendix 3 204

Appendix 4 210

Appendix 5 211

Appendix 6 212

Table One. Timeline.. 215

Order Of Battle At Anzac 25–27 April 1915 218

Further Reading 222

Index 224

ACKNOWLEDGEMENTS TO THE FIRST EDITION

This book had its origins as an Army Staff College paper in 1978 which provided me the opportunity to interview several veterans of the landing, including the late Brigadier Noel Loutit, DSO. As a young lieutenant, he was one of the few men who penetrated furthest inland on 25 April. The veterans' comments were revealing and they set me on the quest to understand what actually occurred during the battle. This book is the result and is dedicated to them. An article in *The Journal of the Australian War Memorial* followed in 1993 and, after a Great War Forum discussion concerning Turkish machine-guns, another was published in *Wartime*, Issue 50. To the forum members who contributed to the discussion, I offer my grateful thanks.

Since then Dr Peter Pedersen, Head of the Research Section at the Australian War Memorial (AWM), not only supported my contentious views, but encouraged me to produce something more substantial, assisting me in obtaining documents and maps, and providing useful comments on the manuscript. Mr Roger Lee and Lieutenant Colonel Glenn Wahlert of the Australian Army History Unit asked me to write this book, and their assistance and encouragement, and that of Dr Andrew Richardson, has been exceptional. They formed an excellent support team and I am most grateful to them for ensuring that this book saw the light of day.

Many people have helped me track down primary sources, without which the book could not have been written. For the ANZAC sources Ashley Ekins, Head Historian of the AWM, with his wealth of knowledge on sources relating to the Gallipoli campaign, uncovered material I would not otherwise have found. Ian Affleck assisted in identifying photos from the AWM's vast collection, and the staff at the AWM's Research Centre provided me every assistance in tracking down Australian sources and maps; it was a pleasure to work with them.

Peter Hart of The Imperial War Museum went out of his way to track down sources in the United Kingdom that proved invaluable and provided feedback on the manuscript. In New Zealand the Director and staff at Archives New Zealand, and the Chief Librarian and staff at the Alexander Turnbull Library in Wellington kindly helped me access New Zealand Expeditionary Force documents and photographs, particularly Ms Gillian Headifen, who made the search for primary sources and the acquisition of photos so much easier. Mr John Crawford, the New Zealand Defence Force historian, Professor Glyn Harper at Massey University, and Ms Dolores Ho, archivist at the Queen Elizabeth II Army Museum, provided me every assistance in accessing source material.

For the Ottoman sources, David Cameron generously gave me a copy of the translation of Sefik Aker's very detailed account of the *27th Regiment*'s fighting at Anzac from 25 to 27 April; it was pure gold. Dr Ed Erickson of the United States Marine Corps Staff College at

Quantico, Virginia, kindly provided invaluable information on Turkish material and made deft adjustments to the manuscript. Harvey Broadbent of Macquarie University assisted with Turkish photographs and confirmed a number of issues relating to the Ottoman actions on 25 April, as did Professor Haluk Oral of Bahcesehir University in Istanbul and Dr Mesut Uyar at the Australian Defence Force Academy. Sedar Ataksor provided photographs and information relating to his grandfather, Captain Halis.

My Duntroon classmates Major General Paul Stevens, AO, Brigadier John Wilson, CSC, Brigadier Adrian D'Hage, AM, MC, and the late Colonel Phil Bunyan all provided suggestions that improved the manuscript and assured me that my analysis was not unreasonable.

In preparing the manuscript for publication, Cathy McCullagh's deft editorial hand has improved the book considerably, Mark Wahlert constructed the magnificent 3D pictorials of the Sari Bair Range and organisation charts, Eric Olason produced the superb maps, Catherine McCulloch of the Department of Defence did a cracking job of resurrecting my photos of Gallipoli taken in 1988, and Iain Davidson kindly supplied the photo of the New Zealand Expeditionary Force badge on the back cover. Finally, I am enormously grateful to Denny Neave, my publisher, and all the staff at Big Sky Publishing.

Last, but not least, I am indebted to my wife Judy, who has forgone much over the past two years without complaint as research and writing took over our social life. She has been a true best mate, and I could not have completed this volume without her extraordinary support.

Any errors in the book are mine alone.

ACKNOWLEDGEMENTS TO THE SECOND EDITION

In the first edition of this book I wrote that 'this is not a definitive history of the battle — no history of an event ever can be. History is a continuing dialogue as new information emerges and writers bring their own emphasis and specialist knowledge to bear on the subject.' Over the past two years new information on the Ottoman side of the battle has become available, as have several previously unpublished photographs in the AWM's archives taken very early on the morning of 25 April, including a remarkable shot of Anzac Cove taken within an hour and a half of the initial landing. This new information does not change the thrust of the original narrative and analysis, rather it reinforces much of my contention.

When Dr Roger Lee of the Australian Army History Unit decided to undertake a third printing of *The Landing at Anzac, 1915* for the centenary of the battle, to be issued alongside Professor Mesut Uyar's account of the Turkish action at Anzac on 25 April 1915, the opportunity arose to produce a second edition incorporating some of the new information and photographs. Further, the word limit placed on the first edition was now relaxed, allowing me to expand the story in a few chapters and include more participants' accounts and information that I had reluctantly cut from the original manuscript. Overall, however, the narrative is largely unchanged. The principal inclusions provide a more detailed analysis of some issues, including the initial strategy, based on a paper I delivered at the Chief of Army's History Conference in October 2103, a postscript commenting on the changed nature of the battlefield 100 years after the event, further detail in some of the appendices, a section discussing the initial casualties based on the new photographs, and additional maps.

I am indebted to several people who provided new information and discussed the first edition with me. Foremost among these is Professor Mesut Uyar of the University of New South Wales, Canberra. Mesut is a former Turkish Army officer, a veteran of the war in Afghanistan and a scholar with extensive knowledge of the Gallipoli campaign and the Ottoman primary sources. He has been most generous in sharing his knowledge with me and allowing me access to additional Turkish sources that were not available to me when I first wrote this book. I am also indebted to Dr Christopher Pugsley, former Senior Lecturer of War Studies at the Royal Military Academy, Sandhurst, for his paper on British command and control in the twentieth century, to Keith Mitchell who produced the additional maps, Catherine Job for her generosity in providing detailed information on the 1st Field Company from a study she is currently undertaking, Mr Bill Refshauge for his unpublished paper on the extent of the misplaced landing, John Crawford, the New Zealand Defence Force historian who has helped enormously in providing sources on the New Zealand Territorial Force and in supplying additional personal diaries written by New Zealand soldiers, Carolyn Carr, Chief Librarian of the New Zealand Defence Force Library, the Director and staff at Archives New Zealand, and the Chief Librarian and staff at the Alexander Turnbull Library, particularly Gillian Headifen, who provided access to diaries and papers of New Zealand participants. My thanks also to Mr Jack Hoey Moore, who graciously allowed me to quote from his father's book *Anzac Jack*. Finally, but certainly not least, my grateful thanks to Dr Roger Lee and his team at the Australian Army History Unit for their sustained and unfailing support, particularly Dr Andrew Richardson, whose enthusiasm and assistance know no bounds.

Again, any errors in this edition are entirely mine.

Chris Roberts
Canberra
22 October 2014

INTRODUCTION

The landing at Anzac is the most celebrated battle in Australian and New Zealand history, and is regarded by many as symbolising the point at which both these young countries gained their nationhood. Indeed Anzac looms larger in the consciousness of the current generations of both countries than any other battlefield. Yet most Antipodeans who trek halfway around the world to visit Gallipoli have only a vague idea of what occurred on this rugged strip of coastline, and much of their understanding remains wrapped in myths and misconceptions. It is often simply the 'Anzac legend' that entices them to visit what they regard as sacred ground rather than any real knowledge of what occurred there.

The Anzac legend was created and thoroughly disseminated well before the campaign itself had drawn to its dismal conclusion. British war correspondent Ellis Ashmead-Bartlett's dispatch, which appeared in newspapers in early May 1915, was written in a heroic, sensational style designed to stir public sentiment and boost morale, and captured the hearts of Australians and New Zealanders alike. The inaccuracies woven through the account survived uncorrected to find their way into the mythology of the battle, and many have been handed down as accepted fact for the best part of a century. Australian war correspondent Charles Bean's report was less dramatic and more accurate, yet it also contained the inevitable inaccuracies of immediate post-battle dispatches. The heroic style flavoured subsequent wartime articles and books such as John Masefield's *Gallipoli*, 'Digger' Craven's *Peninsula of Death*, and an article for the Queensland Education Department's *The School Paper* in April 1916 written under the intriguing pseudonym 'No 94'. The first visual depiction of the landing was the film *The Hero of the Dardanelles*, filmed on Sydney's Tamarama Beach and released in July 1915 as a recruiting tool for the Department of Defence, and is shown in modern documentaries and news items on Anzac Day. It depicted a bloody landing with corpses and wounded littering the shoreline, and set the scene for the popular image of the landing. Others such as Charles Dixon's painting *The Landing at Anzac*, the film *Tell England* (1931), which depicts heavy losses under conspicuous machine-gun fire, and the television series *ANZACS* (1985), which depicts the 8th Battalion fighting its way ashore in broad daylight, only serve to enhance the view of a bloody landing and heavy casualties on the beach. That the initial landing was in darkness and the 8th Battalion landed much later, is ignored in the interests of the overall storyline. These dramatic depictions are not borne out by several photographs taken at Anzac Cove very early on the morning of 25 April 1915. The first full-scale account of the Anzac campaign, Philip Schuler's *Australia in Arms*, published in 1916, emphasised the valour of the troops, but was marred by important distortions of the truth. Such accounts appealed to the citizens of two young nations eager to make their mark on the world. John Masefield's best-selling *Gallipoli* (1919) is also riddled with inaccuracies, but had great popular appeal and has recently been reprinted. However, by 1946, misconceptions surrounding the landing in popular myth had become so colossal that Charles Bean felt compelled to write, 'Neither then nor at any time later was that beach the inferno of bursting shells, barbed wire, and falling men that has sometimes been described or painted.'

Charles Bean wrote the first serious history of the landing in the first volume of his magisterial and acclaimed *The Official History of Australia in the War of 1914-1918*. Like all national histories, it is written primarily from the Australian and New Zealand perspective, although Bean made cursory attempts to ascertain the Turkish involvement. Hurriedly written, the 600-page tome was published within two years of his return to Australia, with some veterans asked for their recollections of the day's fighting six weeks before the manuscript was due at the publishers. Focusing primarily on the participants, it is rich in descriptive detail of the actions of individuals, but less so in providing a clear narrative and synopsis of the battle, and the reader generally feels overburdened with detail. The dawn landing itself is well covered, but events later in the day are blurred, vague and confusing, with separate events running together, and the story largely told in terms of the areas over which the battle was fought rather than in a sensible chronology. Prominent Australian Great War historian Professor Robin Prior regards Bean's Gallipoli volumes as 'virtually unreadable'. Indeed the *Official History* bears all the hallmarks of a history written too soon after the event. The preface to the third edition in 1934 contains corrections and new information, some of which has since been found also to be incorrect. A close reading of Volume I exposes inconsistencies and contradictions, while a comparison with the recollections sent in by some participants reveals that their accounts differ from Bean's version of their actions. The testimony of at least two leaders of the advanced parties contradicts Bean's versions of events in which they played the central role, but are consistent with the account of Lieutenant Colonel Mehmet Sefik, commander of the Ottoman *27th Regiment*, the first unit the men of the Australian and New Zealand Army Corps (ANZAC) encountered. Yet its monumental detail and richness of personal experience places Bean's history almost in the category of a primary source and, regarded as a classic, it has become the standard reference for all matters relating to the landing. Indeed, most subsequent histories base their narrative on Bean's account without questioning it. Like Clausewitz, however, Bean's volume is more often quoted than studied, and only during the last 20 years has his version of events been challenged. A further re-evaluation is now possible with the recent emergence of Turkish primary sources and new publications and articles addressing the Turkish role in the campaign.

The Turkish accounts challenge a number of assertions that have formed the mainstay of the Australian, New Zealand and British histories, and on which the legend has been built. These assertions range from machine-guns greeting the Anzacs as they stormed ashore and the extent of the opposition encountered, to the timings of the Turkish counter-attacks. Photographic evidence from the morning of 25 April also provides a contrasting view, undermining in particular the common perception of heavy opposition and ANZAC casualties on the beach. The accounts of men who landed in the early dawn are often contradictory in their assessment of the reception they received. Albert Facey's dramatic 'first-hand account' of landing with the 11th Battalion on North Beach under heavy machine-gun fire in his memoir *A Fortunate Life* is clearly manufactured as, according to

Facey's service record, he arrived at Gallipoli 12 days after the landing. His service record also refutes his claim of being wounded. Two men of the 11th and one of the 1st Field Company who made the initial landing on North Beach mentioned only rifle fire, while another believed there were no Turkish machine-guns at the beach. Some of the Australian veterans' accounts also support the Turkish version of the events of that memorable day.

The reasons given for the failure of the Anzacs to achieve their objectives on 25 April 1915 are varied and contradictory. Foremost are the misplaced landing; the disorganisation of units caused by the intermingling of the tows; poor maps; inadequate intelligence; and the rugged terrain which hopelessly mixed and delayed the troops before they could reach their objectives. Other contrasting views suggest that the eager Australians overshot their objectives and, hopelessly outnumbered, were driven back by Turkish counter-attacks. Some claim that the covering force commander stopped to reorganise his men and that the enemy arrived in strength before he could push on. Looming large in most accounts is the aggressiveness of Mustafa Kemal, commander of the *19th Division*, who drove his troops to reach the vital ground before the Australians. Several others argue that the covering force objectives were too ambitious. A few highlight the inexperience of the ANZAC troops and their commanders as the decisive factor in the campaign. Interestingly, one author claims that the landing was, in fact, an ANZAC victory.

In 1990, John Robertson suggested in the preface to his superb *Anzac and Empire* that an updated, analytical tactical study of the campaign was long overdue. *The Landing at Anzac, 1915* seeks to address this substantial gap in the analysis of the campaign as it relates to the first four days, and provide a tactical study and analysis of the landing. This account begins by supplying the necessary context for the battle, explaining how the armies of 1915 were organised and equipped, describing the tactical doctrine they followed, the weapons they used and the limitations of their battlefield communications. These armies were vastly different from the armies of today, and also varied considerably from the armies of 1918. Any examination of the landing at Anzac Cove also requires an understanding of tactics and the way that armies operate. Likewise, the training and experience of the opposing forces are important considerations, as is an understanding of the tactical relevance of the ground over which they fought, the rationale behind the Ottoman *5th Army's* defensive posture, and what ANZAC sought to achieve.

In undertaking such a study, *The Landing at Anzac, 1915* not only questions the commonly accepted myths that have coloured the perceptions of several generations, but also seeks to describe the battle from 'both sides of the hill', considering the actions of the Anzacs and also those of their Ottoman opponents. Only then can today's Australians and New Zealanders understand what happened and why, and look back on the actions of those first Anzacs through a lens unclouded by myth, hyperbole and patriotism. However, this is not a definitive history of the battle — no history of an event ever can be. History is a continuing dialogue as new information emerges and writers bring their own emphasis and specialist knowledge to bear on the subject. While *The Landing at Anzac, 1915* has used as much of the available information from Turkish sources as possible, these also contain contradictions, and many more documents from the Turkish archives and memoirs from Turkish participants have yet to be made available in English. In 2015 two books will be published based on Turkish archival primary source material and memoirs which will provide the Ottoman version of events — one by Harvey Broadbent and the other by Associate Professor Mesut Uyar. These volumes and the translated documents at Macquarie University will provide a far more detailed account of the Ottoman response on 25 April and allow English-speaking historians to better research the events of that extraordinary day. Hopefully, future histories and documentaries will place the landing at Anzac in an historically accurate frame, free of the mythology that dominates and distorts the present view of the battle.

CHAPTER 1

THE INSTRUMENTS OF BATTLE

On a stony beach in the pre-dawn darkness, Private Alex Wilson was helping Sergeant Fred Coe remove his pack when the first shot rang out, shattering the silence. There was a brief pause before more shots rained from the heights above. Offshore, machine-guns on the steam pinnaces that had towed strings of boats towards the shore opened fire on the Ottoman riflemen above the beach, adding considerably to the increasing crescendo of fire. So began the most famous battle in Australian and New Zealand history.

The armies that clashed that day, like all the armies intent on destroying one another in 1915, were a blend of the old and the new during an epoch of change in warfare. Battlefield mobility and communications were much the same as when Napoleon swept across Europe a century earlier, and the core of their fighting elements remained the foot-bound infantry supported by horse-drawn field artillery. However, the revolution in weaponry over the previous 60 years had made their battlefield much more lethal, much larger, and far more difficult to control. In the decade prior to the Great War (1914–1918), this fundamental change in firepower had engendered a heated debate over tactics, the employment of cavalry and artillery, and the nature of the future battlefield. Horsed cavalry continued to perform its traditional roles of reconnaissance, flank protection, screening and shock action, but the lethality of the breech-loading, magazine-fed rifle and the emerging machine-gun had largely negated its shock effect, while aircraft provided a more rapid and vastly greater sweep and depth of reconnaissance. The Russo–Japanese War (1904–1905) had provided clear evidence of the power of the machine-gun and the need for artillery to employ indirect fire from cover. The performance of the machine-gun in this conflict had persuaded the German Army to follow the British lead and include machine-guns in its infantry regiments. Despite considerable debate over direct versus indirect fire, many artillery pundits continued to advocate the use of direct fire from close behind the infantry firing line. This was largely a result of the lack of reliable communication between the forward observer and the gun line during mobile operations. However some were swayed by the argument that placing the guns in the infantry firing line boosted the morale of the infantry soldier. While railways had transformed the strategic movement of armies, at the tactical level under favourable conditions they still marched at around 4.8 kilometres an hour, and supplies and ammunition still moved forward in horse-drawn wagons or loaded on pack animals.

For operations, armies were organised and deployed in formations that were, from largest to smallest, the army, the corps, the division and the brigade. The building blocks that comprised these formations were the special-to-purpose units of the arms (infantry battalions, cavalry regiments, artillery batteries, and engineer and signal companies) and the services (medical, transport, supply). Brigades were standard structures that grouped two to four fighting units of the same type (cavalry, infantry or artillery) into a formation of 2000 to 4000 men. In the Ottoman Army the equivalent of the brigade was the regiment. The division (either infantry or cavalry) was a standard, self-contained organisation of two or more infantry or cavalry brigades, supported by artillery brigades and units of the other arms and services. It numbered from 12,000 to 18,000 men depending on the country of origin, and whether it was a cavalry or infantry division. The corps comprised two or more divisions plus allocated corps troops, such as heavy artillery and additional cavalry, engineer, transport and logistic units. Depending on the number of divisions and corps troops allotted to it, the corps numbered from 40,000 to 80,000 men. An army comprised two or more corps plus allocated army troops, and varied in strength according to the number of corps and army troops it commanded, ranging from around 85,000 to 350,000 men.

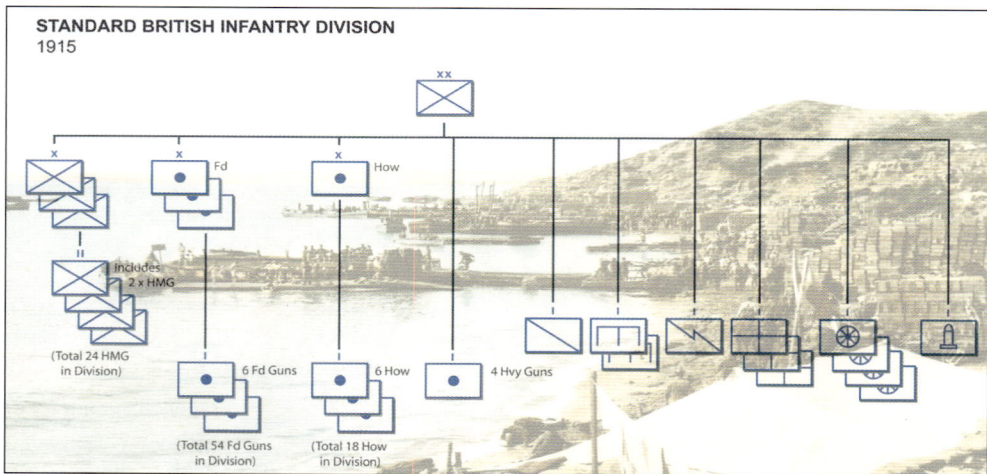

For some armies, operations involving the larger of these formations represented a relatively new experience. Before the war the British Army's purpose was to garrison, protect and police the far-flung empire, notably in India and Africa, and provide ground defence for the British Isles behind the protective bulwark of the Royal Navy. An expeditionary force, based around six infantry divisions, existed on paper for a small continental commitment hanging off the flank of the French armies should the need arise. With mobilisation in 1914, three corps headquarters were raised under a newly formed General Headquarters, British Expeditionary Force (BEF). Consequently, unlike their French, German and Ottoman counterparts, the British had little experience and few officers trained in operations at the corps and army level, while the Australians and New Zealanders had no real experience at any level.

The Australians and New Zealanders followed British doctrine, tactics and organisation, but had no standing army other than a small pool of permanent officers and soldiers undertaking staff and instructional postings, or serving in coastal artillery batteries. As a result, the Australian Imperial Force (AIF) and the New Zealand Expeditionary Force (NZEF) had to raise and train their units, brigades and divisions largely from scratch. It was only in Egypt in December 1914 that their fighting components were grouped into the Australian and New Zealand Army Corps (ANZAC). The standing armies of the Ottomans, on the other hand, had been organised into armies, corps and divisions since the 1870s, and were augmented to full strength on mobilisation by reservists who had completed their full-time service with the colours. They also had considerable battle experience, having handled these formations in several wars, most recently during the Balkan Wars (1912–1913).

A 1914 British infantry division numbered around 18,000 men, its fighting strength centred on its three infantry brigades, supported by three field artillery brigades, one howitzer artillery brigade and a heavy artillery battery. A cavalry squadron and engineer, signals, medical and transport units completed the structure. An Ottoman infantry division numbered some 12,000 men, its fighting strength its three infantry regiments and a field artillery regiment. The Ottoman division also boasted a cavalry squadron and engineer, medical and transport support.

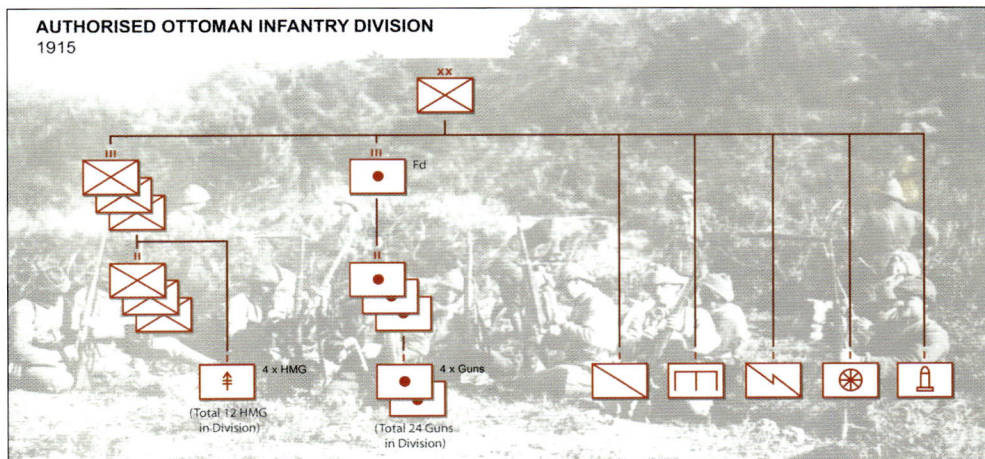

AUTHORISED OTTOMAN INFANTRY DIVISION
1915

INFANTRY

The infantry was the mainstay of the armies. The ANZAC infantry brigades comprised four infantry battalions, while the Ottoman infantry regiments had three battalions and a machine-gun company of four Maxim heavy machine-guns. However, in 1915, due to severe shortages of these weapons, only one or two regiments per division were allocated a machine-gun company.

An ANZAC infantry battalion, numbering just over 1000 men, had four rifle companies and a machine-gun section of two Maxim guns, providing a total of eight guns per brigade compared to the four guns in an Ottoman regiment. The Ottoman infantry battalion of 1100 men had four rifle companies and no machine-guns. The ANZAC rifle company,

Rifle, Mauser, 7.65mm Gewehr 98, Model 1903

Calibre:	7.65mm
Length:	1.25m
Weight:	4.1kg empty
Action:	Bolt action
Capacity:	5 round fixed box magazine
Range:	Sighted to 2000m
Sights:	Curved tangent rear sight with V notch and fixed post front sight
Loading:	5 round charger clip

The Mauser 7.65mm *Gewehr* 98 model 1903 was the standard rifle used by the Ottoman forces during the Great War. Based on the standard German Mauser *Gewehr* 98, it was chambered for the 7.65mm x 53mm Mauser cartridge for the Ottoman forces. It was a very accurate and reliable weapon. Its bolt action was not as smooth or as fast as the British SMLE and, given its smaller five-round magazine, it had a lower rate of fire than the SMLE at the rapid rate. Nonetheless, with the ability to load five rounds from a stripper clip with one downward thrust of the thumb, in the hands of trained soldiers it was capable of delivering 20 to 25 rounds per minute at the rapid rate. An Ottoman platoon of 80 trained riflemen armed with a Model 1903 was capable of delivering some 1600 rounds per minute.

While its effective range was officially considered 500 metres, in the hands of a competent sniper it was accurate out to 1000 metres or more.

Rifle, SMLE 0.303-inch No. 1 Mk III*

Calibre:	0.303-inch (7.7mm)
Length:	1.13 m
Weight:	4.11 kg
Action:	Bolt action
Capacity:	10 round detachable box magazine
Range:	Sighted to 2000 yds (1829 m)
Sights:	Sliding ramp rear sight with U notch and fixed post front sight. Also fitted with a 'dial' long-range volley sight on the side of the weapon.
Loading:	5 round stripper clip

The rifle, short, magazine, Lee-Enfield (SMLE) No. 1 Mk III* was the standard British rifle in 1914. It was a very accurate and reliable weapon and is considered by many to have been the best rifle used during the Great War. One of the most widely produced weapons of its day (over 17 million), the SMLE was manufactured in some 27 models and was the Australian Army's rifle until 1959, used throughout the Great War, World War II, the Korean War and the Malayan Emergency.

The smooth, fast bolt action of the SMLE, its ten-round box magazine and the ability to load five rounds from a charger clip with one downward thrust of the thumb made this a deadly weapon in the hands of well-trained riflemen. The British Army's test at the rapid rate required a soldier to hit a No. 2 figure target 15 times in one minute at a range of 300 metres. Many men exceeded this with 25 or more hits. The record was 38 hits in one minute by Sergeant Percy Snoxall in 1914, beating the previous record of 36 hits in one minute. A British platoon of 50 trained riflemen armed with the SMLE was capable of delivering over 1200 rounds per minute at the rapid rate. British infantry were trained to open fire on an assaulting enemy at 600 yards (548 metres).

While its effective range was officially considered 550 metres, in the hands of a competent sniper it was accurate out to 1200 metres or more.

with a strength of 227 all ranks, had four platoons each of 54 all ranks, and an Ottoman rifle company, numbering 265 all ranks, had three platoons, each of 85 all ranks. While the ANZAC platoon had four sections of 12 riflemen under a corporal, the Ottoman platoon had nine squads, each of eight riflemen and a non-commissioned officer (NCO).

Unlike modern battalions, the 1915 infantry battalion was a rifle unit pure and simple. Its 1000 riflemen, armed with magazine-fed, breech-loading rifles, formed the basis of infantry tactics and delivered the infantry's main firepower, which was both substantial and accurate over long distances. The German Mauser and British Lee-Enfield rifles were capable of delivering between 20 and 30 rounds per minute. In the hands of well-trained troops they were deadly. The British Army's annual rapid fire classification test required an infantryman to hit a Figure 2 target 15 times in one minute at a range of 300 yards (275 metres). Many exceeded this, scoring 25 or more hits. The record was 38 hits in one minute, attributed to Sergeant Percy Snoxall in 1914, breaking the previous record of 36 hits in one minute. Such accuracy and speed was attained by superb marksmen under ideal conditions and, during debates and trials conducted prior to the war, British officers argued that massed, rapid fire was more effective than marksmanship. At 20 rounds per minute, when circumstances required, a 50-man platoon could deliver 1000 rounds per minute while each of the four rifle companies, with every man on the firing line, could fire over 4000 rounds per minute for short periods, provided the ammunition lasted. Likewise, the 80 odd riflemen in an Ottoman platoon could fire some 1600 rounds per minute, approximately the same number of rounds per minute the four guns in the machine-gun company could deliver. This high volume of fire was achieved because the Lee-Enfield magazine held ten rounds and the Mauser held five. The bolt, worked by two quick actions of the hand, ejected the spent round and replaced it with a live one, and the ammunition was carried in five-round chargers, enabling all rounds to be loaded into the magazine in one downward thrust of the thumb. The tendency by some writers to attribute the heavy casualty rates in the first year of the war to machine-guns overlooks the devastating rifle fire a battalion was capable of producing, similar to that of the British infantry at Mons, Le Cateau and Ypres.

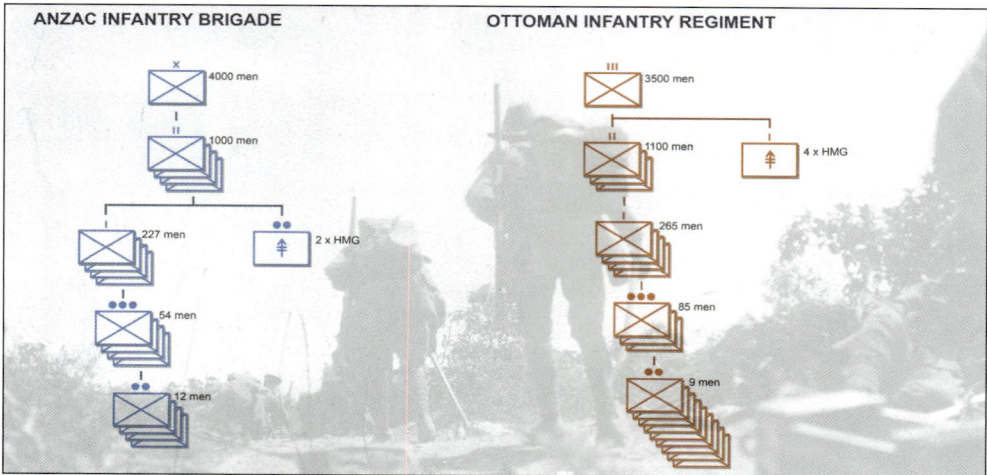

ANZAC INFANTRY BRIGADE — OTTOMAN INFANTRY REGIMENT

The problem confronting all armies in the decades before the war was how to close with the enemy against such a high volume of fire without sustaining devastating casualties. This had been one of the most significant problems confronting the infantry commander since the mass introduction of the rifle in the 1860s. In 1862, during the American Civil War, Confederates at Fredericksburg armed with muzzle-loading rifles capable of firing only two to three rounds a minute had stopped repeated mass Union assaults dead in their tracks, slaughtering vast numbers of men within 100 metres of the Confederate line. Eight years later at Mars-le-Tour and Gravelotte, French infantry armed with the breech-loading, single-shot Chassepot, which was capable of 15 rounds a minute, drove German infantry assaults to ground 500 metres away. By 1914 the magazine-fed, breech-loading rifle had made the infantry attack infinitely more deadly over longer ranges. In defence, infantry lying in line engaged an advancing enemy with withering rifle fire supported by artillery and machine-guns. British infantry were trained to engage at 550 metres, the 'effective' range of the Lee-Enfield.

The solution to the problem of how to close with enemy defenders appeared to lie in suppressing those defenders with a deluge of sustained rifle fire, supported by artillery and machine-guns, while the attacking infantry went forward in section rushes, an early form of fire and movement. The assaulting infantry battalion deployed in two groups — a firing line and a general reserve — with platoons and sections in an extended line with two to three metres between men. In the attack, half the firing line laid down a heavy covering fire as adjacent sections and platoons advanced in short rushes to take up a new fire position from which to cover the advance of the other sections and platoons. In theory and on exercises, once the enemy fire was subdued, the attackers charged home with the bayonet. If an enemy flank presented itself, it was engaged in front by the firing line, while the reserve manoeuvred onto the flank and turned the position.

MACHINE-GUNS

In 1914 machine-guns were by no means prolific in any army, with British and German infantry divisions each possessing a mere 24 guns. While the authorised number for an Ottoman infantry division was 12, shortages meant that many divisions possessed far fewer than their entitlement. At Gallipoli the *7th*, *9th* and *19th divisions (III Corps)* were each short one company, while the *3rd* and *11th divisions (XV Corps)* had only four machine-guns each.

Although they were highly effective weapons when brought into action, in reality, all armies were still coming to terms with the machine-gun and, in the years leading up to the war, there was considerable debate on its employment. In 1914 machine-guns, which were significantly heavier weapons, were employed quite differently to the way they are used today, and their employment resembled that of artillery batteries and sections, rather than integral elements of the rifle platoon as they were to become later in the war when the lighter Lewis gun was introduced. Both the ANZAC and the Ottoman guns were mounted on a tripod and, with its water cooling system, the Ottoman gun (MG09) with a heavier tripod weighed over 62 kilograms, although some Ottoman machine-guns had heavier wheeled mounts much like a miniature gun carriage. Together with its boxes of ammunition, the gun was carried in a wagon or by pack animal to provide tactical mobility. When dismounted and manhandled by the crew, these guns were considerably less mobile. Although the British Vickers gun (1912) was lighter and more reliable, the Australian and New Zealand battalions used Maxim guns chambered for the .303 round at Gallipoli. Fed with a 250-round belt, the Maxim was capable of firing 400 to 500 rounds per minute at the sustained rate; however they had an enormous appetite for ammunition and a propensity to overheat which led to jamming. Consequently, training emphasised traversing fire in short bursts of five to ten rounds, while rapid fire against concentrated targets involved bursts of 30 to 50 rounds. British and German pre-war doctrine generally agreed on their employment on the battlefield in both attack and defence, and either frontally or on a flank. The difference lay in the preferred methods of control and deployment of the guns, and in this the Ottomans followed German doctrine.

A Turkish machine-gun company deployed as a battery showing three of the four guns. The fourth gun is out of picture to the right. Each pair of guns (a platoon) is supported by a range-finder team, with the company commander located between the two platoons. Following German doctrine the Ottomans preferred to keep the guns grouped as a battery under the control of the infantry regiment commander with both guns in a platoon given the same target. While a platoon could be deployed separately, the guns were kept grouped as a pair given the tendency of the Maxim to jam (AWM A00577).

The British regarded the machine-gun as a powerful auxiliary, well adapted for close cooperation with the infantry, and a weapon of opportunity delivering concentrated fire against favourable targets. They incorporated the machine-gun within the battalion in a section of two guns under the battalion commander's control, where the gun was considered better able to support the infantry. However the British also recognised the utility of massed guns, and allowed two or more sections to be grouped as a battery under the brigade machine-gun officer, where they were used as a powerful reserve for the brigade commander. At the ANZAC landing, for example, the Australian 2nd Brigade brigaded the guns of the 6th and 8th battalions, while those of the 5th and 7th remained under battalion control.

The Ottoman machine-gunners comprised a separate branch to the infantry. They grouped four guns in a company which was assigned to an infantry regiment (brigade) where they were used as a mobile reserve or for general support directed by the regimental commander. They were not averse to splitting the company into two platoons (each of two guns) in

HEAVY MACHINE-GUN, MAXIM

Calibre:	Ottoman (MG09) 7.65mm, British 0.303-inch (7.7mm)
Length:	1.175m
Weight:	Ottoman 62kg (gun body 26.5kg, tripod 31.5kg, water and water canister 4kg)
Action:	Recoil
Capacity:	250 round cloth belt
Range:	Sighted to 2000m; extreme range 3600m
Sights:	Flip up graduated rear sight with fixed post front sight
Rate of fire:	450–500 rounds per minute
Crew:	4 men plus additional ammunition bearers

The Maxim heavy machine-gun was used by the Ottoman Army and ANZAC at Gallipoli. The ANZAC Maxim used the 0.303 round and the Ottoman gun, the German export variant MG09, used a 7.65mm round. The British Maxim was mounted on a lighter tripod than the Turkish, which was generally mounted on the heavier German tripod, although others had a wheeled mount. While the British Army introduced the lighter and more efficient Vickers machine-gun into its units in late 1912, the Australians and New Zealanders retained the old Maxims, receiving a few Vickers guns late in the campaign before being re-equipped with Vickers when they returned to Egypt in early 1916. The Ottomans had four Maxims in a machine-gun company attached to the infantry regiment (three battalions), while the Anzacs had two in each infantry battalion.

The Maxim was a heavy, cumbersome weapon which was normally carried in a wagon with spare barrels and first line ammunition. When manhandled it broke down into a four-man load: the gun, the tripod, the water canister and tubing, and two ammunition boxes. Although the cyclic rate of fire was 450–500 rounds per minute, sustained fire led to overheating of the barrel and jamming. Thus training emphasised short bursts of five rounds and, when traversing fire, bursts of ten rounds. The mount was provided with traversing and elevation mechanisms with rough and fine adjustments and could be used in the direct and indirect fire modes.

The tendency of the gun to jam led to the policy of employing the Maxim in pairs sited alongside each other. While the British integrated the gun within the infantry battalion under the commanding officer's control, the Ottomans, using German doctrine, preferred to use Maxims in a four-gun battery. The British also allowed the guns to be brigaded under the brigade machine-gun officer in a four, six or eight-gun battery, while the Ottomans deployed them in two platoons each of two guns under the regimental commander, although contemporary photographs later in the war showed that they generally retained the battery deployment in line as their preferred method.

close support of the battalions, but again this occurred under the control of the regimental commander. Due to the Maxim's tendency to jam, deployment of single guns was actively discouraged, and in some cases forbidden. Thus while the British preference was to employ the guns at battalion level, the Germans and Ottomans preferred to employ the company as a battery at regimental level, where it was considered their tactical mobility and combined firepower could be better utilised and ammunition resupply was easier.

In both armies, when used in sections (or platoons), the guns were deployed in pairs and sited alongside each other with a spacing of 17 to 20 paces, although contemporary photos taken early in the war show the guns sited closer together. When used as a battery they deployed much the same as an artillery battery in line abreast, with each pair assigned a specific target supported by a range-finder. In defence, while the guns could be placed in the firing line at the outset, the pre-war doctrine of both armies advocated holding them back as a fire reserve that could 'respond quickly to a threatened point' and 'with decisive effect'. The German regulations cautioned that, while machine-guns were excellent defensive weapons, employing them in a static defence (pre-positioned in the firing line) deprived them of their mobility, whereas using them in active defence (identifying the threat and then deploying them to where the need was greatest) better utilised this scarce and valuable resource. Thus commanders were urged to use their machine-guns as a reserve and deploy them once the point of greatest threat had been identified. Regulations stressed that suitable positions should be reconnoitred beforehand to enable the guns to be brought into action quickly.

The Ottomans also employed pre-Maxim era Nordenfelt guns, sited primarily in their coastal defences given their lack of tactical mobility. The Nordenfelt was a multi-barrelled mechanical volley-gun rather than an automatic machine-gun. Mounted on a heavy base, it was produced in various calibres with from two to 12 barrels; those captured at Cape Helles on 25 April were 1-inch, four-barrelled guns. Fed by a vertical hopper magazine carrying a column of rounds for each barrel, they were fired much like a multi-barrelled rifle by pulling a handle back and forth to eject the spent cartridges and insert and fire the new. The rate of fire depended on the speed with which the handle was operated.

ARTILLERY

In 1914 horse-drawn field guns and their smaller sibling the mountain gun were anti-personnel weapons which supported their own infantry in defence and attack by engaging enemy troops with shrapnel. The shrapnel shell encased between 230 and 375 metal balls, depending on the calibre. A time fuse burst the casing in the air above the infantry, showering the balls forward and down into the massed ranks of men. The German-supplied Ottoman shells also included a version with both high explosive and balls, which could be set for airburst (with the high explosive head landing in the middle of the shrapnel impact area) or for ground burst with the shrapnel thrown outwards. When the shell burst above closely grouped infantry in the open, either standing or lying down, shrapnel balls inflicted widespread casualties, with the beaten zone of a single shell approximately 20 metres wide and up to 275 metres deep.

MOUNTAIN GUN, KRUPP QF 75MM, MODEL 1904

Calibre:	75mm
Barrel Length:	1.05m
Gun Weight:	420kg with shield, 387kg without shield
Action:	Single motion wedge breech mechanism with hydro-spring recoil system
Range:	4800m
Ammunition:	5.53kg shrapnel shell with 230 x 11g balls
Battery first line:	128 rounds per gun
Fuze:	Time and percussion
Crew:	6 men

The Krupp quick-firing 75mm mountain gun was a German light artillery piece designed for mountain warfare. Carried on pack animals, the gun was broken down into four loads: the barrel, the cradle, the carriage and recoil barrels, and the trail, wheels and axle. It fired a lighter shrapnel shell than field guns with fewer balls per shell. On coming into action the gun had to be unloaded and assembled either on the gun line or in dead ground just to the rear. It was normally used in the direct fire role. The guns were organised and employed in four-gun batteries or could be detached into two-gun sections.

The *9th* and *19th divisions* each had two batteries of these guns. This was the gun employed against the Anzacs on 25 April rather than the heavier 75mm field gun so often depicted. The battery sited on Lone Pine at the time of the landing lost three of its guns, captured by the Australians by 6.15 am. The remaining gun came into action on Hill 165 at around 9.30 am. Another battery arrived to support the *27th Regiment* at 10.30 am, going into action at 11.00 am, while a third battery accompanied the *57th Regiment* and went into action on Scrubby Knoll sometime between 11.00 am and noon. The fourth battery came forward with the *72nd Regiment* between 4.00 and 4.30 pm.

(John Lafferty image)

Turkish mountain battery deployed for action, showing the Krupp QF 75mm mountain gun model 1904. Nine of these guns supported the Ottoman infantry from around 11.00 am on 25 April (Ed Erickson image).

Unlike modern artillery, the field and mountain guns deployed close behind the infantry firing line using direct fire where they could see the enemy infantry from the gun line. Less frequently they employed indirect fire from behind folds in the ground. Whereas with direct fire the gunners could see the target and adjust their fire by direct observation, the problem with indirect fire lay in communication between the forward observation officer, who could observe the target, and the gun line, which could not. The only means of adjusting fire in the indirect role was through indicating corrections by flags, or using telephone cable laid between the two. Clearly, the use of telephone cable in mobile warfare was not always practical.

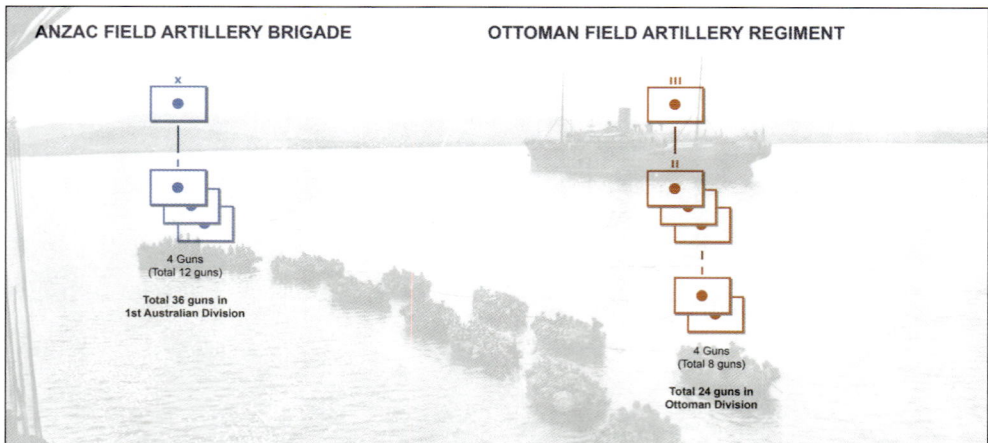

Theoretically, the quick firing (QF) field guns could punch out up to 20 rounds per minute. However, the limited amount of ammunition carried with the guns and in battery first line holdings ensured much slower rates of fire. Rapid fire was used only in emergencies as the guns could not sustain long periods of rapid fire because of crew fatigue and damage such as increased barrel wear. The field gun, which was horse drawn, was extremely mobile. Moving into action, the teams galloped up to the gun line, swung their pieces around and, in a matter of minutes, were ready to fire, the ammunition limber positioned alongside the gun. As the name implies, the mountain gun was a small, light gun half to a third the size of a field gun and designed for mountain warfare. It was broken down into its component pieces — barrel, wheels, shield, trail, etc — and carried on pack animals. Its mobility was limited to the pace of the infantry, and the gun took longer to bring into action than a field gun as it had to be unpacked and assembled before it was ready to fire. The mountain gun fired a lighter shell than the field gun and its ammunition was also carried by pack animal, reducing the number of shells carried within the battery.

The standard British field gun in the infantry division was the QF 18-pounder (84mm) Mk I, with a range of 6000 metres. Australian and New Zealand field artillery brigades each had 12 of these guns, organised in three batteries each equipped with four guns, rather than the six of a regular British battery, giving a total of 36 guns in the division. Battery first line holdings were 176 rounds per gun. The 1st Australian Division, however, lacked the heavier QF 4.5-inch howitzers and 60-pounder guns of the British infantry division. However, ANZAC did have two Indian Army mountain batteries as corps troops, each armed with six 10-pounders (70mm) with battery first line holdings of 137 rounds per gun, while the New Zealand Field Artillery Brigade also had a four-gun battery of QF 4.5-inch howitzers, carrying 108 rounds per gun.

At Gallipoli the Ottoman divisional artillery was a mish-mash of field and mountain guns ranging from the old 87mm field gun with a range of 6800 metres and dating from 1885, to various models of the QF Krupp 75mm field gun (with a range of 5900 metres) and the QF Krupp 75mm M1904 mountain gun (4800 metres). The divisional artillery regiment comprised three battalions each of two batteries with four guns per battery, giving a total of 24 guns in the division, often with different varieties of guns in each regiment. The *9th Artillery Regiment* (*9th Division*), for example, had four batteries of QF 75mm field guns and two of QF 75mm mountain guns, while the *39th Artillery Regiment* (*19th Division*) had two batteries of QF 75mm field guns, two of QF 75mm mountain guns and two of the old 87mm field guns. Battery first line ammunition holdings ranged from 128 shells per mountain gun to 155 for field guns.

COMMUNICATIONS

Compared to current communication tools such as the mobile phone, satellite communications and electronic tablets, battlefield communications in 1914 were archaic. The revolution in weaponry and the growth of mass armies over the 60 years preceding the war resulted in considerably larger, more lethal battlefields, but the technical development in communications had not kept pace. The increased lethality of the battlefield meant commanders could no longer ride horses along the firing line and observe at first hand what was happening across the battlefield. Like the soldier, commanders had to take cover, which considerably restricted their view unless they occupied a prominent position that overlooked the battlefield, or at least gave them observation of much of their firing line. Radio was in its infancy — sets were bulky, unreliable and generally only operated down to corps headquarters, although the 1st Australian Division had a radio section. Within the infantry division, the only means of communication were by semaphore (flags), heliograph (mirrors), couriers on bicycles, horse or motorcycle carrying messages, and by telephone when static operations permitted cable to be laid. Direct voice communication, other than by telephone, between division and brigade, and brigade and battalion was impossible. Within the battalion and at company level, bugle calls and runners represented the principal means of communication although, during the battle, runners could be killed or lose their way and crucial messages lost. By the time they got through, the information could well be out of date. Platoon instructions were passed by voice, either by the platoon and section commanders shouting instructions, or by information passed along the line from one man to the next. These messages could be misconstrued or completely misunderstood, particularly in the din and excitement of battle, which probably led to the oft-quoted distortion of 'Send us reinforcements, we are going to advance,' to 'Lend us three and four pence, we are going to a dance.'

Thus, for senior commanders, communication and obtaining an accurate battle picture were slow and sporadic unless they took positive action to acquire such information. Often, real-time information was available only at battalion and company level, and this was usually a microcosm of events immediately to their front that generally bore little resemblance to the overall situation and could significantly overemphasise local difficulties and crises. Incorrect or out-of-date information could be passed up or down the chain of command giving senior commanders a false battle picture. In battle it was difficult for them to maintain close control of events and required a high level of training and experience from all ranks. The trick for senior commanders was being sufficiently well forward to observe as much of the battlefield as possible but not so far forward that they were pinned down and unable to see the overall picture. They also had to implement effective command and control arrangements for the passage of information up and down the chain of command, and across their sector of the battlefield. Only then could they gain a reasonably accurate battle picture or effectively gauge the tempo of the battle and quickly identify areas of threat and opportunity in which to employ their reserves.

COMMAND AND CONTROL

Command is 'the authority invested in a commander to direct and control a military force' and is the function 'by which a commander makes decisions, conveys his intent and impresses his will upon his subordinates'. It is fundamentally concerned with leadership, a capacity to determine a course of action to achieve an objective, provide clear direction to staff and subordinates, and in the execution of the operation the ability to positively respond to unexpected difficulties, take calculated risks, make timely decisions, and manoeuvre his forces to achieve the intended objective. Moltke the Elder wrote that no plan survives first contact with the enemy, and it is the function of commanders at all levels to adjust to changing circumstances with the purpose of achieving the objective of the operation.

Command also encapsulates the function of control, which is primarily (though not exclusively) a staff responsibility. Control is the facilitation of command and is effected through formal and informal structures, processes and systems, which are not always tangible and clearly defined. For a commander, control does not mean micro-management, but is concerned with influencing activities by intervening when necessary to ensure his intent, or the objective, is attained. Control is about imposing the commander's will on events and the enemy, as and when required.

Field Service Regulations, Part 1, *Combined Training*, 1905 outlined the British command philosophy:

> It will often happen that local circumstances, impossible to foresee, may render the precise execution of the orders given to subordinate leaders not only unsuitable but impracticable. Moreover, when it is impossible, as must often be the case, to issue more than very general instructions, the attainment of the object aimed at must be left to the initiative and intelligence of these leaders.

> Decentralisation of command, and a full recognition of the responsibilities of subordinates in action, are thus absolutely necessary; and leaders must train their subordinates not only to work intelligently and resolutely in accordance with brief and very general instructions, but also to take upon themselves, whenever it may be necessary, the responsibility of departing from, or from varying, the orders they may have received.

In one of its guiding principles, the same manual dictated that such departure was justified 'if the subordinate who assumes the responsibility is conscientiously satisfied that he is acting as a superior would order him to act if he were present.'

Field Service Regulations, Part 1, *Operations*, 1909 (reprint 1914) reinforces the decentralised approach in detailing the issue of operation orders: 'The general principle is that the object to be attained, with such information as affects its attainment, should be briefly but clearly stated; while the method of attaining the object should be left to the utmost extent possible to the recipient, with due regard to his personal characteristics', adding that, '**The object of an operation order is to bring about a course of action in accordance with the intentions of the commander, suited to the situation, and with full co-operation between all arms and units**' (emphasis in the original).

Thus, the British practised a philosophy of decentralised command not dissimilar to the German *aufstragtaktic* or directive control and, while a subordinate could alter his orders, this depended on the situation on the ground. Such a change had to be in accordance with achieving his commander's intent — the task or objective to be attained. This flexibility and decentralisation of command reflected the changing nature and increasing size of the battlefield, and the inability of senior commanders to exercise the direct control over their force that commanders such as Napoleon, Wellington, and Lee had enjoyed during the first six decades of the nineteenth century. Whether the Ottoman Army, which trained under German doctrine, adopted the German philosophy of command is unknown, although the events of 25 April demonstrated that, at the very least, the Ottomans had a similar approach.

CHAPTER 2

GENESIS OF THE CAMPAIGN

STRATEGIC HUMILIATION

On the eve of war, Winston Churchill, First Lord of the Admiralty (the political head of the Royal Navy), requisitioned two new British-built battleships which were almost ready for delivery to the Ottoman Navy. While his actions were justified in maintaining the Royal Navy's superiority in dreadnought battleships over the Imperial German Navy, they were contractually legal, and the British provided compensation, the Ottoman authorities were outraged. During the first week of the war, the German battlecruiser SMS *Goeben* and the light cruiser SMS *Breslau*, under Admiral Wilhelm Souchon, evaded units of the British Mediterranean Fleet and, on 10 August, entered the Dardanelles, the narrow strait separating the Gallipoli peninsula from Asia Minor. The next day, amid a flurry of diplomatic activity, the ships were sold to the Ottoman Empire as replacements for the requisitioned British ships and Souchon was named Commander-in-Chief of the Ottoman Navy. Three days later, the British Naval Mission, which had been advising the Turks, was dismissed. Germany had scored a diplomatic coup and a strategic success of the first magnitude. The already strong relations between the two nations were further strengthened and German influence in Constantinople rose. For the British, and for Churchill and the Admiralty in particular, the German escape and their diplomatic triumph represented a humiliating failure that was to have tragic repercussions.

Control of the Dardanelles and the Bosphorus, the narrow entrance to the Black Sea at Constantinople, was of immense strategic value. Together they provided the only all-weather sea route through which the British and French could provide succour to their Russian allies and vice versa. Closing this supply route to the Triple Entente (Britain, France and Russia) had been one of the German government's objectives. The Ottoman government was rent by indecision over the European war; some factions advocated joining the conflict — albeit with conflicting views over which side to join — while others advised adopting a neutral stance. Russia was the natural enemy of the Ottoman Empire and thus many Turks were reluctant to side with the Allies. However, they recognised that an alliance with a victorious Entente would protect Ottoman territory and interests from Russian imperialistic designs. On the other hand, joining a winning Germany and Austria-Hungary would provide territorial spoils at the expense of the Russians. It was this delicate balance that was upset by Churchill's decision and Souchon's ships. Although the Ottoman government had ordered mobilisation in August 1914, the Turks had remained steadfastly neutral, and the nations of the Entente were eager that they either remain so or join the Entente.

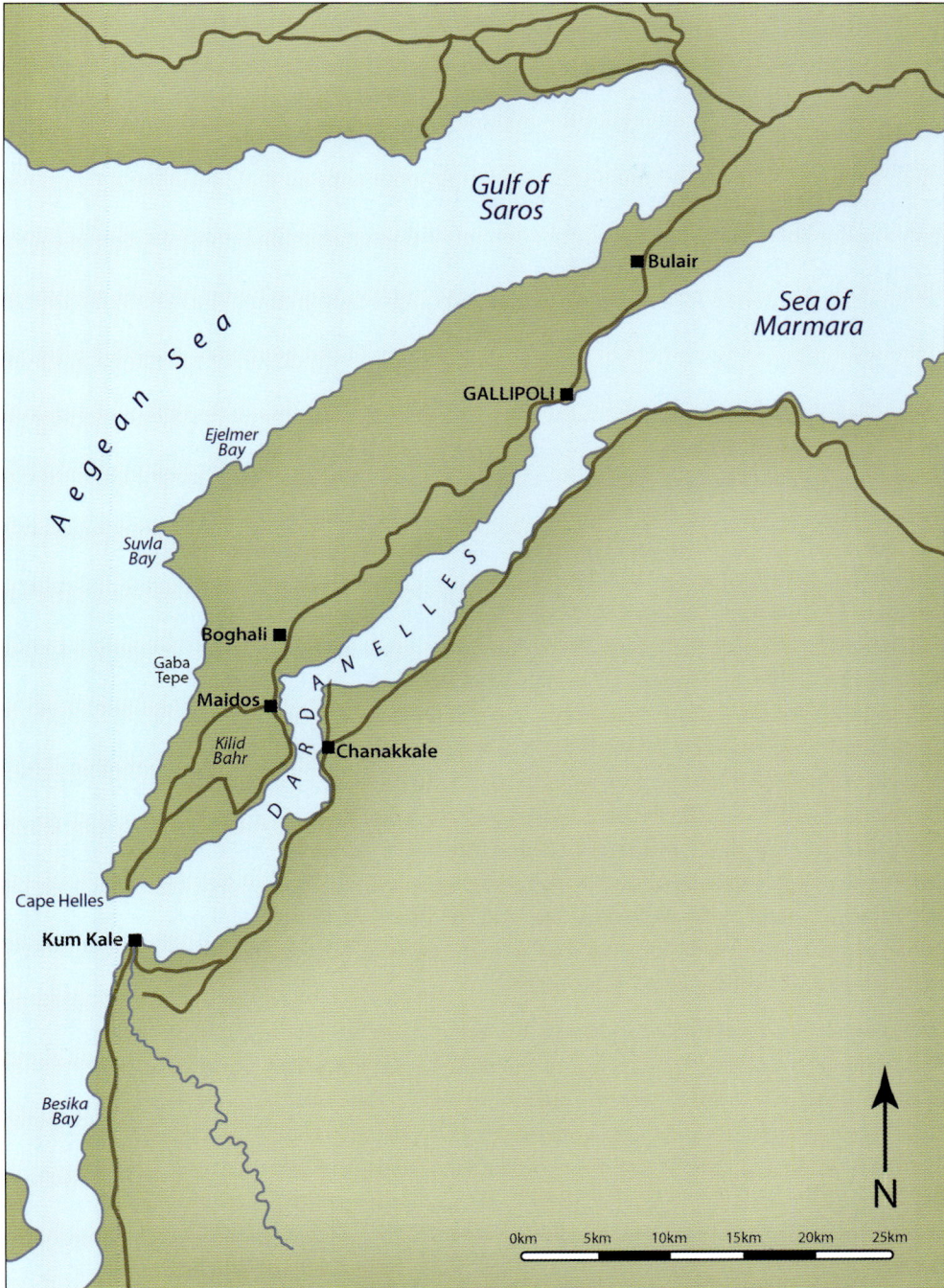

The Gallipoli peninsula and the Dardanelles. The Gallipoli peninsula is some 84 kilometres long and 18 kilometres across at its widest point. The area between Bulair and Boghali is rough, mountainous country which drops onto the narrow, open plain between Gaba Tepe and Maidos (Eceabat). The steep-sided Kilid Bahr Plateau gradually slopes to open agricultural land as far as Cape Helles. Separating the peninsula from Asiatic Turkey, the Dardanelles is 61 kilometres long and varies in width from six kilometres at its southern end to 1.2 kilometres at the Narrows opposite Chanakkale.

FIXATION WITH THE DARDANELLES

European opinions of Ottoman naval and military capabilities were generally poor. Churchill's view of 'scandalous, crumbling, decrepit, penniless Turkey' reflected the prevailing attitude in Britain which was reinforced by reports from the British Military Attaché and officers visiting Turkey. Indeed the capture of the Gallipoli peninsula had been considered as early as August 1914, well before the declaration of war against the Ottomans. When neutral Greece offered to place her naval and military resources at the disposal of the Entente, Churchill immediately asked the Chief of the Imperial General Staff (CIGS) to examine the feasibility of seizing the Gallipoli peninsula using a Greek army. The CIGS considered the operation 'feasible, but extremely difficult'. However, the Greek offer had a number of attached conditions which did not include a Gallipoli venture and the idea was abandoned.

Ultimately, it was Souchon's ships that triggered the Ottoman Empire's entry into the war on the side of the Germans. On 29 October 1914, with German government support and acting on instructions from Colonel Enver Pasha, the Ottoman Minister for War — but without the authority of the Ottoman Cabinet — Souchon led a flotilla into the Black Sea and attacked the Russians. Dismayed, the Ottoman government ordered the flotilla's withdrawal, but the damage was done and Russia declared war on Turkey. In an impulsive response which British Admiral Sir Roger Bacon later described as 'an act of sheer lunacy' and Admiral Sir John Jellicoe considered 'an unforgivable error', Churchill personally cabled Admiral Sir Sackville Carden, Commander of the British Mediterranean Fleet, ordering him to bombard the forts at the entrance to the Dardanelles. Carden's attack was launched on 3 November, two days before Britain formally declared war. This achieved little, other than the destruction of one fort when a magazine blew up, and tangible encouragement for the Turks to hasten their defensive preparations on the peninsula. Nor did it improve Churchill's already shaky position as First Lord of the Admiralty following the debacle of sending the largely untrained and ill-equipped Royal Naval Division (RND) to the defence of Antwerp, several naval disasters at sea, and the Navy's lacklustre performance in meeting public expectations, exemplified by the German Imperial Navy bombarding a cluster of east coast towns and slipping away unmolested.

The concept of a Dardanelles operation was raised again in mid-November when the British War Council considered the defence of the Suez Canal. Churchill argued that the best way to defend this vital seaway was through a combined naval-military operation to take the Gallipoli peninsula, optimistically commenting that the operation, 'if successful, would give us control of the Dardanelles, and we could dictate terms to Constantinople.' How holding the Dardanelles would enable the Allies to dictate terms to the Ottoman government was not articulated, given they were already blockading the mouth of the strait without any tangible effect on the Ottoman government. Field Marshal Lord Kitchener, Secretary of State for War, responded that no British troops could be made available for a Dardanelles campaign and that there was a severe shortage of shells even to support the army in France.

By late November 1914 the old regular British Army had largely been destroyed in its first exposure to a modern, industrial war on a grand scale, culminating in the frightful losses at the First Battle of Ypres. The BEF was being sustained by the Territorial units (part-timers) that had been rushed to France in late 1914 and early 1915. Kitchener's principal problems were twofold: first, obtaining sufficient numbers to maintain the BEF on the Western Front against a future German attack; and second, providing sufficient troops to defend the United Kingdom against a possible invasion, an issue of considerable concern at the time. The New Armies created with the rush of enthusiastic volunteers during the early months of the war would not be ready until the next summer at the earliest and, realistically, much later. Racing off to open another front with insufficient resources and significant logistic difficulties made little sense, despite the allure of highly questionable strategic results.

The Dardanelles campaign was raised yet again in late December 1914 when, in response to the stalemate on the Western Front, the British government had begun the search for an alternative theatre of war in which to employ the New Armies. Maurice Hankey, Secretary to the War Council, presented a memorandum proposing a coalition among the Balkan states, Greece, Bulgaria, Romania and Russia, to 'weave a web around Turkey to end her career as a European power'. The ultimate objective was to occupy Constantinople, the Dardanelles and the Bosphorus. Opening up this sea route, Hankey argued, would enable wheat to be exported to the allies. The oft-mooted purpose of the operation of supplying ammunition and arms to Russia is not mentioned in Hankey's memorandum largely because the British were unable to maintain sufficient ammunition to the BEF on the Western Front, a situation that would result in the shells scandal of 1915. In his memorandum Hankey proposed that Britain contribute three army corps to the enterprise. This received some support within the War Council, particularly from Churchill and Lloyd George, the Chancellor of the Exchequer, despite several glaring difficulties: the British Army was struggling to maintain four corps in France and Belgium; the withdrawal of three of them would seriously weaken the Western Front and open a breach with the French; the proposed members of the coalition were deeply suspicious of one another; and several of them remained neutral. The memorandum received no endorsement.

The stakes were raised on 2 January 1915 when the Russians requested a demonstration against the Ottoman Empire to relieve pressure on the Caucasus front. Kitchener discussed with Churchill the possibility of a purely naval demonstration, noting that 'the only place [it] might have some effect in stopping reinforcements going east would be the Dardanelles.' The next day, in a rambling memorandum, Admiral of the Fleet Lord Fisher, First Sea Lord of the Admiralty (the professional head of the Royal Navy), argued for an immediate combined operation against the Ottomans. In a grandiose plan reflecting fanciful ideas rather than the realities of the situation, he proposed that the Indian Corps and 75,000 British troops be withdrawn from France for an attack on the Asiatic shore south of the Dardanelles; the neutral Greeks would capture the Gallipoli peninsula; the neutral Bulgarians would march on Adrianople (a major city in north-western Turkey); and the neutral Romanians would join the Russians and Serbs in an attack against Austria. At the same time, the Royal Navy should 'force the Dardanelles'.

A NAVAL OPERATION

Churchill seized on the final point in Fisher's proposal and immediately sought Carden's advice on whether forcing the Dardanelles by naval gunfire alone was feasible. Carden replied that the Dardanelles forts could not be rushed, but 'might be forced by extended operations with large numbers of ships.' Asked for a detailed plan, Carden proposed a four-stage step-by-step operation with a probable time-frame of a month. This was enough for Churchill who, against Fisher's advice, took the proposal to the War Council on 13 January 1915. Kitchener reiterated that no troops were available, estimating that 150,000 would be required for the operation, and adding that further study would be required to ascertain the exact number. He considered, however, that a massive naval demonstration was worth attempting, noting that it could be cancelled should the bombardment prove ineffective. This only served to fuel Churchill's enthusiasm.

In reality, Kitchener and Churchill were proposing two different operations: Churchill sought a naval attack to force the Dardanelles and overawe Constantinople, while Kitchener advocated a naval demonstration that could be abandoned if it proved ineffectual. This lack of clarity of the objective continued to pervade future discussions. Swayed by Churchill's enthusiasm and Kitchener's support for a naval bombardment, the Council gave planning permission for the Admiralty 'to prepare for a naval expedition in February to bombard and take the Gallipoli peninsula with Constantinople as its objective.' The Council neglected to consider how the Navy would realistically 'take the Gallipoli peninsula'. When advised of the proposal, the French agreed to provide a naval squadron.

Fisher continued to object to a purely naval attack with a verve that equalled Churchill's passionate advocacy for the attack. Nevertheless, much to Fisher's dismay, the War Council formally approved the operation on 28 January 1915. This contradicted accepted naval wisdom that attacks by warships against forts without military support rarely produced worthwhile results. Many in the Navy believed that a combined naval-military operation was the only realistic option. The decision had strong political motives. Given the stalemate on the Western Front, the Council believed a circuit-breaker was required. In addition, the promise made to the Russians to provide a demonstration had to be kept, and Churchill was driven by the need to restore his own prestige and that of the Admiralty. Ironically, the demonstration was no longer required as, by 5 January 1915, the Russians had defeated Ottoman forces in several battles, although they had neglected to advise the British.

Further concerns arose in the Balkans where the Serbs were now in need of urgent assistance. Britain and France each proposed to send one infantry division to Salonika to protect Greece's communications while the Greek Army marched to Serbia's aid. Kitchener agreed to release the 29th Division as Britain's contribution. The project was eventually dropped, but the need to assist Serbia remained a major concern, and the Dardanelles venture began to acquire a new justification.

In mid-February a naval memorandum added fuel to the fire: not only would landing parties be required to finish off the forts, but if the straits were to be used by merchant vessels, both shores must be held by ground troops once the fleet had passed through. In the light of Kitchener's agreement to release the 29th Division for Salonika, the decision was taken that the 29th and ANZAC were 'to be available in case of necessity to support the naval attack'. On 18 February 1915 the French advised that they would provide an infantry division. The next day Kitchener changed his mind and insisted that the 29th Division could not be released, but that ANZAC, while relatively untrained, could still be sent to assist the Navy. ANZAC was to be used to support the Royal Marine Light Infantry (RMLI) in securing the forts once they had been reduced and in garrisoning the peninsula, not for an amphibious assault. Churchill now weighed in and advocated that at least 50,000 troops be made available at three days' notice to reach the Dardanelles. No decision was made, and the purely naval assault went ahead as planned.

HMS *Ocean*, one of the Canopus class pre-dreadnought battleships assigned to reduce the Turkish fortifications covering the Dardanelles. Launched in 1898, she carried four 12-inch guns, twelve 6-inch guns, ten 3-inch guns, and six 1.8-inch guns. Only the 12 and 6-inch guns would have been useful against the forts. She and her fellow pre-dreadnoughts were considered expendable. *Ocean* sank on 18 March after striking the Turkish minefield laid parallel to the southern shore (Wikipedia Commons).

A FLAWED STRATEGY

The expectation that the Navy could subdue the forts, take the peninsula, force the Dardanelles, and then compel the Ottoman government to capitulate simply by having the fleet stand off Constantinople was extraordinarily unrealistic. Carden's force comprised 17 battleships, the battlecruiser *Inflexible*, two cruisers, two light cruisers and several destroyers. While impressive on paper, 16 of the battleships (12 British and four French) were pre-dreadnoughts dating from between 1895 and 1906, most of which were

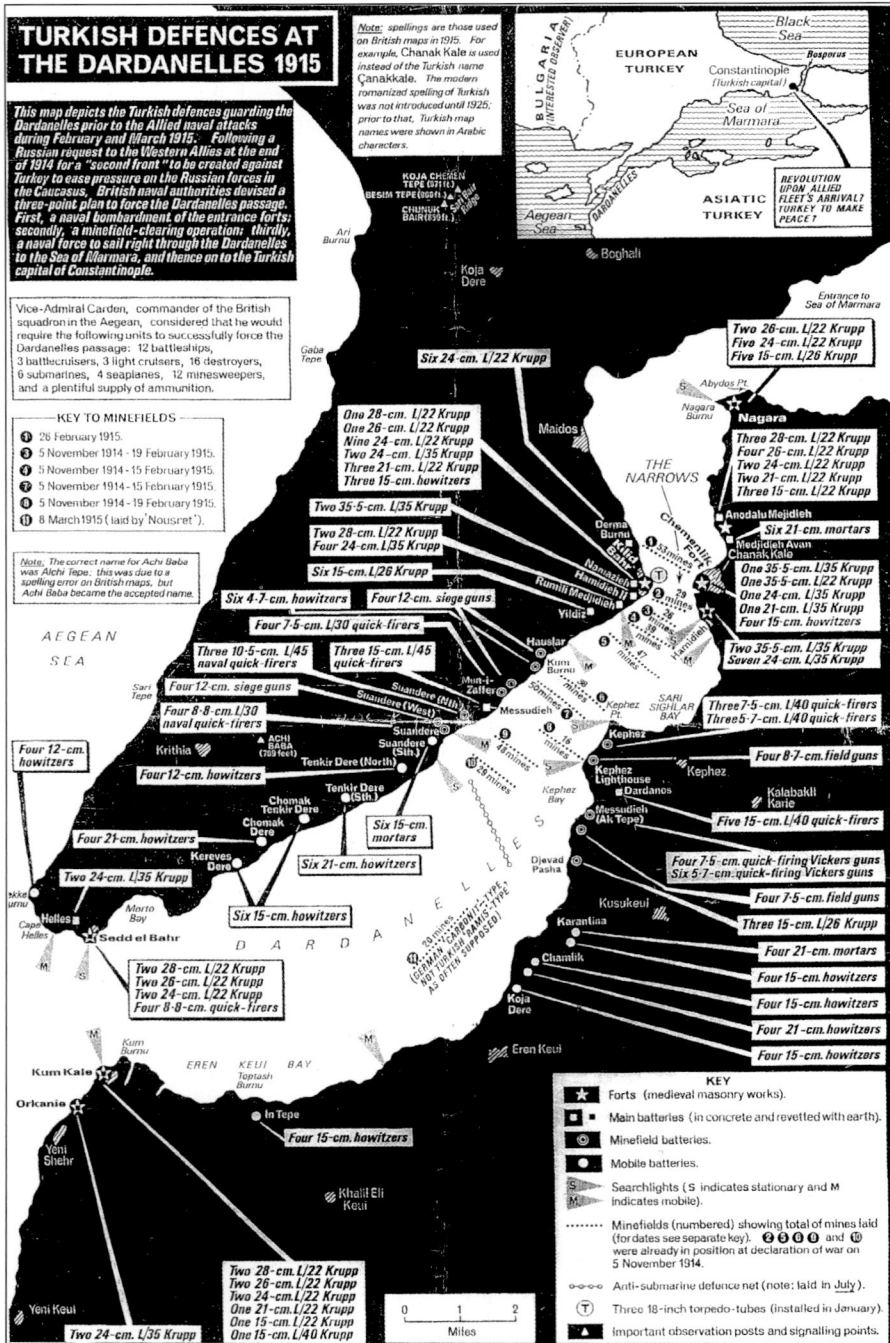

TURKISH DEFENCES AT THE DARDANELLES 1915

This map depicts the Turkish defences guarding the Dardanelles prior to the Allied naval attacks during February and March 1915. Following a Russian request to the Western Allies at the end of 1914 for a "second front" to be created against Turkey to ease pressure on the Russian forces in the Caucasus, British naval authorities devised a three-point plan to force the Dardanelles passage. First, a naval bombardment of the entrance forts; secondly, a minefield-clearing operation; thirdly, a naval force to sail right through the Dardanelles to the Sea of Marmara, and thence on to the Turkish capital of Constantinople.

Vice-Admiral Carden, commander of the British squadron in the Aegean, considered that he would require the following units to successfully force the Dardanelles passage: 12 battleships, 3 battlecruisers, 3 light cruisers, 16 destroyers, 6 submarines, 4 seaplanes, 12 minesweepers, and a plentiful supply of ammunition.

The Dardanelles artillery defences. The *Chanakkale Fortified Area* Command controlled over 300 guns ranging from heavy 35.5cm guns in forts to 4.5cm mobile guns along both shores covering the southern portion of the Dardanelles. These defences were supplemented by 344 mines in ten minefields strung across the strait in the narrow confines below the Kilid Bahr Plateau. An 11th minefield was later laid parallel to the southern shore. It was this minefield that did so much damage during the main naval attack on 18 March.

considered expendable. Only the recently launched *Queen Elizabeth* and the battlecruiser *Inflexible* were truly modern warships. Furthermore, the minesweepers required to clear the minefields were unarmed North Sea trawlers, operated by their civilian crews who were unwilling to work under fire. Confronting them was a formidable obstacle.

The French pre-dreadnought battleship *Bouvet*. Launched in 1896, she carried two 12-inch guns, two 10.7-inch guns, eight 5.4-inch guns, and eight 3.9-inch guns. *Bouvet* was one of the four French battleships assigned to the naval operation (Wikipedia Commons).

The Dardanelles is 61 kilometres long and ranges from one to six kilometres wide. As such, the entire length of the waterway can be covered by gunfire. In the narrower portions there is little or no room for manoeuvre under gunfire. The strongest defences were in the lower half, where the *Chanakkle Area Fortified Command (CAFC)* controlled over 300 guns ranging from 35.5cm (13-inch) to 4.5cm (1.7-inch) pieces, arrayed along both shores of the strait. Of these, over 100 of the heaviest calibres were in fortified batteries, with the strongest concentration around the Narrows, where any warship presented a perfect target. While some of the older forts comprised masonry constructions that were more susceptible to gunfire, many were new, more resilient concrete fortifications fronted with earthen glacis. Furthermore, the low trajectory of the naval guns made destroying the guns within the forts more difficult. The remaining guns were corralled in 25 mobile batteries positioned between Cape Helles and the Narrows, and could move to various firing locations to avoid shelling from the ships. Supplementing them were ten minefields — with a total of 344 mines — laid across the waterway in the restricted waters approaching the Narrows. The notion that Carden's antiquated ships alone could destroy these defences and allow unimpeded sailing up the strait was highly questionable — more so the belief that they could achieve this in a month. Even in the unlikely event that they achieved their mission and slogged their way up the Dardanelles, on entering the Sea of Marmara the surviving vessels would have to fight the Ottoman fleet, including the modern ex-German battlecruiser *Goeben* manned by its German crew, which had the advantage of being able to cross the Allied fleet's 'T' as it emerged from the narrow strait.

Even had the Anglo-French fleet been able to overcome these enormous challenges and appear outside Constantinople, it was unlikely that the Ottoman Empire would have been persuaded to capitulate. This belief is based on the assumption that, once a nation's capital is threatened or captured, it will immediately surrender. Such a view ignores the numerous examples in which this simply did not occur. For example, the Russians did not surrender to Napoleon in 1812; the Confederates failed to capitulate when Richmond was threatened in 1862, simply moving the seat of government when the city fell in 1865, as did the French when the Prussians besieged Paris in 1870, and the Germans threatened it in 1914. Indeed it was highly likely that the Ottoman government would do the same and continue directing the war from Anatolia. Furthermore, there is evidence that the Turks fully intended to defend their capital against a fleet that had been ordered not to fire on the city. An expected capitulation under these conditions was wishful thinking in the extreme.

THE ARMY IS DRAWN IN

Employing Carden's four-stage plan, the Anglo-French fleet began its operation on 19 February 1915. That same day, without the consent of the War Council, Churchill trumpeted the 'success' of the opening day's bombardment in a press announcement, despite the fact that Carden's attack had caused little or no damage. Hankey recorded the effect of this ill-informed press release: 'The announcement had a remarkable effect on the attitude of the War Council. When the decision had been reached to undertake the naval bombardment it had generally been assumed that the attack could be broken off in the event of failure. But when the War Cabinet met on February 24th, notwithstanding that the Outer Forts had not yet been finally reduced, it was felt that we were now committed to seeing the business through.' Kitchener considered that 'the publicity of the announcement has committed us'. The next day he directed Lieutenant General Sir John Maxwell, General Officer Commanding (GOC) the Egyptian Expeditionary Force (EEF), to warn ANZAC to be ready to embark on 9 March 'to assist the navy ... give any co-operation ... required ... and to occupy any captured forts.' In response, the partially trained 3rd Australian Infantry Brigade embarked for Lemnos Island on 2 March 1915.

As the British Official Historian noted, what the government required was a reliable assessment of whether the Dardanelles was worth the effort. Such an assessment should have been based on a detailed strategic analysis and a balanced consideration of the rival claims on the forces made available. The Admiralty called for larger numbers of troops, BEF headquarters in France argued that none could be spared, and the British General Staff in London was not consulted. In reality, this was strategic direction based on wishful thinking supported by operational planning on the run. No effort was made to present a pragmatic assessment of the value of the operation or the resources required for its success.

The French pre-dreadnought *Bouvet* capsizing after striking the Turkish minefield parallel to the southern shore of the Dardanelles. *Bouvet* sank in less than in three minutes and only 48 men from her complement of 710 survived (Wikipedia Commons).

By 9 March 1915 the naval effort had made little headway. The outer forts at the mouth of the Dardanelles had been silenced through a combination of naval gunfire and RMLI landing parties placing charges on several of the guns, but the subsequent stages were proving far more difficult. On 10 March Kitchener changed his mind again and advised the War Council that the 29th Division was available to support the Navy. However, despite naval opinion that troops would be required to continue the attack, Churchill now considered that the Navy could penetrate the Dardanelles without the Army's help. Despite this, the next day General Sir Ian Hamilton was appointed to command the Mediterranean Expeditionary Force (MEF). With a hastily arranged staff and instructions from Kitchener that any large-scale land operations were only to be contemplated if the fleet failed to penetrate after every effort had been exhausted, he departed London on 13 March 1915. Recalling the effect of Churchill's press release on 19 February, Kitchener added that, '[h]aving entered the project of forcing the Straits, there can be no idea of abandoning the project.' For the Army, the possibility of the Dardanelles becoming an unwanted, alternative theatre of operations was quickly assuming reality.

Churchill now decided to rush the Dardanelles, ignoring the fact that stage two of the four-stage operation was nowhere near completion. Carden, contrary to his previous advice, agreed and replied that he would now attack the forts at the Narrows (stage three) with his entire force, while silencing the inner batteries and clearing the minefields (stage two) under cover of this attack. Then, suffering a nervous breakdown, he requested leave, which was hardly an endorsement of his advice.

HMS *Irresistible*, a pre-dreadnought Formidable class battleship, abandoned and sinking after striking the Turkish minefield that also claimed *Bouvet* and *Ocean*. Launched in 1898, she carried four 12-inch guns, twelve 6-inch guns, sixteen 3-inch guns and six 1.8-inch guns, and a crew of 780 men, most of whom were rescued (Wikipedia Commons).

Hamilton arrived in theatre on 17 March and conferred with Carden's replacement, Admiral Sir John de Robeck, who advised that he 'proposed to exhaust every effort to reduce the Dardanelles by naval means before calling on the military for assistance.' On 18 March, while Hamilton and his staff undertook a reconnaissance of the Aegean coast of the peninsula, the Anglo-French fleet steamed into the Dardanelles determined to blast its way through, only to suffer ignominious defeat. The fleet lost three battleships sunk and three so badly damaged that they were out of action for some time — including the battlecruiser *Inflexible*. Its strength had been reduced by a third as a result of devastating gunfire and well-positioned minefields. After the war, Churchill claimed that, following the 18th March battle, the Turkish batteries had almost exhausted their ammunition and another determined effort would have seen the Navy through — a claim not supported by Turkish archival sources. According to Erickson (*Gallipoli: The Ottoman Campaign*), only four of the 14 permanent forts had engaged the fleet on 18 March. While ammunition in these batteries had been depleted, it had not been exhausted, and there were substantial quantities in the remaining forts, including those of the inner defences covering the Narrows. Nor had the minefields been breached and, with one minefield alone having sunk or seriously damaged four of the six battleships lost on the 18th, it could reasonably be expected that the ten minefields strung across the strait and the unsuppressed forts would account for a considerable number of the remaining 11 battleships in any subsequent attempt to force their way through.

While de Robeck was ready to make another attempt with ships alone, at a conference on 22 March Hamilton convinced him that the fleet could only pass through once the peninsula had been captured by ground forces. The fact that the Ottoman batteries along the Asiatic shore would not be occupied was ignored. On 27 March Churchill reluctantly acquiesced and cabled that a combined naval-military operation was now essential.

Just as the Navy had been forced into a purely naval attack, the Army had now been drawn into a new theatre of war it neither wanted nor had the resources to commit. Rather than arriving at the need for the campaign through measured analysis and pragmatic consideration, the campaign had evolved through wishful and, at times, impulsive thinking in search of highly questionable strategic outcomes, based on a poor opinion of Ottoman capabilities and an attempt to salvage political reputations.

CHAPTER 3
THE OPPOSING ARMIES

MEDITERRANEAN EXPEDITIONARY FORCE

An ad hoc formation in every sense of the term, the MEF was cobbled together in March 1915 under a hastily formed General Headquarters. Comprising formations and units in various stages of training and with varying capabilities, its soldiers came from Britain, France, India, Ceylon and the Antipodes. The best trained were the British 29th Division and the French Corps Expeditionnaire d'Orient (CEO), but even these were new formations with new staffs and with little opportunity to exercise at brigade and divisional levels. The 29th was created in January/February 1915 from regular units that had been garrisoning the empire, and which had been brought home to fight in France. The CEO was an infantry division purpose-raised for the campaign from a mixture of French, Algerian, Senegalese and Foreign Legion units drawn from the depots in Africa and France. Added to these was the RND, which was a mixed bag comprising four battalions of well-trained RMLI and five of raw Royal Naval Reserve (RNR) volunteers excess to requirement and now training as infantry. The RND had no artillery and was short of support troops. The final component of the force was the partially trained ANZAC.

Australians recently arrived in Egypt establish their camp at Mena in December 1914 (AWM CO2588).

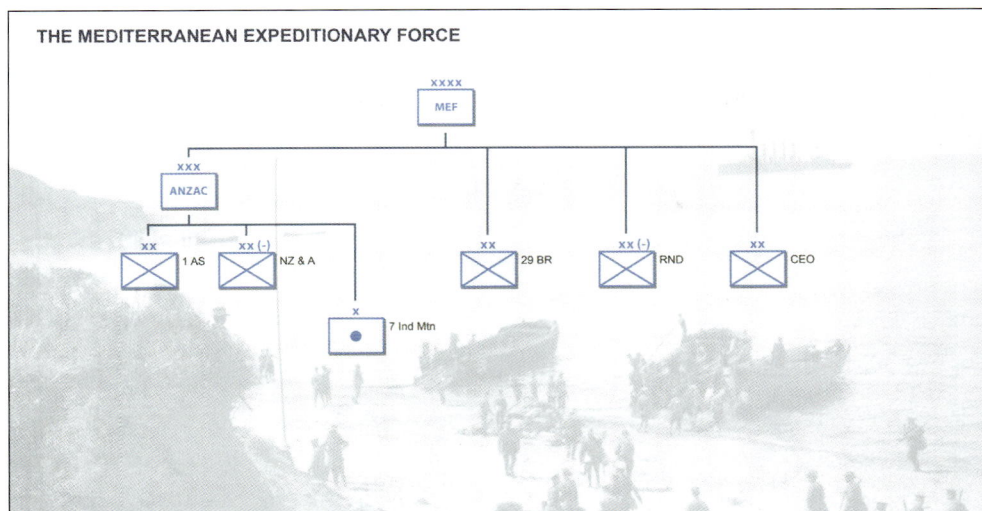

THE MEDITERRANEAN EXPEDITIONARY FORCE

ANZAC

Neither Australia nor New Zealand fielded a full-time active army, preferring initially to rely on a system of voluntary part-time units of the militia (paid) and the volunteers (unpaid) supported by a small permanent staff and instructors, and regular garrison artillery in the coastal fortifications. There was no formal training system as exists today, although there were schools of musketry in both countries. Australia also had schools of military engineering and artillery which trained men in the technical skills of their corps. There was no formal officer training, although each year a permanent officer at captain/major level was selected to attend the British Army Staff College. For the vast majority, however, training was completed under the auspices of local units with irregular training regimes based around the weekly evening parade and the odd weekend camp, at which attendance was intermittent. Standards varied according to the experience and knowledge of unit officers and instructors, some of whom were ex-British Army regulars. Many, however, were largely self-taught, either from reading official manuals, texts such as Hamley's *Operations of War* and James's *Modern Strategy*, and books on military history, or simply learning from their self-taught elders. Former drill masters who had served in the British Army provided the fundamentals of foot and arms drill and weapons handling. Any effort to learn tactical manoeuvres was generally limited to annual camps, although not everyone attended these. The irregular and ad hoc nature of training prevented the building of any serious military capability, even among individuals, and some units resembled an exclusive club rather than a military unit.

The standard was so poor in New Zealand that it became a festering issue in Parliament, leading in December 1909 to the scrapping of the old volunteer force and the introduction of part-time, compulsory military training. Boys between the ages of 12 and 18 would serve in the junior and senior cadets and, once they had turned 18, would join the newly created Territorial Force (TF) until they were 21, later extended to 25 years on Lord Kitchener's recommendation in his report to the government of the same year. The situation was no better in Australia. In his carefully worded report to the Australian government in 1909, Kitchener commented that the volunteers and militia were 'inadequate in numbers, training, [and] organisation ... to defend Australia' and that the training was 'too fast' with manoeuvres undertaken without the necessary systematic recruit and individual training essential to teaching the fundamental skills of soldiering. Consequently, in 1911 Australia followed New Zealand's lead, scrapping the inefficient voluntary system and adopting part-time, compulsory military training.

Australian cadets aged 12 to 17 years undertook physical training and drill and, for the senior cadets, small bore musketry training. Youths aged from 18 to 26 served part-time in a new and revamped force based on regional units administered by military districts. In Australia the training obligation in the new Citizen Military Force (CMF) was 16 days per year for the light horse and infantry. Service was undertaken at 90-minute, weekly night parades, occasional half-day parades, and an annual camp of eight to 12 days, longer for members of the artillery. However, those living more than five miles from a designated training area were exempt: of 155,000 youths registered for training in 1911 only 92,463 or 60% were liable for service. This regime provided only the most basic level of training, focusing primarily on individual skills and lower level unit drills. Officer training in handling units and formations under field conditions was limited. While the Permanent Force provided a small pool of instructors spread thinly on the ground, responsibility for the bulk of the training fell on each unit's officers and NCOs, largely drawn from members of the old voluntary system.

In New Zealand, a considerable number of British Army NCOs was recruited to assist in drilling and training the new TF, together with several British officers, including Major General Sir Alexander Godley, who was appointed to command the New Zealand Defence Force. In the short period before the outbreak of war, he and his British staff and instructors made a considerable contribution to its development. While a few British officers were seconded to the Australian Army, the Commonwealth tended to rely more on its own Permanent Force personnel. To provide a home-grown, professionally trained permanent officer corps, candidates were selected for entry to the newly established Royal Military College, Duntroon, through a selection program and competitive examinations which applied to applicants from both countries. This provided trained junior officers for their first appointment in the Permanent Forces, but no formal higher level officer training was introduced in either country.

Overall, while the introduction of part-time compulsory training substantially raised standards, it still fell far short of the proficiency required of forces undertaking combat operations. Sir Ian Hamilton's 1914 report to the New Zealand government, in his capacity as Inspector-General of Overseas Forces, commented: 'The land forces of New Zealand are not perfect, or anywhere near perfect. In some respects development may be backward. But at least I am able to report broadly that the progress made during the past three years in giving shape to a real national army in New Zealand has been singularly rapid.' While acknowledging the high intelligence, quality and promise of the men undertaking training, he identified a significant weakness in the proficiency of the officers. This is unsurprising given the markedly higher level of skills and increased knowledge they had to master and practise themselves, as well as train and administer their men, and the limited time and opportunities available to them to do so. Hamilton added that, while 'the higher leaders showed aptitude and training … the junior leaders were keenness personified, but a proportion, perhaps one-half, had neither a thorough grip over their men nor a mastery of the situation, nor, again, a practised eye for country.'

Similarly, in his 25 June 1914 report on the defence forces of New Zealand, Godley wrote: 'The knowledge and efficiency of the officers and non-commissioned officers of the Territorial Force has shown a marked improvement: this is due in great measure to the special courses in instruction of various kinds … Still there is much room for improvement.' In his rather more frank annual report on the Australian Military Forces, dated 30 May 1913, Major General Kirkpatrick, while acknowledging a steady improvement throughout the force, described fundamental deficiencies in training and proficiency within each of the arms and services. In a similar observation to Hamilton's concerning officers, he remarked of the infantry, 'the company officer was often lacking in self confidence, and in control of men' and, more generally, while 'the commanders showed improvement in the conception of a plan, … they sometimes forgot the difficulties attendant upon a sudden change of plan.' Given that the cadets at Duntroon undertook four years' full-time training for their first appointment as junior officers, it is not surprising that the part-time Territorial and CMF officers, with perhaps 20 days a year, lacked the proficiency required of them.

While this represented tangible progress towards the formation of a better defence capability, compared to the full-time professional and conscript armies of Europe and the Ottoman Empire, the Australians and New Zealanders were still very much amateur armies. One contemporary writer described the part-time force as 'little more than an organised schedule of human material, mainly excellent, which would become available for training only at the outbreak of war.' In practice most had only a smattering of knowledge on soldiering and lacked much of the collective training that welds individuals into effective fighting units.

The *Defence Act* in both Australia and New Zealand stipulated that the CMF and TF could only be called out for the defence of their respective countries. Consequently, on the outbreak of war, when the Australian and New Zealand governments each offered Britain a contingent of troops, they had to rely on volunteers to raise a separate force for overseas war service. Their confidence in making the offer was justified: the rush of volunteers to serve in the AIF and NZEF was overwhelming. In the first four months Australia recruited sufficient men for 16 infantry battalions, 10 light horse regiments, nine field artillery batteries and the appropriate number of support troops — enough for an infantry division, plus an extra infantry brigade and three light horse brigades. From a much smaller population New Zealand fielded an equally impressive response: an infantry brigade, a mounted rifles brigade, a field artillery brigade, and an extra mounted rifles regiment.

The 1st Australian Division was the centrepiece of the AIF. Following the standard British structure it numbered around 17,500 men. Its fighting strength comprised the 1st, 2nd and 3rd infantry brigades and the 1st, 2nd and 3rd field artillery brigades. However it lacked the field howitzer brigade and heavy artillery battery that were standard in British divisions, and the field batteries had four guns rather than the six of regular British batteries. Minor units provided engineer, signals, medical, transport and supply support, while a light horse regiment — the 4th Light Horse — provided the divisional reconnaissance capability. The excess battalions (13th to 16th) raised in the rush to enlist made up the 4th Infantry Brigade, while the 1st to 3rd and 5th to 10th light horse regiments formed the 1st, 2nd and 3rd light horse brigades.

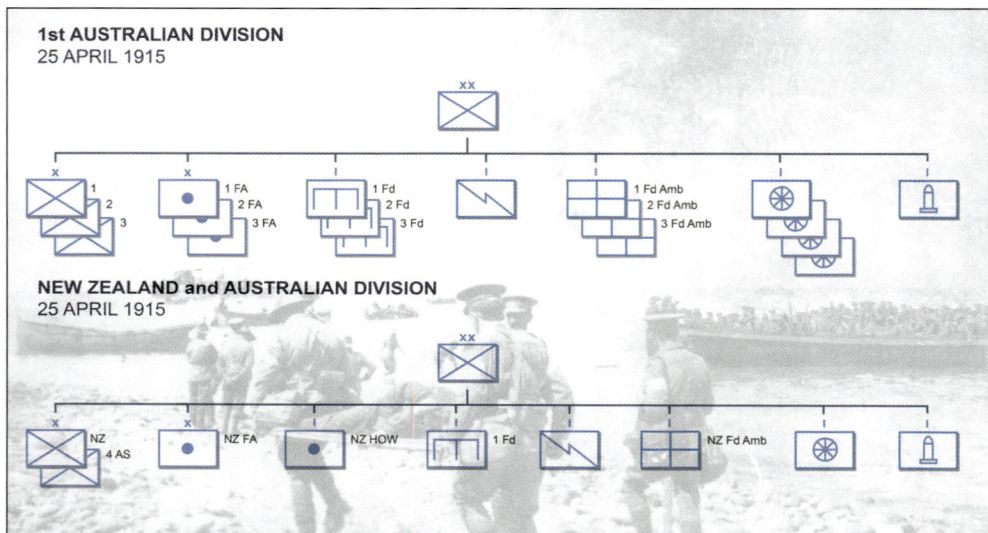

The NZEF consisted of three separate brigades. The Auckland, Wellington, Canterbury and Otago battalions formed the New Zealand Infantry Brigade, and the Auckland, Wellington, and Canterbury Mounted Rifles comprised the New Zealand Mounted Rifles Brigade. The Otago Mounted Rifles remained an independent unit. The gunners formed the New Zealand Field Artillery Brigade and, like the Australians, each of its batteries had four guns.

Despite the volumes written on the Gallipoli campaign, the precise composition of each force has yet to be analysed in detail. The New Zealanders initially sought to enlist men from the TF. Working under their respective military districts, each of the 17 TF infantry battalions was tasked with recruiting a company to fill its military district's battalion of the infantry brigade. Likewise, the 12 TF mounted rifle regiments were each asked to recruit a squadron for the expeditionary force. While a good many TF men rushed to enlist, ex-British regulars living in the country, ex-militiamen and others with no previous military training were also recruited. The Otago Battalion's historian recorded that three-fifths of its men had no previous military experience.

Australian infantry training in Egypt in early 1915 occupy a rudimentary trench. This and the following photo show the concentrated formations adopted during the early stages of the war (AWM PS0760).

Australian recruiting was organised through the military district headquarters in each state. The original intention was that half the force would be drawn from the CMF, but this was overlooked in the haste to recruit. According to Charles Bean, the 1st Australian Division had only 2300 compulsory trainees. Of the remainder almost 4000 were former volunteers and militiamen, some 2300 were British ex-regulars or ex-TF men, and over 6000 men had no prior military experience. On the other hand, 607 of its 631 officers had previous military training, including 15 British Army officers on attachment to the

Permanent Forces, and 84 serving or retired professional officers. The remainder were ex-militia or CMF officers. Just over 100 had seen active service in the South African War or other colonial conflicts. In the 4th Brigade's battalions, which were raised in late September-early October, previous military experience appears to have been less common — the 15th Battalion's war diary records that 85% of the men had no previous military experience. The recruits came from all occupations and, contrary to Charles Bean's image of an AIF from the bush, most were from the cities and major towns. In the 1st Australian Division's 12 infantry battalions, between 24% and 28% of the men listed their next of kin as residing in the United Kingdom. Considering those who had emigrated with their parents during the latter third of the nineteenth century, it is estimated that well over a third, and possibly more than 40% of the initial AIF were born in the British Isles, and a good many of those who had been born in Australia had British-born parents. Similar ratios are likely to have characterised the NZEF.

In professional armies, recruits would undertake extensive training over several months to provide them with a solid grounding in the individual skills necessary to make them competent soldiers before they were posted to their units. There they would be involved in collective training programs to develop a cohesive force well practised in conducting the various phases of war. For example, during the Vietnam War, Australian recruits spent five months undertaking a rigorous and systematic recruit and special-to-branch training regime before joining their units, and then completed collective training in platoon, company and battalion exercises that welded them into cohesive, well-oiled units before they were deployed overseas. In the Second World War, the 6th Australian Division, raised in September 1939, spent 16 months training before entering combat in 1941. This was not to be the case with the original Anzacs. Compared to modern training requirements, those of the AIF and NZEF lacked any sense of orderly progression. The AIF and NZEF volunteers went straight from the recruiting office to units that were still being organised, were housed in makeshift accommodation and were trained by newly appointed officers and NCOs, many of whom were as inexperienced as their troops.

Most units were formed during the third week in August and did not reach full strength until the first or second week in September, during which time the focus was on administration, establishing camps, equipping the men, and elementary drill. Lieutenant Charles Fortescue of the 9th Battalion wrote, 'There were no drill instructors available, no schools of instruction to train NCOs and officers and no time to train these even if schools were available. The unit was there and it had to train itself.' Training varied from unit to unit. The 5th Battalion's companies appear to have each spent one day on the Williamstown rifle range before sailing, completing Part I of Table B of *Musketry Regulations* (30 rounds of ammunition per man for grouping and initial application shooting); while the 3rd Battalion spent a total of seven days on the Long Bay rifle range which, given the number of men to be trained and the limited range facilities, would have achieved little more. The 8th Battalion's commander noted that 'Training was necessarily hurried, rank & file displayed remarkable aptitude, not sufficient time devoted to elementary training … musketry practice inadequate.'

The NZEF had even less time for training prior to embarkation on 22 September. The Auckland Battalion's historian remarked that 'they learned to form fours, to march reasonably, and make the proper connection between rifle and bayonet. The most exciting experience was the march to Manurewa, some fifteen miles.' The Wellington Battalion's training 'consisted largely of physical exercises and route marching to get the men fit and hard, with a little musketry and steady drill, to get cohesion in the unit.' While waiting in Wellington Harbour to sail, the battalions of the New Zealand Infantry Brigade undertook limited training when they could get ashore. Each battalion also participated in manoeuvres in the nearby Kiopara Hills, highlighting Kitchener's earlier criticism of training as 'too fast'. They were not a success. The post-manoeuvre report highlighted serious deficiencies in training and a marked lack of knowledge at all levels.

Australian infantry occupying a trench during training in Egypt early 1915. Field exercises often comprised a battalion moving from camp in the early evening, digging in during the night and in the dawn confronting another battalion attacking the position. Note how closely the firing line was packed in the early stages of the war (AWM PS0728).

Farewelled by large, cheering crowds on the docks, the NZEF, the 1st Australian Division and the 1st Australian Light Horse Brigade sailed in mid-October for the rendezvous at Albany in Western Australia where, on 1 November, the combined convoy began its five-week journey to Egypt. On board, where space was tight, training was limited to lectures, drill, physical training, rifle exercises and, on the odd occasion, musketry practice from the stern of the ship when it took its turn to pull astern of the convoy. For many it was the inexperienced leading the inexperienced. One Australian officer noted that they received instruction one day and imparted their knowledge to their men the next. Second Lieutenant Spencer Westmacott of the Auckland Battalion wrote, 'We took the *Field Service Regulations*, reading them paragraph by paragraph in turn, officers as well as men in the ranks ... Needless to say we learnt a great deal ourselves at these classes.' Arriving in Egypt in early December, they set up camp near Cairo, the Australians under the shadow of the Great Pyramids at Mena, and the New Zealanders at Zeitoun, where serious training could now begin in earnest.

Accompanied by a small but carefully chosen staff from India, Lieutenant General Sir William Birdwood took command of the Antipodean forces on 21 December 1914 and organised them into a corps of two divisions: the 1st Australian Division, and the New Zealand and Australian (NZ&A) Division. The latter was a division in name only. Formed in January 1915 by lumping the remaining Australian units with the New Zealanders, it comprised the New Zealand Infantry Brigade, the New Zealand Mounted Rifles Brigade, the 1st Australian Light Horse Brigade, and the soon to arrive 4th Australian Infantry Brigade. The orphan Otago Mounted Rifles found a role, albeit briefly, as the divisional reconnaissance unit, and the New Zealand Field Artillery Brigade and a recently arrived New Zealand battery of 4.5-inch howitzers rounded out its fighting capability. As well as having only 16 guns, the division was short of engineers and logistic units, although these were soon brought up to strength by New Zealanders living in England.

Training in the desert initially focused on the soldiers' individual military skills, but the urge to do more quickly took hold and, by 17 December, the 3rd Battalion was practising night operations. After his initial inspection, Birdwood considered the Anzacs' training decidedly backward, commenting that they 'had not been drilled in bayonet fighting, no digging and very little musketry'. The corps artillery commander remarked that the artillery 'was practically untrained' and Lieutenant William Dawkins of the 2nd Field Company, a recent Duntroon graduate, wrote: 'Our infantry are our weakest point in the division.' While Bridges sought to remedy these deficiencies through a more progressive system, it was still rushed, and Godley pushed the NZEF to battalion and combined training early in the New Year. It was quite unlike the systematic and progressive training from recruit to individual branch skills to unit collective training that is the benchmark today. On 4 January Lieutenant Colonel William Malone, commanding the Wellington Battalion, wrote: 'Start battalion training today. The Brigadier is in a hurry to rush us along at schemes and [at] the top of the work [sic]. I am determined to begin at the bottom. He has been used to troops who, before they go to their Regiments after enlisting have had 6 solid months recruits [sic] training, a very different thing to ours, where the men have only been 4 months together and 2 of them at sea on a transport with no room to work.' Nonetheless, as early as 11 January 1915, the New Zealand battalions were involved in combined arms training with sections of artillery and battalion attacks intermixed with individual training in musketry, route marches and drill. On 26 January, training for the New Zealand Infantry Brigade abruptly ceased when it was sent to occupy the Suez Canal defences in anticipation of an Ottoman attack. There Private William Ham became New Zealand's first battle casualty, dying of wounds on 6 February. The brigade remained garrisoning the canal until 26 February, having lost a full month's training.

By mid-February brigade and divisional exercises were being conducted, although these were tame affairs lasting only a few hours with the troops returning to camp in the heat of the afternoon, or undertaking defensive exercises overnight and returning to camp the following morning. The training programs provided little opportunity for commanders, particularly at battalion level and above, to train and exercise their units and formations under the realistic or arduous conditions they would confront on the battlefield. There were no lengthy exercises and most lasted from four to six hours followed by a debrief. At the individual level ammunition restrictions affected musketry training, with issues steadily reduced from 120 to 75 rounds per rifle, insufficient to complete the British Army's Table A of *Musketry Regulations*, the recruits' course for the regular army, which was allocated 200 rounds per man. Machine-gunners had their allocation cut from 2000 rounds to 75 rounds. Bridges reported that only around half the 1st Division's soldiers were eventually classified as proficient.

On 27 February the 3rd Australian Infantry Brigade had its training cut short when it was ordered to support the naval operation in the Dardanelles. Arriving at Lemnos on 4 March, the 9th Battalion disembarked but, with water supplies limited, the other battalions were forced to remain in the cramped quarters of their transports. Subsequent training involved disembarkation practice, assaults up hills and the inevitable route marches, and focused on preparing them for the role of occupying the forts once the Navy had subdued them. Captain Dixon Hearder of the 11th Battalion wrote, 'About three times a week we used to go ashore ... [a]nd indulge in sham fighting or hill climbing, anything to keep fit, and return about 4pm.' If Lance Corporal George Mitchell's diary is any indication, between 4 March and 21 April his company of the 10th Battalion spent a total of 16 days ashore, plus two half days familiarising themselves with embarking and disembarking from HMS *Prince of Wales* before leaving Lemnos. It was hardly sufficient to prepare a force for serious offensive operations.

Back in Egypt, the remainder of ANZAC continued a haphazard program of short brigade and divisional field exercises intermixed with individual training, musketry and route marches, alongside parades and reviews for visiting dignitaries. In March Malone was highly critical of the standard of performance and, when Birdwood expressed the view that the New Zealanders had improved 'enormously', the ever-critical Malone disagreed and told him so. Sent to umpire an exercise between the 2nd Light Horse Brigade and the New Zealand Mounted Rifles Brigade on 17 March, he considered it 'a poor show and neither Brigadiers [sic] in my opinion seem to have a sound knowledge of their work.' Even considering Malone's propensity to criticise everyone but his own battalion, it was an observation that applied to many of the battalion and brigade commanders, and indeed to much of ANZAC. However, by the end of March the troops were toughened and beginning to show distinct improvement and Birdwood reported favourably on the standards achieved. Nonetheless, both divisions and their brigades were far from fully trained and efficient formations when, in early April, they embarked for the Dardanelles.

Ottoman infantry on the way to the front. Widely disparaged, they proved hardy, well-trained and tough opponents. Most had already seen from one to three years' full-time service in the active army, and many were combat veterans of the Balkan Wars (Harvey Broadbent image).

THE OTTOMAN ARMY

Widely regarded as a ragtag army and considered of little consequence by Western military observers, the Ottoman Army had trained under the influence of a German Military Mission since 1882. This was a full-time conscripted army which had adopted German doctrine and tactics, had a formal system of training schools for each branch of the service, and formal officer education in the form of the Ottoman Military Academy which prepared officers for their first appointment. The Ottoman Military College prepared middle-ranking officers for General Staff appointments while selected senior officers received further education at the prestigious German War Academy. Prior to the Balkan Wars, conscripts served three years full-time in active units and then spent further time in reserve (*Redif*) units.

While some reform had been instituted in 1908, their crushing defeat in the Balkan Wars had stung the Ottomans into further action. Sweeping reforms and radical restructuring of the Army were introduced six months after the war concluded. Implementing them with great urgency, the Ottoman High Command was committed to rebuilding the Army into an effective fighting force. A new German Military Mission under General Otto Liman von Sanders arrived to assist, but much of the reform was completed under the driving leadership of Colonel Enver Pasha, the new Minister for War and de facto Commander-in-Chief.

Under the new scheme, conscripts served two years full-time in the active army for infantry and cavalry and three for artillery, followed by 16 years in the reserve. In December 1913, the old system of mobilising reserve divisions was abolished, and all *Redif* units were removed from the order of battle. In their place only active units were maintained, but at a cadre strength of around 40% of their authorised war strength. On mobilisation, the trained reservists would report to reception centres and be allocated to an active unit.

Almost 1300 senior officers were involuntarily retired in January 1914, to be replaced by officers who had demonstrated their competence during the recent wars. In March Enver Pasha issued a comprehensive instruction for training the Army. It demanded strong leadership from the front, demonstrated proficiency in individual training for all junior leaders and soldiers before being graduated into units, hard and realistic training exercises, and aggressive battle tactics. By August 1914 the enormous reconstruction effort had been largely completed. There were five active armies (*First* to *Fourth* and *Sixth*) controlling 13 corps and 33 infantry divisions. Additional troops existed in cavalry and independent infantry divisions, together with several other commands and fortified areas. While most of the reforms were in place and the Army showed signs of improved efficiency, it was still not ready for war.

Further training was required, and serious deficiencies in materiel and weapons remained. Some 280 field guns were needed to bring the divisional artillery regiments up to war establishment, and 200 machine-guns to fully equip the authorised number of machine-gun companies. This equated to 70 field batteries and 50 machine-gun companies short of establishment — deficiencies that could not be readily addressed. While the Army had a long-serving professional officer corps with a hard core of battle-experienced men who had passed through a progressive system of training schools, it lacked that strong element of long-term, professional NCOs who were the glue between the junior officers and the soldiers. They would be drawn from reservists recalled to the colours on mobilisation.

Conscious of his country's lack of preparedness, Enver Pasha ordered mobilisation on 2 August 1914 when hostilities broke out in Europe, but refrained from entering the war. Reservists streamed in and were allocated to the active divisions over the next six weeks bringing them up to war strength. Many were combat veterans of the Balkan Wars, while the conscripts already in the units had between six months and two years' full-time training under their belts. A period of intensive training ensued, and was under way when the Black Sea provocation in late October brought the Ottoman Empire into the war. Nonetheless, the Ottoman Army had retained its reputation for inefficiency. Churchill's view summarised British attitudes: 'A good army of 50,000 men and seapower, that is the end of the Turkish menace.' Lieutenant Colonel Andrew Skeen, one of Birdwood's staff officers, considered the Turks 'an enemy who has never shown himself as good a fighter as the white man.' These were views that would be tested in April 1915.

Ottoman *III Corps* Headquarters in the field on the Gallipoli peninsula. Esat Pasha, the Corps Commander, is seated at the table (Turkish General Staff archives, courtesy Harvey Broadbent).

OTTOMAN *III CORPS*

Regarded as the best in the Ottoman Army, *III Corps* had performed well in the Balkan Wars and was the only corps to escape the reorganisation of 1913, retaining its three organic infantry divisions, the *7th*, *8th* and *9th*, intact. Commanded by the energetic Major General Esat Pasha, it achieved full mobilisation within the requisite 20 days, the only corps to meet its deadline. Esat was tasked with defending the Gallipoli peninsula. The *9th Division* was immediately detached to support the *CFAC* which controlled the forts and the mobile artillery regiments arrayed on either side of the Dardanelles. However, the corps lost its organic *8th Division* for service in the Sinai. In its place *III Corps* was given the new *19th Division*, reactivated in January 1915. The *9th* and *19th divisions* were to face the initial British and ANZAC landings in April 1915.

The *9th* was a veteran division with a good record from the Balkan Wars and its units were recruited from ethnic Turks. The *26th* and *27th infantry regiments* were local to the Dardanelles region, both with their home stations at Gallipoli, while the *25th Regiment* drew its men from further afield. The *27th*, which fought at Anzac, drew most of its men from the Chanakkle and Gallipoli districts, almost all of them illiterate but tough agricultural workers. In contrast to the Anzacs, around 75% were married with families — this regiment was truly defending home and hearth. Lieutenant Colonel Mehmet Sefik, the regimental commander, considered them 'loyal ... bold, zealous ... devoted ... well brought up for war.' The *9th Division* was generally well equipped, although the *26th Regiment* lacked a machine-gun company. The *9th Artillery Regiment* had two battalions of Krupp QF 75mm field guns and one equipped with Krupp QF 75mm mountain guns.

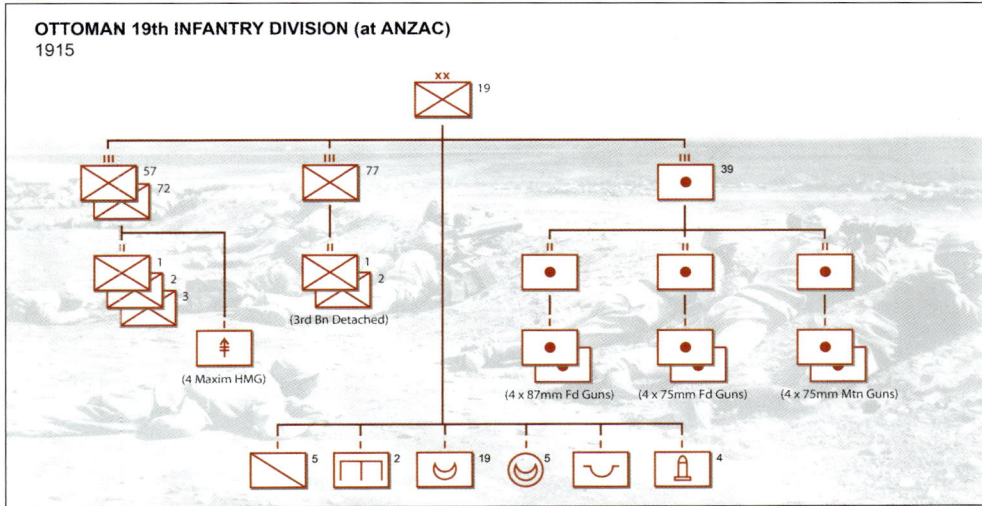

The *19th Division* was less cohesive. Its *57th Infantry Regiment* was Turkish, while the *72nd* and *77th* were considered 'Arab', although recent scholarship indicates that up to a third were ethnic Turks. The *57th* was reactivated in January 1915, its *1st Battalion (1/57th)* created using the fourth companies of the *19th Infantry Regiment*'s battalions which had been training since August 1914. The *2nd (2/57th)* and *3rd battalions (3/57th)*, also raised in January, drew their men from reservists and volunteers. Originally a *26th Division (VI Corps)* formation, the *77th Regiment* was mobilised in August 1914 at Aleppo, Syria. Two-thirds of the men were Arab, while the remainder were Turks from the reserve pools in Thrace. The *72nd Regiment*, part of the independent *24th Division*, was also mobilised in Syria in August 1914. Both regiments were reassigned to the *19th Division* in February 1915. Only the *57th* and *72nd regiments* possessed a machine-gun company. Two of the *39th Artillery Regiment*'s battalions were equipped with different types of field guns (87mm and QF 75mm), however one of the field batteries, although manned, had no guns, and the third battalion was equipped with QF 75mm mountain guns.

Once on the peninsula, these regiments were given three tasks: improving the old seaward defences, many of which had been constructed during earlier crises; undertaking anti-invasion drills; and continuing the unrelenting program of individual and collective training required to shape units and formations into effective fighting forces. With most of its troops already trained soldiers, many with combat experience, *III Corps* had a head start on ANZAC and the luxury of an uninterrupted training program. The Turks also had the advantage of training on the ground they would defend.

COMMANDERS

War is a ruthless and bloody business. Good, strong command is an essential ingredient of successful operations. It demands tough, confident leadership, a readiness to accept calculated risks, an ability to overcome adversity, the capacity to quickly react to changing situations and remain committed despite the odds and, however repugnant, an acceptance that victory comes with casualties. It also requires sound professional knowledge. These attributes are not common to every officer and the knowledge and confidence required is not easily gained. They are developed through regular study and training under realistic and unrelenting conditions in which uncertainty and the unexpected are injected to test commanders under the most difficult conditions. This rarely occurs in peacetime, and only when Army commanders insist on it. Inevitably it takes the furnace of the battlefield to weed out those who lack the knowledge, judgement, nerve and hard-headedness required for victory.

Of the eight senior ANZAC commanders who participated in the landing, four were serving British Army officers. The amiable, popular and ambitious Birdwood was the most experienced, having served in several campaigns on the North West Frontier of India and as Kitchener's Military Secretary during the guerrilla phase of the South African War. He later commanded an Indian brigade and was a senior staff officer in India when appointed to command ANZAC. Commanding the NZ&A Division, the aloof, quick-tempered and sharp-tongued Major General Alexander Godley had seen active service suppressing a native rebellion in Mashonaland and against the Boers in South Africa. An enthusiastic hunting man, he had foregone attendance at the Staff College to volunteer for service in South Africa where he had been with Baden-Powell at the siege of Mafeking. Appointed Commandant of the New Zealand Military Forces in 1910, he displayed considerable organisational ability overseeing the implementation of the new compulsory training scheme and raising the NZEF when the European war erupted. New Zealand-born Colonel Francis Johnston, commanding the New Zealand Infantry Brigade, graduated from Sandhurst with the sword of honour in 1891 and had seen action with the North Staffordshire Regiment during the Sudan campaign (1898) and during the South African War. In New Zealand on furlough in 1914, he was appointed commander of the Wellington Military District and given command of the New Zealand Infantry Brigade on the formation of the NZEF. The habitually pessimistic Colonel Ewan Sinclair-MacLagan commanded the 3rd Australian Infantry Brigade. He saw active service with the Border Regiment in India and was later wounded and awarded the Distinguished Service Order for gallantry as a company commander in South Africa. Recently promoted temporary lieutenant colonel, he was on secondment as the Director of Drill at the Royal Military College, Duntroon, when war broke out and Bridges selected him to raise the 3rd Infantry Brigade. Of all the Australian officers in command appointments he was the most experienced. Other than Birdwood, none of these officers had commanded above company level, and their combat experience had largely been earned in colonial wars against restive natives and agile Boer farmers.

Shy, humourless and brusque Major General William Bridges, commanding the 1st Australian Division, was an Australian Permanent Forces officer. Commissioned into the

LIEUTENANT GENERAL SIR WILLIAM BIRDWOOD, KCMG, CB, DSO, CIE

General Office Commanding Australian and New Zealand Army Corps (ANZAC)

An ambitious soldier characterised by an indifference to danger and an informal manner, Birdwood was popular with the Anzacs and genuinely reciprocated their affection. Graduating from the Royal Military College, Sandhurst, in 1885, he served with the 12th Lancers and the 11th Bengal Lancers on numerous campaigns on the North West Frontier of India. He was on Kitchener's staff during the South African War and commanded the Kohat Brigade on the North West Frontier in 1908. Promoted to major general in 1911, he was appointed Secretary to the Army Department, Government of India, in 1912. Kitchener gave him command of the Australian and New Zealand forces assembling in Egypt where he raised ANZAC in December 1914. A mediocre tactician who sometimes failed to grasp the bigger picture, Birdwood left his staff to complete their work while he visited his troops.

At the landing he allowed Bridges to run the covering force battle and, on coming ashore mid-afternoon, he accepted the stalled situation as he found it and returned to his transport offshore. On being called ashore that night he was horrified when Bridges and Godley urged an immediate evacuation. Initially refusing to accept their advice, he reluctantly acquiesced after a lengthy discussion, but rather than making the decision himself he referred their request to Hamilton. The latter's refusal to countenance what would have been a disastrous move ended the debate.

Throughout the campaign Birdwood was often seen in the trenches chatting with his troops. A teetotaller and non-smoker, he refreshed himself daily by swimming in Anzac Cove in spite of enemy fire, winning the admiration of his soldiers. When Bridges died in May, Birdwood temporarily took command of the AIF until he was formally appointed to the post in September 1915. When the evacuation of the peninsula was again debated in November, Birdwood was the only senior officer who opposed it.

With the expansion of the AIF and NZEF in early 1916, Birdwood took command of I ANZAC and led the corps on the Western Front until November 1917, when he took command of the newly formed Australian Corps. Relinquishing command to Monash in May 1918, he was promoted general and appointed GOC Fifth Army. His success as a commander lay in his leadership and his ability to select able subordinates and high quality staff rather than any tactical or organisational talent. Nonetheless, he set high standards and competently led I ANZAC and the Australian Corps as they developed into first class fighting formations.

Birdwood toured Australia and New Zealand in 1920 where he received a rapturous reception from his former soldiers before returning to the Indian Army, becoming its commander-in-chief in 1925. He retired in 1930 and died in England in 1951.

New South Wales Permanent Artillery in 1885, he was appointed Chief Instructor at the School of Artillery in 1893. During the first six months of the South African War he was attached to a British cavalry division. Widely respected within Australia, he had played a leading role in the formation of the new Australian Army, was the founding Commandant of the Royal Military College and held the Army's top post of Inspector-General when war broke out. His military reputation had been made as a competent administrator and policy staff officer. His temperament, however, discouraged initiative and frank advice from his subordinates. Hamilton, meeting him during a pre-war visit to Australia, had concluded that he would be an excellent chief of staff, but an unlikely leader.

Sydney lawyer Colonel Henry MacLaurin, commanding the 1st Australian Brigade, was the youngest and least experienced of the three brigade commanders drawn from the CMF. Recently promoted lieutenant colonel, he was commanding the 26th Infantry Regiment (CMF) at the time he volunteered for the AIF (an Australian CMF and New Zealand TF infantry regiment equated to a battalion). A Victorian lawyer and politician, the hard-working and abrasive Colonel James McCay commanded the 2nd Australian Brigade. Commissioned into the Victorian Rifles in 1886, he had been a capable Minister for Defence during 1904–05 and had commanded the Australian Intelligence Corps, a part-time organisation, from 1907 to 1912. Commanding the 4th Australian Brigade, Colonel John Monash was a civil engineer and dedicated militia officer with a formidable intellect. Commissioned into the Victorian Garrison Artillery in 1885, he had risen to command the 13th Infantry Brigade (CMF) in 1913, and had earned warm praise from Sir Ian Hamilton during its annual manoeuvres. None of these brigade commanders had seen active service or had much formal training; they were largely self-taught in military matters under the relatively ineffective militia and volunteer system. Monash had supplemented his knowledge with a keen study of military history.

The battalion commanders were all part-timers and had come up through the old militia and volunteer systems. Most, including Lieutenant Colonels George Braund (2nd Battalion), David Wanliss (5th Battalion), Harry Lee (9th Battalion), Lancelot Clarke (12th Battalion) and William Malone (Wellington Battalion), were commanding CMF or TF units when war broke out. Others had also served in the South African War, including Lieutenant Colonel Harold 'Pompey' Elliott (7th Battalion), who had won a Distinguished Conduct Medal while serving as an NCO. At least one, Lieutenant Colonel Walter McNicoll, who was appointed to command the 6th Battalion in early April 1915, had fewer than ten years' part-time service. They were a mixed bag. Lee had spent his entire part-time service in small Queensland regional centres with little opportunity to acquire the knowledge and proficiency required for battalion command; thus his experience was largely administrative. Some, like Malone, Braund and Lieutenant Colonel Stanley Weir (10th Battalion), were keen students of soldiering and demanded hard training and high standards from their officers and men. Others, like Lieutenant Colonel Arthur Plugge of the Auckland Battalion, were less sure of the fundamentals of soldiering but keen critics nonetheless, as Spencer Westmacott was to discover. Having been given charge of the battalion's scouts, Westmacott had trained them according to the current field manual. While exercising them in accordance with the manual

MAJOR GENERAL SIR ALEXANDER GODLEY, KCMG
General Officer Commanding New Zealand and Australian Division

Godley graduated from the Royal Military College, Sandhurst, in 1886 into the Royal Dublin Fusiliers. An enthusiastic horseman, he was passionate about fox hunting and polo. In 1896 he served in a mounted infantry battalion suppressing the Mashonaland Rebellion and, two years later, was accepted into the Staff College at Camberley. Relinquishing his studies, he volunteered for the impending South African War where he served with Colonel Baden-Powell during the Siege of Mafeking, and later as chief staff officer to Lieutenant Colonel Herbert Plumer in the Rhodesian Field Force. Following the war he served in staff and mounted infantry appointments in Aldershot Command.

Godley was promoted temporary major general and tasked with establishing the New Zealand Territorial Force. In this he demonstrated considerable organisational ability and energy and, within three years, had laid a sound basis for the force and provided it with up-to-date equipment and weapons. In August 1914 he raised the NZEF and, with the creation of ANZAC in December 1914, Godley was appointed GOC New Zealand and Australian Division. Although he had seen active service and held field commands as a junior and middle-ranking officer, his training for command at formation level was limited.

Godley took little part in the fighting at the landing, coming ashore at around 3.00 pm with Birdwood, who left Bridges in charge of the battle while Godley largely assumed observer status. That evening he supported Bridges' recommendation for immediate evacuation of the entire force.

Following the landing Godley took charge of the left-hand sector of the ANZAC line where he became known for his indefatigable tours of the lines, although his aloofness, short temper and sharp tongue made him unpopular with his men. To those who worked with him closely, however, he was regarded as a decent, fair, courageous and supportive man who allowed them to perform their duties without undue interference. During the August Offensive Godley commanded the operation to seize the heights of the Sari Bair Range and proved a feeble field commander, failing to control and direct the battle as the situation required.

In March 1916 he commanded II ANZAC and was promoted lieutenant general in September. When the Australian Corps was formed in November 1917, II ANZAC became XXII Corps with Godley retaining command. Throughout the war he retained command of the NZEF and displayed great interest in the health, training and general welfare of the New Zealand troops. An unspectacular divisional and corps commander, his greatest achievements were the establishment of the New Zealand Territorial Force and the raising and training of the NZEF, although he was less impressive in divisional and corps command. Promoted general in 1923, he retired in 1933 and died in England in 1957.

without criticism from Godley, he was berated by Plugge for employing them incorrectly. In the face of 'such contradictory evidence', Westmacott decided to 'drop out as scout officer at the first opportunity'. Time would show that some battalion commanders were to find the exigencies of field command and active service too onerous, and were relieved of command or retired through ill health only months into the campaign.

The Ottoman *III Corps* commanders were all professional soldiers with recent combat experience in large-scale, modern warfare. The Corps Commander, Esat Pasha, was a graduate of the Ottoman Military Academy and the Ottoman Military College, had attended the German War Academy, and had trained with several German units. He commanded a regiment during the Greco–Turkish War (1897) and the provisional *Yanya Corps* during the First Balkan War where he led a spirited defence of the city of Ionnina before being forced to capitulate. Hailed a hero on his return from captivity, he took command of *III Corps* in December 1913. Colonel Halil Sami, commanding the *9th Division*, had initially commanded a regiment and then been appointed Deputy Commander of the *31st Division* during the Balkan Wars. Considered a capable officer, he was promoted to divisional command following the 1913 purge. Lieutenant Colonel Mustafa Kemal, commanding the *19th Division*, first saw combat during the Italian–Turkish War (1912) where he proved himself a skilful combat leader. In the First Balkan War (1912–13) he served as the Chief of Operations of the *Gallipoli Provisional Army* during the fighting in Thrace, and was with the Ottoman forces that recovered most of eastern Thrace from the Bulgarians during the Second Balkan War (1913).

At regimental (brigade) level, both Lieutenant Colonel Mehmet Sefik of the *27th Regiment* and Major Avni of the *57th* had recent combat experience — Avni as Chief of Staff of the *21st Infantry Division* in the Balkan Wars, and Sefik in the Greco–Turkish, Italian–Turkish and Balkan Wars, when he had commanded a *Redif* division in the fight for Salonika. The battalion commanders were junior officers compared to their ANZAC counterparts, and were all majors and captains, the ranks associated with company commanders in the ANZAC battalions. They had experienced modern combat and, while some may have fought as battalion commanders, others had probably fought as company commanders. Major Halis, a combat veteran of the Libyan and Balkan Wars, had taken command of the *3rd Battalion, 27th Regiment (3/27th)*, as recently as September 1914.

MAJOR GENERAL MEHMET ESAT PASHA

Commander *III Corps*

An Albanian born in 1862, Esat graduated from the Ottoman Military High School in 1884 and served in regimental appointments before attending the Imperial Military Academy in 1887. His graduation from General Staff College with high distinction three years later earned him immediate admission to the German War Academy followed by training with several German Army units and formations. He then served on the Ottoman General Staff and as an instructor at the War Academy. As a colonel he commanded a regiment during the Greco–Turkish War of 1897 and, by 1907, he was a major general and Chief of Staff, *Third Army*. He was commanding the *23rd Division* at Yanya when the First Balkan War broke out, and was immediately given command of the *Yanya Corps*. He vigorously defended the city of Ionnina for several months until he was forced to capitulate in March 1913, returning from captivity in December to a hero's welcome and command of *III Corps* at Gallipoli. Under his leadership the corps established itself as one of the most combat-worthy in the Ottoman Army and the only one to meet its mobilisation targets on time in 1914.

With his headquarters at Gallipoli, he deployed the *7th Division* to cover the Bulair Lines near the isthmus and the *9th Division* to the southern half of the peninsula. When the *19th* was assigned to him, he placed it in reserve near Maidos in lieu of the *8th Division*. His initial plan was to defend well forward on the beaches with local reserves close behind, but when General Liman von Sanders took responsibility for the defence in March 1915, the dispositions were changed to defend the coast lightly with strong central reserves.

Learning of the landings early on 25 April, Esat sailed to Maidos and set up a forward headquarters at Mal Tepe around noon. Soon afterwards he established two fronts to control the fighting on Sari Bair and at Cape Helles, assigning the Sari Bair front to Lieutenant Colonel Mustafa Kemal, Commander *19th Division*, and leaving Colonel Halil Sami, Commander *9th Division*, in control of the Cape Helles front. Leaving his commanders to fight their separate fronts, he turned his attention to organising reinforcements. As Liman von Sanders believed an assault might still be made against the Bulair Lines, reinforcements were drawn from *XV Corps* on the Asiatic shore and assigned to Esat's command.

In October 1915 he was appointed Commander *First Army*. In January 1918 he took over the *Fifth Army* at the Dardanelles and in June assumed command of the *Third Army* on the Caucasus front. Following the Armistice, Esat served as Inspector-General of the mostly demobilised *Second Army* until his retirement in November 1919. In 1920 he was the Navy Minister in the short-lived cabinet of Hulusi Salih Pasha. Esat died in Istanbul in 1952.

CHAPTER 4

DEFENDING THE DARDANELLES

A DEFENSIVE DILEMMA

Ottoman defensive preparations on the Gallipoli peninsula were well established. Indeed, as recently as February 1913, heavy fighting against the Bulgarians had occurred in the Bulair Lines around the isthmus. In August 1914, Lieutenant Colonel Perrinet von Thauvenay of the German Military Mission began updating the defensive plan, with *III Corps* tasked to reinforce *CFAC* and defend the peninsula. The *26th* and *27th regiments* already at Gallipoli began moving into coastal defensive positions in late August and early September. Considerable effort was devoted to implementing all elements of the plan. Defences along the coast were improved and new roads built to facilitate the rapid movement of reserves. Defensive manoeuvres were practised by day and night and, by November, combined arms training between infantry and artillery was also being conducted. While Churchill's ill-considered naval bombardment on 3 November served to accelerate this program, the real impetus came after the 18 March attempt to force the Narrows which resulted in the creation of the Ottoman *Fifth Army* under the command of Liman von Sanders. *CFAC* and *III Corps* were placed under his command, as were *XV Corps*, the *5th Division* and an independent cavalry brigade. His area of operations was extensive, running from the Gulf of Saros west of the isthmus, through the Gallipoli peninsula to the Asiatic shore south of the Dardanelles.

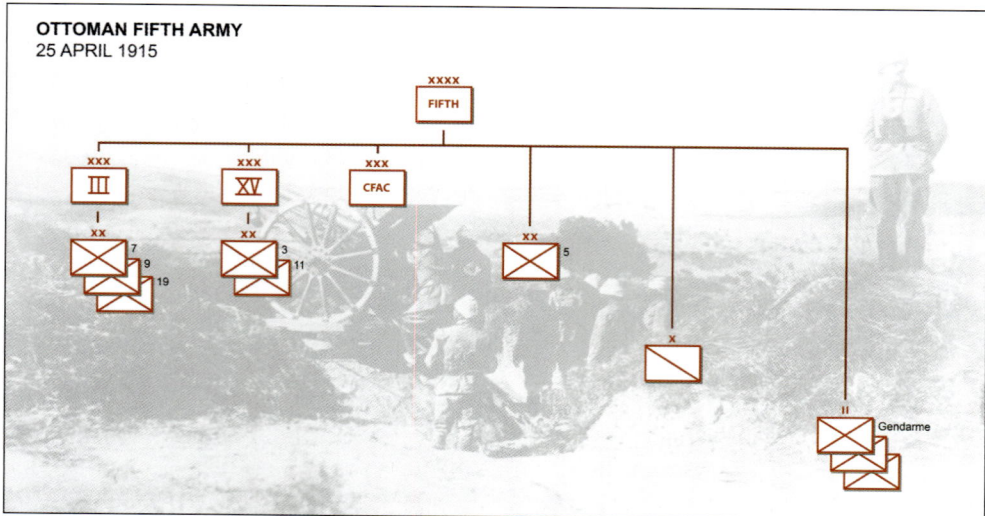

Defending a long coastline is a difficult task and there are rarely sufficient forces to cover all possible landing sites in depth. Generally, two options are open to the defender. The first involves defending forward, placing most of the force on and close behind the beaches across the whole front, with a small reserve held centrally. The intent is to defeat the enemy at the shoreline and deny him a foothold. Supporters of this view argue that the enemy is most vulnerable trying to get ashore and that, once a beachhead is established, it is difficult to eject him. The critics counter that, in trying to defend everywhere, the commander effectively defends nowhere as, at the operational level, the defence is spread thinly across the whole front. Should the enemy achieve overwhelming strength at the point of landing — as is likely — and break through, the reserve may be too small and too far away to achieve an effective counterpunch. Furthermore, only a small portion of the entire defensive force can react to the invasion within a relatively short period. The bulk of the force is defending a shoreline that is not under threat, and cannot or may not be moved quickly to concentrate against the invasion force. In addition, there is always the uncomfortable thought that the initial landing may be a feint intended to draw in the defending forces.

The second option is to defend lightly forward and hold strong reserves back in central locations. Getting the balance right is the challenge. This option is designed to provide a screen to disrupt and delay the enemy landings and contain the invading force before it can break out of the bridgehead. The enemy force can then be hit with a powerful reserve to either seal off the lodgement or overwhelm it and drive it back into the sea. This requires quick and aggressive action in committing the reserves before the enemy can consolidate a suitable beachhead and break out of it. Critics argue that this significantly increases the enemy's chances of success as the reserves may be interdicted, making subsequent ejection of the enemy almost impossible. A delay in committing the reserve until confirmation that the landing is not a diversion may also benefit the enemy. Supporters of this option accept that a foothold will be gained, but argue that a much more powerful force can be deployed quickly against the actual invasion site to seal it off and prevent the enemy from achieving his intent. Numerical superiority, or at least parity, can be established at the threatened point more quickly, and strong counter-attacks can be executed before the enemy has time to consolidate his gains. Both options have their merits and disadvantages. When resources are limited priorities must be determined.

Initially the Ottomans chose to defend forward, with the bulk of their battalions deployed along the coast, each infantry regiment allocated a sector for defence. On assuming command of the *Fifth Army* in late March, however, Liman von Sanders opted to defend the coast lightly and hold strong central reserves, consequently ordering a redeployment of his forces and allocating them according to his assessment of the most likely invasion sites. The most dangerous area and, in his opinion, the most likely with its long beaches, was the isthmus and the head of the Gulf of Saros. A successful landing there could quickly isolate the forces on the peninsula, and it also provided the shortest route to Constantinople. His next priority was the Asiatic shore south of the mouth of the Dardanelles. Cape Helles, at the tip of the peninsula, with its restricted landing beaches, was his third most likely site, and the fourth priority was the Aegean coast between the Cape and Suvla Bay. Accordingly, he deployed the cavalry brigade to screen the northern shore of the Gulf of Saros, the *5th Division* defended

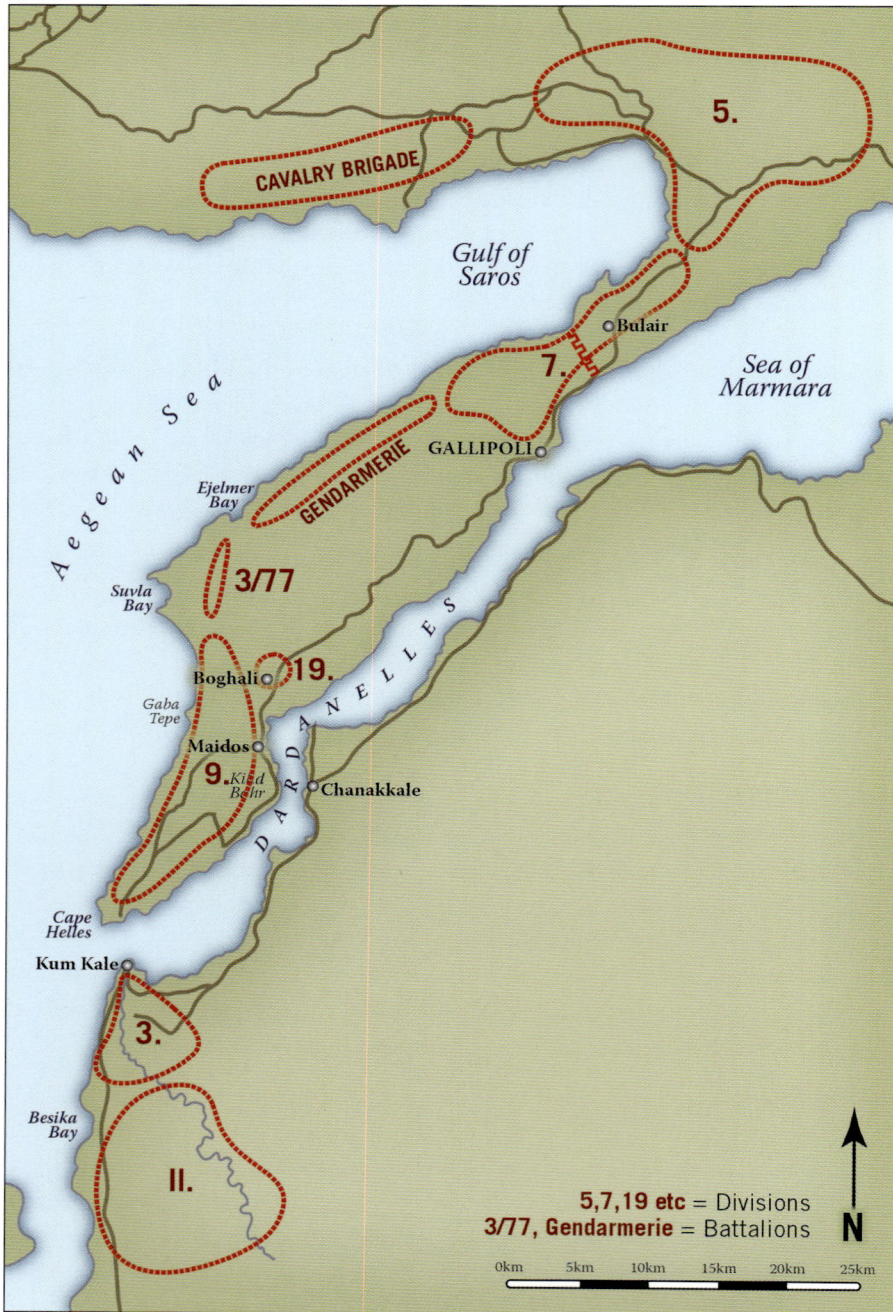

The Gallipoli peninsula showing the Ottoman *Fifth Army* dispositions on 25 April 1915. In the north the *5th Division* covers the head of the Gulf of Saros, while *III Corps* defends the peninsula with the *7th Division* occupying the Bulair Lines on the neck of the peninsula. Further south a *Gendarmerie battalion* provides a screen along the rugged coast of the Aegean, and the *3rd Battalion, 77th Regiment*, covers the hills inland from Suvla Bay. The *9th Division* is assigned the southern peninsula while the *19th Division* is the *Fifth Army* reserve at Boghali. On the Asiatic shore *XV Corps*, with the *3rd* and *11th divisions*, defends the coast south of Kum Kale.

the head of the Gulf, *III Corps* retained responsibility for the peninsula, and *XV Corps* was deployed to the Asiatic shore. Within *III Corps*, the *7th Division* continued to defend the old Bulair Lines on the isthmus, the *9th Division* retained responsibility for the southern half of the peninsula, while the *19th Division* was designated the *Fifth Army* reserve reporting to Liman von Sanders himself.

THE SOUTHERN PENINSULA

Within the *9th Division*'s area, the peninsula gradually widens from Cape Helles like an elongated triangle to the Kilid Bahr Plateau where it is 12 kilometres wide at its broadest point. It then narrows at the valley between Gaba Tepe on the Aegean coast and Maidos (modern day Eceabat) on the Dardanelles, before widening again into the great hill masses south-east, east and north-east of Suvla Bay.

From the cape the ground slopes gradually like a long glacis for nine kilometres to the Achi Baba Ridge. Anyone holding Achi Baba has observation over the glacis approaches, and from the south it is the only ground of tactical importance before reaching the Kilid Bahr Plateau. From Achi Baba the ground drops quickly along spurs and broken country for three kilometres to the foot of the Kilid Bahr Plateau, which sits like a great bastion astride the peninsula. Horseshoe shaped, roughly nine kilometres by six, and rising steeply to an average elevation of 170 metres, it is a strong natural defensive position. Its greatest value is that it overlooks the narrowest portion of the Dardanelles and the narrow coastal plain to the west, and its fortifications housed the heavy artillery batteries that covered both the Narrows and the approaches to it. Further north the plateau dominates the low valley, some three to six kilometres wide, running between Gaba Tepe and Maidos. The valley offers an easy avenue of approach to the Kilid Bahr Plateau from the Aegean Sea, but its narrowness also makes it vulnerable. Overlooking this valley to the north is the Sari Bair Range, a large massif running north-east from the coast for six and half kilometres to the narrow valley through which runs the Gallipoli–Biyuk Anafarta–Boghali–Maidos road. Sari Bair dominates not only the Gaba Tepe–Maidos Valley and the northern approaches to the Kilid Bahr Plateau, but also the land communications down the peninsula. An invasion force attempting to reach the plateau via the Gaba Tepe–Maidos Valley is vulnerable to any defending force holding the range. While the southern ridges of the range fall relatively gradually to this valley, the northern or seaward slopes are a different matter. They drop sharply to a valley running due east from the coast south of Suvla Bay through the village of Biyuk Anafarta to the Gallipoli–Maidos road. This valley was the *9th Division*'s northern boundary. Further east and north-east lies the large mass of hills occupying the width of the peninsula all the way to the isthmus.

The coastal frontage of this area is 32 kilometres. Two small beaches, separated by a broad headland, are at the tip of the peninsula, while on the Aegean coast sheer cliffs interspersed with the odd landing spot extend north for around 20 kilometres. Further north, long beaches extend to Gaba Tepe, a small promontory jutting into the Aegean Sea. From there Brighton Beach runs north to Anzac Cove; both Brighton Beach and the cove lie at the foot of the Sari Bair Range. North Beach extends from the cove all the way to Suvla Bay.

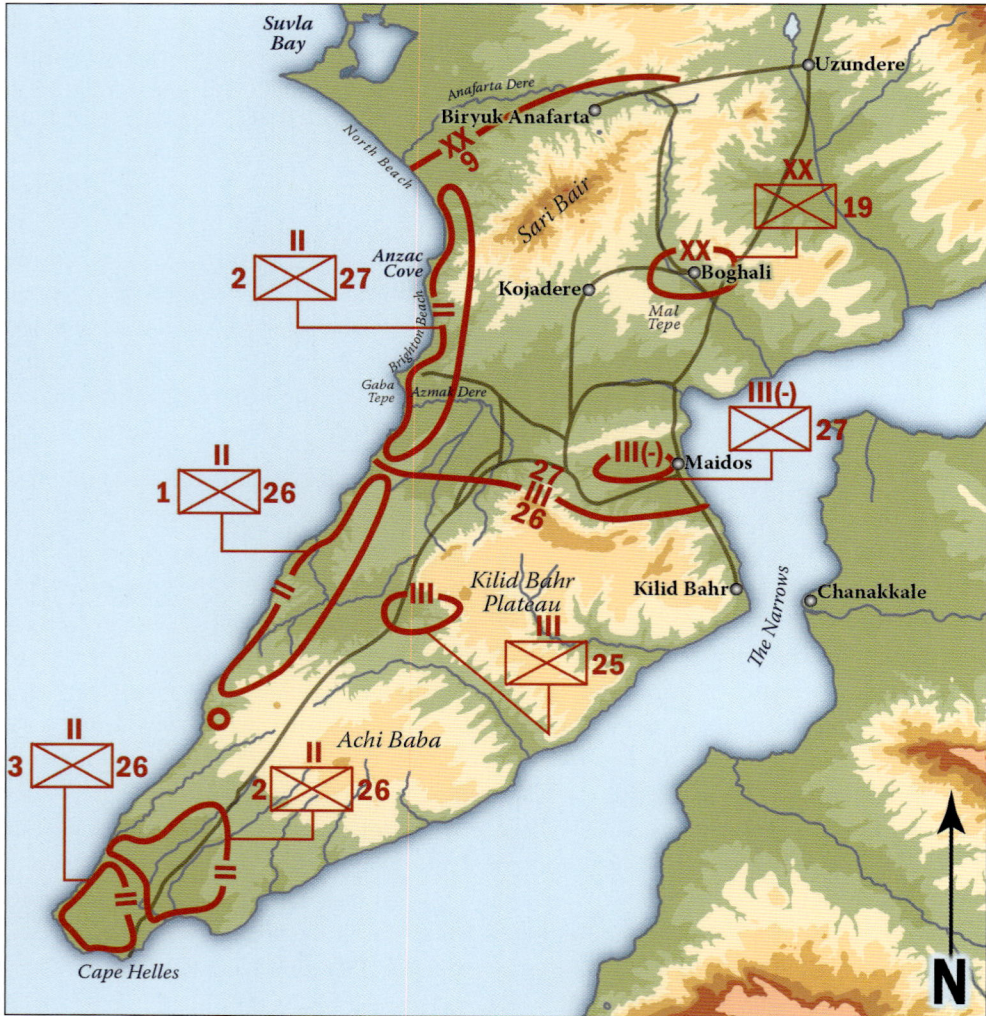

The southern peninsula showing the dispositions of the *9th Division* on 25 April. The peninsula was divided into two sectors between the *26th* and *27th infantry regiments*. In the south the *26th* deployed the *2nd* and *3rd battalions* at Cape Helles mounting the strongest defences, with the *1st Battalion* providing a screen along the Aegean coast. The *27th Regiment*'s *2nd Battalion* screens 12 kilometres of coast either side of Gaba Tepe and the foot of the Sari Bair Range, while the remainder of the regiment is in reserve near Maidos. Behind the *1/26th*, the *25th Regiment* is the *9th Division* reserve. To the south-east of Sari Bair, the *19th Division* is encamped around Boghali, providing the *Fifth Army* reserve.

DEFENDING THE SOUTHERN PENINSULA

The *9th Division* had nine infantry battalions, two machine-gun companies, and four field and two mountain gun batteries. Following Liman von Sanders' defensive concept, four infantry battalions were deployed along the coast and around Cape Helles, and five battalions and the machine-gun companies were held in reserve. One battalion of the *27th Regiment* held the Sari Bair coastline and the beach south of Gaba Tepe, while the *26th Regiment*, which lacked a machine-gun company, held the remaining coast down to and around Cape

Helles. The remainder of the *27th* was in reserve near Maidos, and the *25th Regiment* was concentrated around Serafim Farm on the south-western edge of the Kilid Bahr Plateau. The *3rd Battalion, 9th Artillery Regiment* (*3/9th Arty*), consisting of two mountain batteries, was allotted to the *27th Regiment*, while the two field artillery battalions (*1/9th Arty* and *2/9th Arty*) supported the *25th* and *26th regiments*. In a prescient decision, Liman von Sanders moved the *Fifth Army* reserve, the *19th Division*, with another eight battalions and two machine-gun companies, from Maidos to Boghali, just south-west of the Sari Bair Range. One battalion from the *19th Division*, the *3rd* of the *77th Regiment* (*3/77th*), was detached to guard the coast from Suvla Bay to Ece Bay in the north. In the few weeks remaining, training continued at a frenetic pace with an emphasis on practising defensive arrangements and anti-invasion exercises by day and night.

THE ANZAC BATTLEFIELD

The Sari Bair Range thrusts inland from the Aegean Sea to a height of 300 metres at Hill 971, the highest feature on the range four kilometres from the coast. From there it runs another two kilometres to a broad bluff 150 metres high overlooking a low saddle, through which the Maidos–Boghali–Biyuk Anafarta road runs. The range is a commanding feature. Its tactical importance lies in its extensive fields of observation over the surrounding country, and its dominance of the roads to the north and north-west of Maidos, which itself is a major ferry point across the Dardanelles. With artillery observation posts on the heights, field guns on its southern flanks could command the whole of the Gaba Tepe–Maidos Valley, providing an interlocking field of fire with guns on the northern side of the Kilid Bahr Plateau. Ottoman forces occupying the range would pose a direct threat to the flank of any force attempting to push across the valley from Gaba Tepe. Thus an Allied force seeking to isolate or attack the Kilid Bahr Plateau from the west, north-west and north had to secure Sari Bair.

From the coast to the broad bluff, numerous ridges and spurs shoot out from Sari Bair like the bones of a fish. On the northern side they drop sharply, intermingled with cliffs and a mass of tangled gullies. The first four spurs from the coast end as foothills overlooking the southern half of North Beach; further inland they loom over the Anafarta Valley. While North Beach provides excellent landing sites, the northern slopes of the range are so broken and tangled as to preclude establishing a suitable beachhead and make egress from the beach extremely difficult. The narrow, steep and tangled ridges are difficult to ascend, provide excellent delaying positions to the high ground, and can be held by relatively light forces. On the southern side of the range the ridges are broader and descend gently like long fingers to the Gaba Tepe–Maidos Valley. Movement along the crests is easy and they provide suitable approaches to the spine of the range.

The most significant of these ridges slips off the range 500 metres east of Hill 971 and runs almost due south for four and a half kilometres to Mal Tepe, a 160-metre-high hill two and a half kilometres from the Dardanelles. This ridge dominated the road junctions in the area and the 1915 north-south land communications down the peninsula. Holding

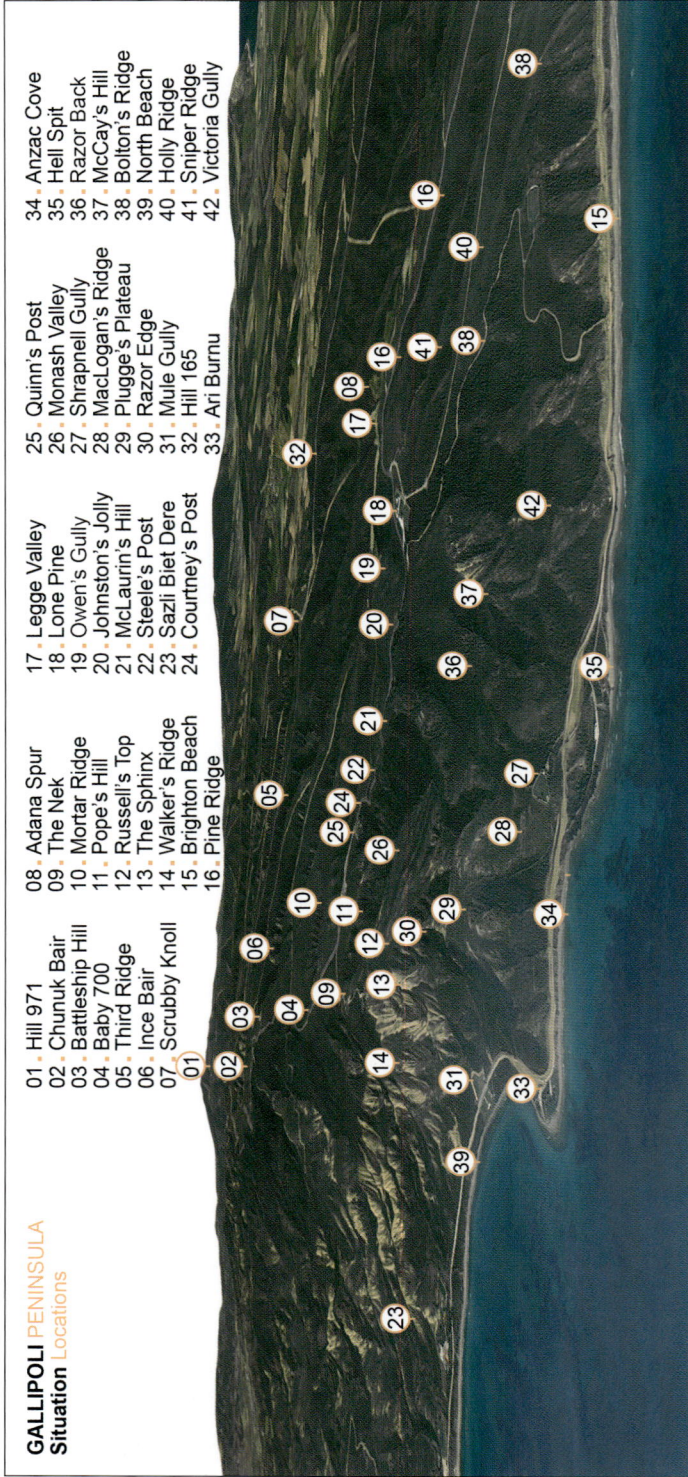

The Sari Bair Range showing the locations of the features mentioned in the text.

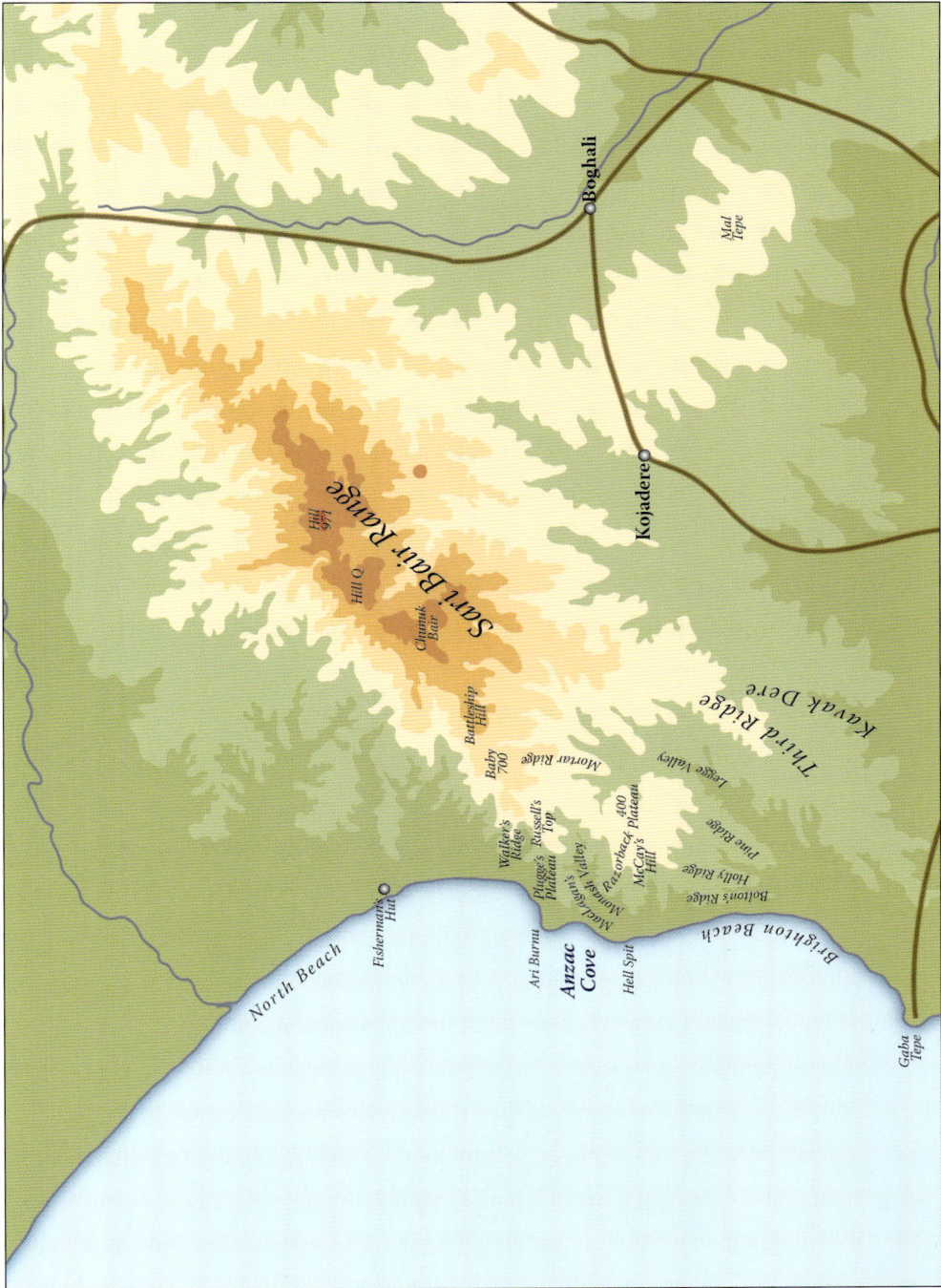

The Sari Bair Range showing the main features. Anzac Cove is 470 m wide and lies 3.1 km north of Gaba Tepe. Distances from the cove: to the western edge of the 400 Plateau is 800m; due east to Second Ridge is 1 km; due east to the crest of Third Ridge is 2.4 km; to Baby 700 is 1.6 km; to Battleship Hill is 2.1 km; to Chunuk Bair is 3.1 km; to Hill 971 is 4 km. The crest of Third Ridge is 1 km from the western edge of the 400 Plateau, and from the northern point of the cove to the Fisherman's Hut is 1.2 km.

Mal Tepe and the ridge to the heights would interdict these communications and cut off the forces on the Kilid Bahr Plateau. Mal Tepe also provides observation over the kink in the Dardanelles and its narrowest sections, enabling the accurate adjustment of naval and artillery gunfire over this portion of the waterway and the main ferry points between the peninsula and the Asiatic shore.

From Hill 971, the spine of the range runs south-west towards the coast through Hill Q to the broad height of Chunuk Bair where the range bifurcates and the prominent Third or Gun Ridge branches off to the south. These three heights are the vital ground. Whoever holds them controls the Sari Bair Range. Hill 971 covers the upper reaches of the Mal Tepe Ridge, and Chunuk Bair covers the upper reaches of Third Ridge — any force holding these can take an enemy line along the two ridges from the flank. The heights also provide observation over the Gaba Tepe–Maidos Valley and the main road junctions, enabling accurate adjustment of artillery and naval gunfire onto positions sited in these areas.

Slowly curving around to the west from Chunuk Bair, Third or Gun Ridge descends to the coast ending at the Gaba Tepe promontory, six kilometres away. Numerous long spurs run off either side, giving its seaward slopes a corrugated landscape. It is the other prominent ridge flowing off the southern flank of the range, and any defender holding it sits directly on the flank of an invasion force moving along the Gaba Tepe–Maidos Valley. For the Allies, the ridge offered an avenue of approach to the vital ground and a good position for a flank guard or covering force against any Ottoman forces approaching from Maidos.

Continuing south-west from Chunuk Bair, the main range descends through another two broad, rounded crests — Battleship Hill and the slightly lower Baby 700 — where the range bifurcates again into First and Second ridges. Dominating the upper reaches of both ridges, Baby 700 is the ground of tactical importance for any force occupying either ridge. Immediately before the bifurcation, Mortar Ridge flows off the inland shoulder of Baby 700 heading due south for 1000 metres. While Mortar Ridge offers little tactical value, it provides depth to the upper reaches of Second Ridge, but to hold it a force must hold Baby 700. From the foot of Mortar Ridge, the large Legge Valley separates Second and Third ridges and intersects the coast just north of Gaba Tepe.

The 400 Plateau looking south across the upper reaches of Monash Valley from First Ridge (Russell's Top) (John Lafferty image).

Second Ridge, with its steep, almost precipitous seaward slopes, runs south-south-west from Baby 700 for 1000 metres before broadening out into a two-lobed upland known as the 400 Plateau. From there the ridge divides, like the fingers of a hand, into several smaller ridges and spurs. Two go west: the Razorback which drops into Shrapnel Gully, and McCay's Hill, which juts over the northern end of Brighton Beach. Next, Bolton's Ridge heads south-west before turning south overlooking Brighton Beach for almost 1300 metres. Inland of Bolton's are six roughly parallel spurs. Branching off Bolton's Ridge, the significant Holly Ridge closely parallels it for 800 metres. Then three short features, Silt Spur, Sniper's Ridge and Weir Ridge, run south off the southern lobe of the plateau. Finally,

The Sari Bair Range from the north, showing the rugged country which drops sharply to the north off the main range. Ari Burnu and Plugge's Plateau are on the far right. Moving left, the image illustrates the sharp drop to the Razor Edge and then the Sphinx and Russell's Top to The Nek (trees) above which looms Baby 700 and then Battleship Hill, Chunuk Bair, Hill Q and Hill 971 on the left skyline (John Lafferty image).

Pine Ridge slides off the south-eastern corner of the plateau and cuts south-west for 1000 metres. Overlooked by Third Ridge, Battleship Hill and Baby 700, Second Ridge is of little tactical value apart from its extension, Bolton's Ridge, which looms over the northern half of Brighton Beach and provides a steep ascent for any invader coming ashore there. Once atop Bolton's, however, Second Ridge provides an avenue of approach to the vital ground via Baby 700 and Battleship Hill.

Pope's Hill, a short spur, juts out from Baby 700 like an appendix into the head of Monash Valley between Second and First ridges. It has little tactical value other than providing an enfilade (flanking) position to any force moving along First Ridge and down Second Ridge from Baby 700. From Baby 700, First Ridge crosses The Nek, a narrowing of the crest, and heads south-west for one kilometre as the steep-sided Russell's Top. It then drops to the aptly named Razor Edge, an exceptionally narrow, sharp-sided 250-metre-long feature, along which a man can walk only with difficulty. It then rises again to the small, flat-topped Plugge's Plateau which overlooks Anzac Cove. From Plugge's the ground drops sharply to Ari Burnu, the northern headland of Anzac Cove, while to the south it descends as a long spur — MacLagan's Ridge — enclosing the cove to Hell Spit. The northern side of First Ridge drops sharply in tangled gullies and cliffs, the most prominent The Sphinx, which thrusts out from Russell's Top presenting a perpendicular face to the coast. The only suitable access to Russell's Top from North Beach is along Walker's Ridge which joins the Top 300 metres from The Nek. On the southern side, the narrow, steep-sided Monash Valley separates First and Second ridges. Running from The Nek into Shrapnel Gully, the valley emerges on the coast at the northern end of Brighton Beach below Hell Spit. Climbing out of the valley onto First and Second ridges is often a two-handed exercise. The overall tactical value of First Ridge is limited; however, for any force occupying the seaward slopes of Second Ridge, holding First Ridge is vital to prevent aimed fire into the rear of the force. For a defender, Plugge's Plateau and MacLagan's Ridge tower over Anzac Cove, but neither is a good defensive position due to limited fields of fire and dead ground. For an attacker Anzac Cove, while shielded from Gaba Tepe and North Beach, offers a very limited landing site backed by steep hills, and the Razor Edge makes First Ridge a difficult approach from the beach to the vital ground. Once on Russell's Top, however, the going is easy.

The lower end of First Ridge showing Ari Burnu and Plugge's Plateau from North Beach with the Razor Edge on the left of the photo. The bulk of the *2nd Platoon*, 8th Company, was on the plateau, and a squad of riflemen was on Ari Burnu, the height on the right overlooking the beach. A rifle squad from Ibrahim's *1st Platoon* was in the area of the red seating below Plugge's Plateau. On 25 April the 11th Battalion and A company of the 12th landed on the beach in the foreground (John Lafferty image).

27TH REGIMENT DISPOSITIONS

Lieutenant Colonel Mehmet Sefik deployed one battalion, the *2/27th* under Major Ismet, along 12 kilometres of coastline on what he described as 'security and observation duties', anchoring the centre of the battalion on the old fortifications at Gaba Tepe. Three rifle companies were positioned on the coast, each covering roughly four kilometres of beach. The northernmost, the *8th Company*, was sited between the *9th Division*'s northern boundary, north of the Aghyl Dere, and McCay's Hill, just south of Anzac Cove. From

Second Ridge from Russell's Top. View from Baby 700 on the left to the 400 Plateau on the right, showing how Baby 700 dominates the ridge. Pope's Hill is the spur running off Baby 700 into the head of Monash Valley in the left foreground. The white monument is on Lone Pine, the southern lobe of the 400 Plateau, while McCay's Hill runs off out of the right edge of the photo (author's image).

there the *7th Company*, supported by two half-platoons of the *5th*, occupied the centre, covering the southern portion of Brighton Beach down to the Asmak Dere, just south of Gaba Tepe. On the southern flank the *6th Company* was entrenched along Palamutlu Ridge covering the long stretch of beach south of Gaba Tepe to Semerly Tepe. Positioned centrally behind the beach defences, the remainder of the *5th Company* was in reserve two and a half kilometres east of Gaba Tepe. Ismet's headquarters on the promontory was linked to each of his companies by telephone cable and back to the *9th Division* headquarters at Maidos. The remaining battalions of Sefik's regiment, the *1/27th* and *3/27th*, and his machine-gun company, were held in reserve near Maidos, seven kilometres from Gaba Tepe.

Located squarely across the foot of the Sari Bair Range, Captain Faik's *8th Company* had two platoons on the coast and one in reserve. On the right Second Lieutenant Ibradili Ibrahim's *1st Platoon* was concentrated around the Fisherman's Hut and what later became No. 1 Outpost, 1200 metres north of Ari Burnu. Ibrahim deployed two nine-man rifle squads to each flank, one located near the Aghyl Dere to the north, the other covering the southern end of North Beach, not far from Ari Burnu. On the left, the bulk of the *2nd Platoon*, under Second Lieutenant Muharrem, occupied Plugge's Plateau, with a nine-man rifle squad located forward on the Ari Burnu headland, and another on Hell Spit. While Plugge's provided a fine observation point up and down the coast, it had limited fields of fire as the ground dropped sharply on all sides. Any troops landing immediately below it would occupy dead ground — ground sheltered from direct enemy fire. The *3rd Platoon*, under Sergeant Major Suleyman, was in reserve with Faik on Second Ridge, not far from Baby 700, and one squad of this platoon was detached to McCay's Hill overlooking the northern end of Brighton Beach. Further south, Second Lieutenant Ismail Hakki's platoon of the *7th Company* occupied the southern half of Bolton's Ridge overlooking Brighton Beach, but again the position had limitations, with the beach itself presenting dead ground to troops on the ridge. The remainder of the *7th Company* was deployed around Gaba Tepe itself, which provided good fields of enfilade fire along the beaches either side and the seaward approaches to these.

Turkish infantry cleaning their rifles on the peninsula. Mobilised in August 1914, the *27th Regiment* had spent over seven months training on the ground on which they would fight during 25 April and proved a well-trained and courageous enemy. The *57th Regiment* had spent almost four months training in the Sari Bair area and also fought well, driving the Anzacs back down the main range (Harvey Broadbent image).

For artillery support Sefik placed Captain Sadik's mountain battery of the *3/9th Arty* on the 400 Plateau in direct support of the *2/27th*, with the priority target on Brighton Beach. It was supplemented by two heavier guns at Gaba Tepe. Although the British *Official History* refers to these as two 120mm (4.7-inch) guns, Turkish sources indicate that they were two old 87mm field guns, one of which had a broken elevating lever and thus could not be fired. Both Sefik and Hakki describe the artillery at Gaba Tepe as one old, slow-firing Mantelli gun, the Ottoman term for the 87mm field gun. Further south a battery of four old 150mm

Anzac Cove from the top of Plugge's Plateau. Note the beach is in dead ground to troops standing on the edge of the plateau (author's image).

(5.9-inch) guns lay behind the *6th Company* and the Palamutlu Ridge, but according to Sefik they could only fire out to sea. The second mountain battery of the *3/9th Arty* was held in reserve south of Maidos near the Kilid Bahr Plateau. The Gaba Tepe defences also sported two 1-inch Nordenfelt volley guns capable of covering the southern half of Brighton Beach and the northern portion of the beach south of the promontory.

Officers of the *27th Regiment* later in the campaign. Lieutenant Colonel Mehmet Sefik, Commander *27th Regiment*, in the centre, Captain Halis, commanding the *3rd Battalion*, sits to Sefik's right, and Captain Faik, commanding the *8th Company*, is standing on the right (Sedar Ataksor image).

Officers of the Ottoman *19th Division*; Lieutenant Colonel Mustafa Kemal, the Divisional Commander, is standing fourth from the left with a cigarette-holder in his hand (AWM P01141_001).

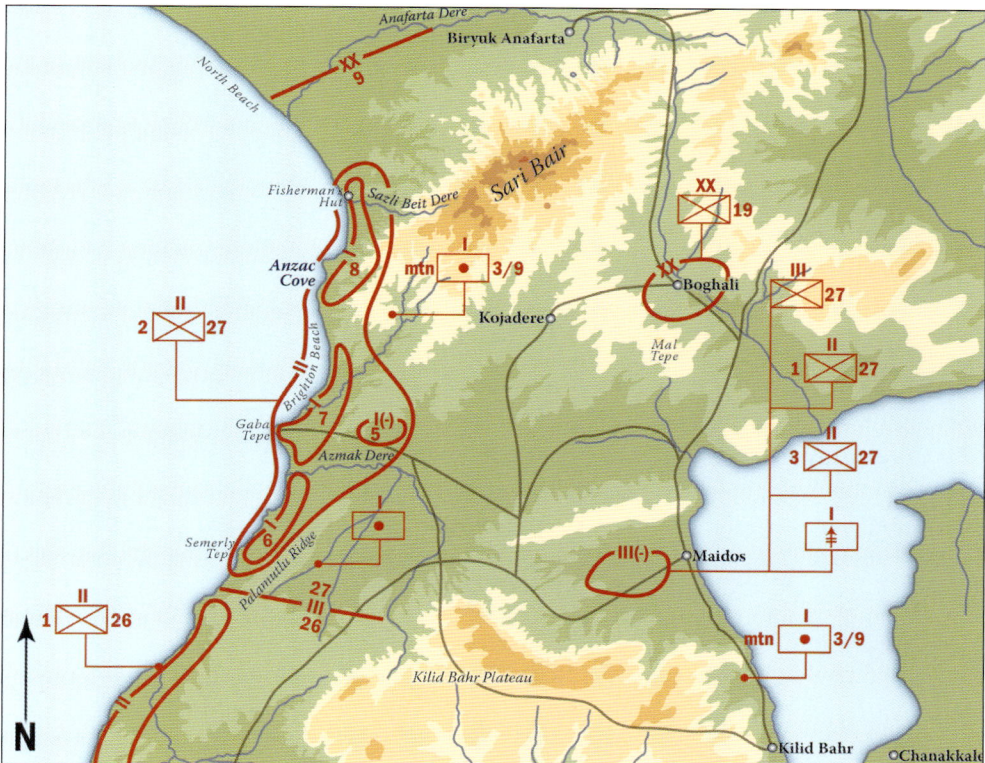

The dispositions of the *27th Infantry Regiment* on 25 April 1915. Deployed forward, the *2nd Battalion* has three rifle companies (*6th*, *7th* and *8th*) covering the 12 kilometres of coast between Semerly Tepe and the Fisherman's Hut, with the *5th Company* in reserve two and half kilometres east of Gaba Tepe. The remainder of the regiment, the *1/27th*, *3/27th* and the machine-gun company are in reserve near Maidos. A battery of four mountain guns of the *3rd Battalion*, *9th Artillery*, is at Lone Pine. The other mountain battery of the *3/9th Artillery* is south of Maidos, and a battery of four 15cm heavy guns is sited behind the Palamutlu Ridge.

Discounting any possibility that the Allies would make a serious landing at Anzac Cove and the beaches north of it, Liman von Sanders and his subordinates expected that an Allied landing in the *27th Regiment*'s area would occur on the beaches either side of Gaba Tepe. The strongest defences, therefore, were around the promontory itself, taking advantage of its enfilade position. Should the Allies land here, the *2/27th* would disrupt and delay them, while the remainder of the regiment marched rapidly to the threatened point to contain the beachhead before it could be expanded. Stronger reserves would then follow, seal off the incursion and drive the invaders back into the sea.

CHAPTER 5

AN AMPHIBIOUS OPERATION

GETTING ASHORE

An amphibious landing on a defended shore is among the most difficult of military operations. The last time the British had undertaken such a landing was Abercrombie's brilliant assault at Aboukir Bay, Egypt, against the French in 1801. Over the intervening century or more, the means of getting ashore had not changed — men crammed into open boats would be rowed the final yards to the beach with no protection whatsoever. What had changed was the vastly increased range and lethality of small arms, exposing the men in the boats to a far deadlier reception.

The attacker employs several means to overcome the difficulties of getting ashore and breaking out of a beachhead. The first involves achieving strategic or at least tactical surprise by landing where the enemy is not expecting an invasion. To preserve the element of surprise, deception and feints are often employed to mask the location of the main landing, forcing the defender to spread his forces across the whole coastline and either deploy his reserves early to the wrong place or withhold deploying them until the situation is clarified. Such deception must be realistic, reinforce the foe's preconceived views on where the landing will occur, and be maintained long enough to cause the enemy uncertainty, thereby delaying the deployment of his reserves. Ideally, the deception should persuade the enemy to regard the actual landing as a feint, and the deception as the true landing, as occurred with Operation Fortitude, the deception operation covering Operation Overlord in 1944.

Second, the attacker seeks to land a numerically superior force capable of quickly breaching the enemy's defensive line. This requires sufficient shipping and landing craft to move large numbers of troops ashore rapidly on a relatively wide front, preferably against a portion of coast that is lightly held. Width improves the chances of breaching a weak point and exploiting this to take the stronger posts from the rear. Once he has broken through the coastal defences, the invader then has to fight for and establish a sufficiently deep and broad beachhead within which to build up his forces for the breakout. In doing so, the initial force ashore seeks to capture a covering position on tactically significant ground that protects the follow-on forces, allowing them to establish themselves ashore without interference from the enemy. The *Field Service Pocket Book 1914* defined a covering position as 'a position to be occupied by an advanced detachment of troops at such a distance from the selected landing that neither anchorage, beach, nor forming up place are exposed to shell fire from the enemy's land forces.' A deep bridgehead allows the follow-on force to land without becoming immediately engaged or suffering undue interference from the enemy. The beachhead also has to be large enough to provide some freedom of manoeuvre for the breakout. Too narrow and shallow a beachhead makes it easier for the defender to concentrate forces to seal it off, interfere with the landing of the main body, and mount counter-attacks to stall and defeat the invasion. Conversely, a broader and deeper bridgehead makes the enemy's task more difficult, forcing him to disperse his reinforcements over a wider area to contain it, and thus having less concentrated strength with which to mount an effective counter-attack.

Third, speed is of the essence. For the invader, quickly securing the ground of tactical importance and a sufficiently deep beachhead, and rapidly building up the force for the breakout is essential. Any delay is likely to hand the initiative to the enemy, allowing him to concentrate his reserves and contain the incursion, as occurred at Anzio in 1944 during the Italian campaign.

Australian infantry practising disembarkation training on Lemnos Island. Conducted under battalion auspices it generally involved rowing ashore followed by a route march (AWM P00821_005).

PREPARATIONS

The naval operation had effectively robbed the MEF of any strategic surprise. Thus, tactical surprise, limited though it would be, rested on the quality of the deception and feints employed. However, time and resources prevented the Allies achieving anything credible over a long period. The concentration of the force in Mudros Harbour and aerial reconnaissance conducted over the southern portion of the peninsula only heightened Ottoman awareness that an invasion was imminent. Success now depended on the operational plan, how well it was executed, the capabilities of the force, and the reactions and capabilities of the Ottoman defenders.

In the weeks following the decision to conduct the military operation, the Allies mounted an extensive reconnaissance program from the sea and by air. Naval vessels carrying military observers conducted cruises along the coast seeking to pinpoint the enemy's defences. At a distance, however, they could gain only a general feel for the coastal entrenchments. Air patrols over the peninsula were more successful and produced quite an accurate picture of the Ottoman dispositions down to artillery battery locations, their entrenchments and the locations of reserves. Any suggestion they should have identified machine-gun positions, as one historian argues that they failed to do, is patently absurd. The map on page 74 illustrates the level of detail recorded in the Kilid Bahr–Sari Bair area. It also shows that the old Turkish maps the Allies used, and which were issued to ANZAC, while not perfect by today's standards, were substantially better than described in popular myth. What the maps in the Sari Bair area did not show, however, was the Razor Edge between Plugge's Plateau and Russell's Top, and this was to have a significant impact on the deployment of troops on 25 April.

On 3 April 1915 ANZAC began breaking camp around Cairo and moving to Alexandria to embark for Lemnos Island to join the 3rd Australian Infantry Brigade in Mudros Harbour. Birdwood, Bridges and their staffs arrived on 12 April, and the next day were briefed on the impending operation, the naval arrangements and updated on the latest intelligence on Ottoman dispositions. Boarding HMS *Queen* on 14 April with the 1st Australian Division's brigade and battalion commanders, they reconnoitred the coastline from Bulair to Cape Helles, paying special attention to Gaba Tepe. Over the next week the troops practised landing operations. However, rather than full rehearsals for the coming operation, these were simply disembarkation practices undertaken at battalion level, generally followed by route marches.

New Zealanders undertaking disembarkation training in Mudros Harbour in the week before the landing (Alexander Turnbull Library).

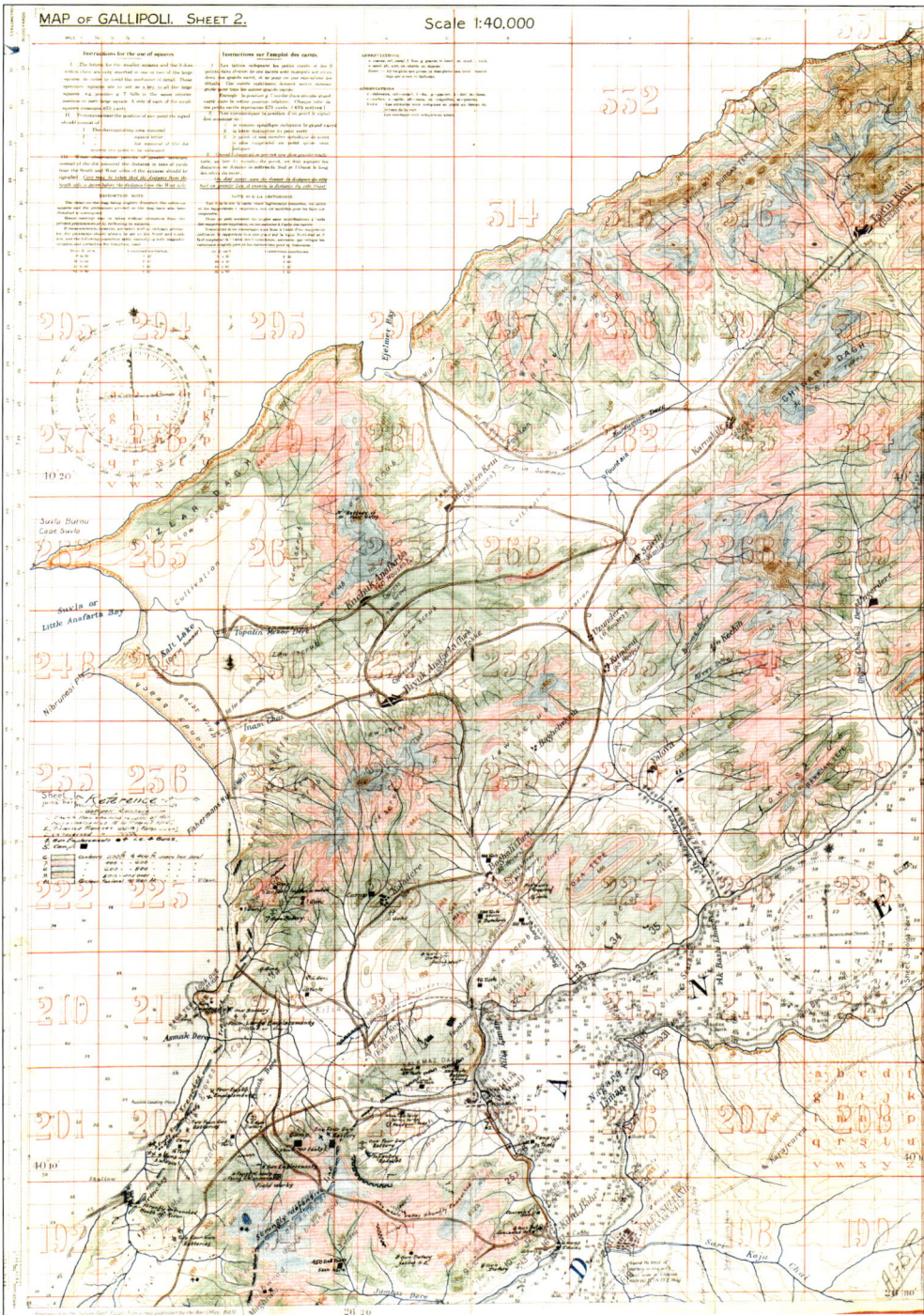

1:40,000 map of the Sari Bair–Maidos area used by ANZAC showing the extensive intelligence on Turkish locations from aerial and naval reconnaissance in the month before the landing. While the map is not perfect by today's standards, it disproves the myth that ANZAC had faulty intelligence and poor maps.

Contrary to some views, the records of the MEF, ANZAC and its two divisions reveal that the landing arrangements were planned in great detail. Conferences between the various levels of command thrashed out the operational plan. Detailed instructions flowed down the chain of command covering all aspects of the landing including the allocation of shipping, timings, the landing of the covering force, positioning of transports off the coast, the disembarkation of the following troops, beach parties, evacuation of the wounded, communications, administrative arrangements, and logistic support for the troops ashore. Given the limited time available, this represented a stupendous effort by staffs that had never worked together before and demonstrated a high degree of thought and competence. What the records also reveal, however, were concerns about the standard of training of the ANZAC troops. Indeed instructions to junior commanders and their troops covered matters that would have been second nature to well-trained troops, such as the conduct of outpost duties and fire discipline.

HAMILTON'S OBJECTIVES

Hamilton's objective was to capture the batteries covering the Dardanelles. To do the job properly required both shores to be cleared, but this task was beyond the capabilities of his resources. He had insufficient troops to clear both shores, and the approach from the Asiatic shore would open up a long and vulnerable right flank through hilly country to attack, and eventually swallow his entire force. Quite apart from this, Kitchener had forbidden him to attack there. The only option left was the peninsula.

One approach was to land on the western coast opposite the Kilid Bahr Plateau, driving straight for the plateau and the heavy artillery fortifications covering the Narrows. Securing the plateau first would not only eliminate these guns, but would also isolate the Ottoman forces in the south, allowing the remaining batteries to be taken by an advance from the high ground to the low. Hamilton would have preferred to land his whole force close to the Kilid Bahr Plateau. However, he rejected this idea primarily because there were insufficient small craft to land a large force simultaneously, the beach space opposite the plateau was cramped, restricting the rapid build-up of men and stores, and his reconnaissance had told him that all the natural landing places except Cape Helles were covered with an elaborate network of trenches, although he was not to know that the coast here was sparsely manned. Furthermore, a landing in this area would have meant that his line of communication between the beach and the plateau was vulnerable to attack on both flanks, and would require the diversion of troops to keep it open. Hamilton eventually decided that his main attack would be at Cape Helles, which he mistakenly believed was lightly held, supported by a subsidiary attack and two feints.

The MEF's mission was 'to assist the fleet to force the DARDANELLES by capturing the KILID BAHR Plateau, and dominating the forts at the NARROWS.' Hamilton sought to achieve this through two landings supported by two feints on the Ottoman flanks. In the first feint the Navy would bombard the Bulair Lines while the transports carrying the RND would demonstrate at the head of the Gulf of Saros to ensure that the *5th* and

7th divisions remained in place. In the second feint, the French fleet would demonstrate off Besika Bay while a regiment of the CEO would effect a temporary landing at Kum Kale on the Asiatic shore at the mouth of the Dardanelles to keep *XV Corps* occupied and prevent the guns there firing on Cape Helles. The main effort would be made by the 29th Division at Cape Helles, with the object of securing the Achi Baba Ridge, the first ground of tactical importance on the way to the Kilid Bahr Plateau, before advancing to capture the plateau. ANZAC would support the main operation by making a subsidiary landing north of Gaba Tepe to secure the Sari Bair Range and sever the road communications north of Maidos.

Given the limited beaches available at Helles, the main assault was to be spread over five small and widely dispersed beaches (S, V, W, X and Y), to be followed by an advance taking the longest route to the Kilid Bahr Plateau in the teeth of what would prove to be the strongest enemy entrenchments on the southern peninsula. The flanks, however, would be secure, and the Navy advised that it could provide fire support from the flanks in enfilade to the advance. Once the 29th Division had secured the Achi Baba feature, it would be reinforced by the CEO for the push to the plateau.

The subsidiary attack would be made by ANZAC against the Sari Bair Range, initially to secure a beachhead between the Fisherman's Hut and Gaba Tepe, with the ultimate objective of taking the Mal Tepe Ridge, cutting the north-south road communications, and hopefully drawing off Turkish reinforcements from the main thrust.

Irrespective of which plan Hamilton adopted, if the Army was confined to the peninsula, it could only do half the job. The obvious weakness was that the batteries on the Asiatic shore remained a threat to any shipping in the Dardanelles. Most of these were mobile guns which could move when engaged, and most of the fortified batteries on that shore were beyond the crook of the Narrows, making them difficult targets for naval gunfire unless the ships lay almost under them. Considering the naval efforts to date, there was no guarantee they would be any more successful in subduing the forts, or getting through the ten lines of minefields, without further significant loss. Even if the Asiatic guns could have been subdued by the Navy, there was the very real probability that, once the fleet passed, Ottoman mobile batteries would return to interdict the waterway and disrupt the transports needed to support any occupation of Constantinople. Thus the Army's operation to assist the fleet was just as flawed as the strategy to force the Dardanelles in the expectation that Constantinople would capitulate to the fleet.

ANZAC PLAN

Hamilton tasked Birdwood to effect a landing between Gaba Tepe and the Fisherman's Hut with the ultimate aim of seizing the ridge running south from the Sari Bair Range to the Mal Tepe feature and, in doing so, sever the north–south road communications. Seizing this line, he wrote, ANZAC 'will threaten, and perhaps cut, the line of retreat of the enemy's forces on KILID BAHR Plateau, and must, even by their preliminary operations, prevent the said plateau being reinforced during the attack of the 29th Division ...' He specified that achieving the first objective would see a brigade-sized covering force establish itself on the Sari Bair Range 'to protect the landing of the remainder of the Army Corps'. He noted that Chunuk Bair and the ridges running from it to the north-west (Chunuk Bair to Walden's Point) and south-west (Third Ridge) to the sea offered 'a strong covering position' although taking Hill 971 was left to Birdwood's discretion. Leaving the covering force on the Sari Bair Range to protect the northern flank, the remainder of the corps would then advance and attempt to seize Mal Tepe. Oddly, he added, 'Should the A&NZ Army Corps succeed in securing this ridge the results should be more vital and valuable than the capture of the KILID BAHR Plateau itself.' Why this was so was never explained, and seems strange given that the whole point of the operation was the capture of the plateau. Although not mentioned in the orders or instructions, the ANZAC landing would also divert Ottoman reinforcements from the principal landing at Cape Helles and thus dissipate their reserves. If a sufficiently deep penetration was made, ANZAC could absorb a significant portion of these reserves and perhaps become the Ottoman forces' main focus, allowing the 29th Division and the CEO a clearer run to the plateau.

Some historians have criticised Hamilton's orders as too vague. From a soldier's perspective, when read in conjunction with the accompanying instructions, they provide a succinct picture of the commander's intent, and gave Birdwood little scope for determining how and where he might effect the landing and establish a beachhead. His orders clearly state that Birdwood first had to secure the Sari Bair Range to protect the subsequent advance to the Mal Tepe Ridge. Sketch Map 1 to Hamilton's Force Order No. 1 shows that the landing was to be made at the northern end of Brighton Beach, and Hamilton stipulated the size of the covering force, the covering position to be attained, and the extent of the beachhead required for the disembarkation of the remainder of the corps (the line Fisherman's Hut to Chunuk Bair to Gaba Tepe). Subsequent actions to secure the corps objective, the Mal Tepe Ridge, were wisely left to Birdwood's discretion, as they would very much depend on the situation facing him once the beachhead was secured. What the critics forget is that orders and instructions are the summary of the essential agreed details of a planning process that starts with a commander's intent, and during which

the respective commanders and staffs thrash out the options, agreed plans, resources and supporting details in a series of conferences that percolate down and become more definitive through each level of command. Many diaries mention the series of planning conferences that occurred between the commanders and staffs at all levels once the force assembled at Mudros Harbour. Given the number of conferences that were held between force, corps and divisional levels, Birdwood and his subordinates would have harboured no doubts as to what was expected. On 16 April Hamilton noted in his diary, 'Birdie came later and we took stock together of ways and means. We see eye to eye now on every point.' The subsequent instructions issued by ANZAC and the series of orders and instructions distributed by the 1st Australian Division and the 3rd Brigade show an increasingly detailed consistency as to what was intended. This was consistent with the prevailing command and control doctrine. In addition, the 1st Division commanders down to and including the battalion commanders undertook an offshore reconnaissance along the Aegean coast that paid particular attention to the Gaba Tepe–Sari Bair area, to gain the best view they could of the terrain over which they would have to fight and to clarify features on the ground. Such is the fallacy of drawing conclusions based simply on one set of orders without considering the military planning process, the level of command at which they are issued, and the subsequent instructions and orders issued to each subordinate level.

Birdwood's task was not an easy one. The northern end of Brighton Beach was backed by the steep slopes of McCay's Hill and Bolton's Ridge, and was in enfilade to Gaba Tepe, although small arms fire from the promontory would be at extreme range. Taking Gaba Tepe would require a hard fight through the defences along Bolton's Ridge and on the promontory itself. More difficult still was the task of securing the beachhead. Having landed and broken through the initial defences, the covering force had to advance across several spurs to reach the covering position before Ottoman reinforcements arrived. Time was critical, and in an instruction to his battalion commanders Sinclair-MacLagan emphasised this: '… by pushing on to our objective, the covering position which we must get to as rapidly as possible …' If the covering force was held up, or had to fight its way forward, the chances of reaching the position before the Ottoman reinforcements arrived

The northern end of Brighton Beach, the intended landing site for the 3rd Brigade. Hell Spit is on the far left and the intended brigade frontage extended from just this side of the spit along some two-thirds of the beach towards the camera. Bolton's Ridge rises steeply above the beach and Lone Pine is on the horizon to the right (author's image).

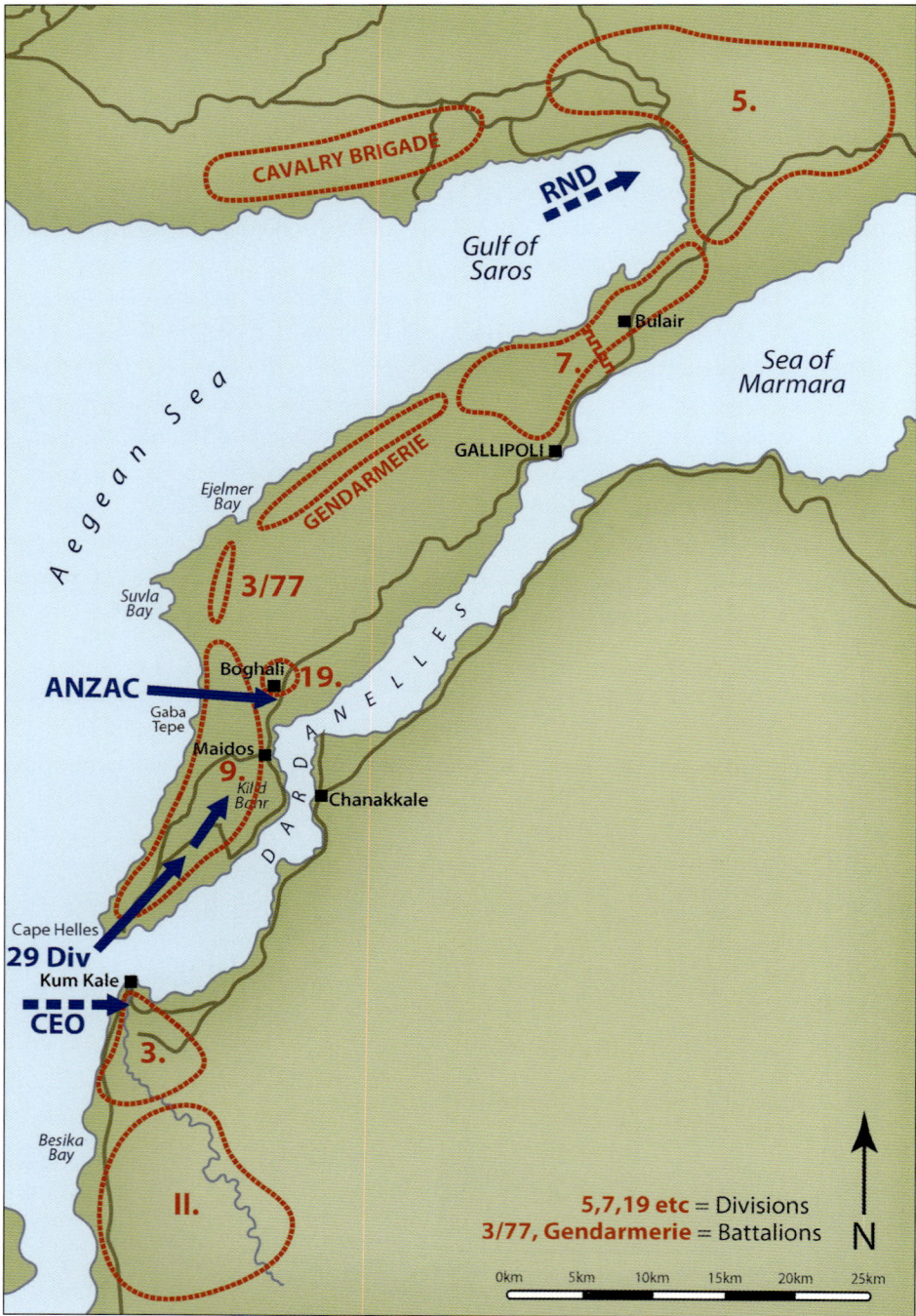

Hamilton's plan. On the Ottoman northern flank the RND are to make a demonstration in the Gulf of Saros, while on the other flank the French are to land a regiment at Kum Kale as a feint to fix the *3rd* and *11th divisions* and stop the batteries there from firing on the main landing at Cape Helles. They will then withdraw. The main assault will be conducted by the British 29th Division at the toe of the peninsula, supported by a subsidiary landing by ANZAC one mile north of Gaba Tepe.

Hamilton's objectives of the main and subsidiary attacks. In the south, landing on five beaches (S, V, W, X and Y), the 29th Division is to secure the Achi Baba feature (broken line). Reinforced by the CEO, both divisions will then advance and capture the Kilid Bahr Plateau (continuous line). To the north, landing on Z Beach, the 1st Australian Division is to secure a covering position along Third Ridge (broken line). Bridges later included the heights of Hill Q and Hill 971 in the 1st Division's tasks. Following this, ANZAC will advance to secure the ridge running from the Sari Bair Range to Mal Tepe (continuous line) to cut the Ottoman north-south road and prevent reinforcements from the north reaching the Kilid Bahr Plateau.

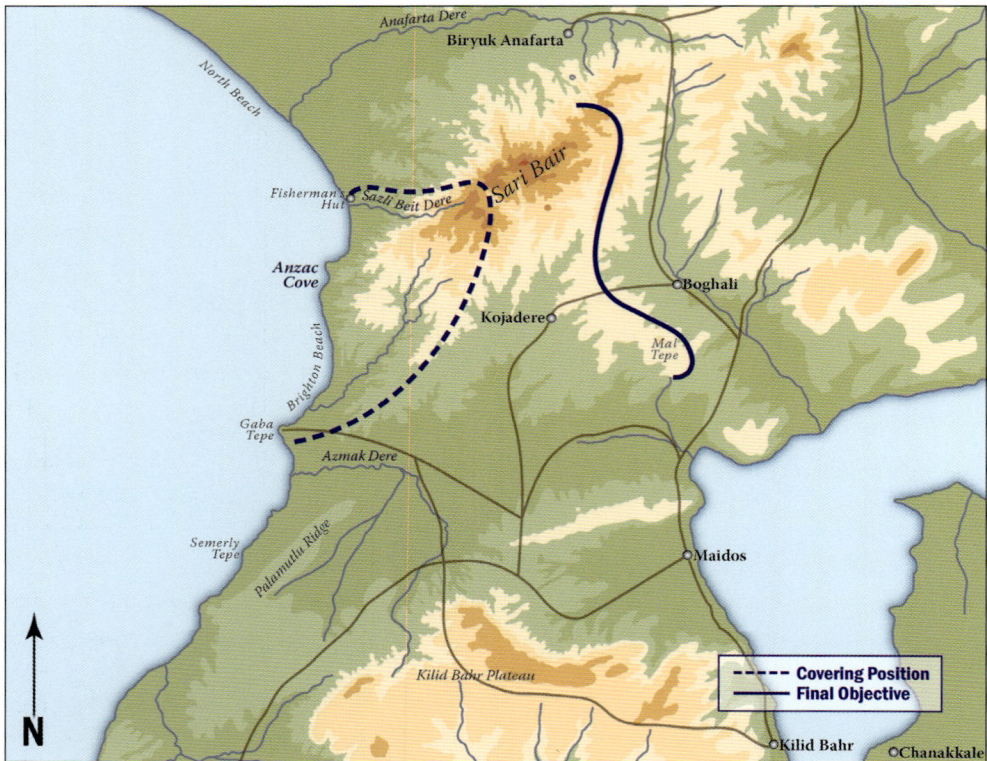

ANZAC objectives assigned by Hamilton and Birdwood, comprising a covering position from the Fisherman's Hut to Chunuk Bair and then along Third Ridge to Gaba Tepe, with the final objective along the ridge from Sari Bair to Mal Tepe.

were very slim indeed. Not everyone was sanguine about the operation. Brigadier General Harold 'Hooky' Walker, Birdwood's Chief of Staff and a no-nonsense British regular, opposed the entire Gallipoli operation, maintaining that it had no chance of success. He would later command the 1st Australian Division and prove to be one of the best divisional commanders in the AIF. Sinclair-MacLagan also had grave doubts about the ANZAC operation, the opposition he expected to encounter, and the ability of his brigade to hold the covering position.

Birdwood assigned the Sari Bair objective to the 1st Australian Division. Directing the covering force to seize Third Ridge from Gaba Tepe to Chunuk Bair inclusive, he reminded Bridges of the advantages of moving on a broad front and occupying the covering position 'as rapidly as possible'. The rest of the division would be landed immediately after the covering force to secure the position and the northern flank in the direction of the Fisherman's Hut.

While some believe that Third Ridge was too long for a brigade defence, the role of a covering force is not to defend a position *per se*. Rather it acts as a light screen or advance guard behind which the main body can disembark without undue interference from the enemy.

Its purpose is to intercept, delay, disorganise and deceive the enemy before he can attack the force being covered. The role of the covering force is to compel the enemy to deploy early at a distance from the beaches, and to buy time for the main body to land and deploy. If pressed, portions of the force may fall back, but in so doing they must force the enemy to fight for ground, and it is clear from Birdwood's instructions that he intended the remainder of the 1st Division to quickly reinforce the covering position. Seizing a broad covering position also increased the difficulties faced by the Ottomans in sealing off the invasion. They would be forced to disperse their reinforcements over an even broader frontage to contain it, robbing them of the ability to concentrate strong forces for the counter-attack. A covering position along Third Ridge would also force the Ottomans to attack from inferior or low ground, except on the main range from Hill Q, but even there it would be a difficult operation on a narrow front.

In reality, Third Ridge provided the first position inland on which a sufficiently deep beachhead could be established. A line along First and Second ridges, and anchored on Baby 700 was too shallow, too small, too narrow and too cramped a position for the remainder of the corps to disembark without being drawn into a fight on the covering position, or to have sufficient room to manoeuvre for the breakout. First and Second ridges were also inferior ground as they were overlooked by the upper reaches of Third Ridge and Battleship Hill. For the Ottoman defenders, a beachhead on First and Second Ridge could be sealed off with fewer troops and the invasion stifled in its infancy. Second Ridge also had the disadvantage that it had no defensive depth; if the Ottomans broke through there was no suitable place to fall back other than the confines of Plugge's Plateau and MacLagan's Ridge immediately above Anzac Cove.

Once he had secured the beachhead, Bridges was given the option to consolidate his position or make a further advance 'depending on the situation'. The 7th Indian Army Mountain Artillery Brigade (two batteries) was assigned to provide early fire support until the heavier field guns could be landed. The NZ&A Division was simply told that it would disembark after the 1st Division, although Godley was directed to visit Birdwood's transport for further instructions before landing, depending on the situation ashore.

To overcome some of the difficulties of an opposed landing, Birdwood sought to achieve local surprise and minimise the defenders' fire by opting for a silent night attack, hoping to land the 3rd Brigade in darkness. The initial date for the assault was 23 April, which gave him almost three hours of darkness between moonset and civil dawn; however, foul weather delayed the landing until 25 April. With a moon waxing to 77% of its disk visible, his window of opportunity now narrowed to just two hours between 2.57 am (moonset) and 4.55 am (civil dawn, when objects can first be distinguished). In addition, by landing along the northern half of Brighton Beach with the left flank under the shoulder of Hell Spit and the right flank some 1000 metres or more north of Gaba Tepe, they would avoid the strongest defences around the promontory. Unbeknown to Birdwood, but to his advantage, the northern portion of the landing would strike the weakest point of any defence — the boundary between two units — in this case that of the *7th* and *8th companies*.

1ST DIVISION PLAN

Bridges nominated Sinclair-MacLagan's 3rd Infantry Brigade as the covering force. Landing in three waves on a 1500-metre frontage, the first wave of six companies would initially seize Bolton's Ridge and McCay's Hill, with two companies of Lee's 9th Battalion (Queensland) on the right, two of Weir's 10th Battalion (South Australia) in the centre, and two 11th Battalion (Western Australia) companies, under Lieutenant Colonel James Lyon Johnston, on the left. The second wave comprised most, but not all, of the remaining two companies of these battalions, and would support the first wave, with all three battalions concentrating along Bolton's Ridge and on McCay's Hill. Clarke's 12th Battalion (Tasmania, South and Western Australia) largely comprised the third wave as the brigade reserve. Having overcome the beach defences, the leading battalions would push inland to the covering position. Two companies of the 9th would swing south and take Gaba Tepe and the southern end of Third Ridge, while the other two headed east to occupy the ridge 1100 metres further up. The 10th would occupy the ridge east of the 400 Plateau, centred 900 metres north of the Queenslanders. Moving along Second Ridge to Baby 700 and then up the main range, the 11th Battalion would occupy the junction with Third Ridge, extending from the northern slopes of Battleship Hill, around the bifurcation on Chunuk Bair and 600 metres down the ridge. The 12th was to rendezvous in Victoria Gully near the head of Bolton's Ridge; once there it would act on Sinclair-MacLagan's orders.

Birdwood intended to use the remainder of the division to secure the covering position. Bridges decided to do this by seizing the vital ground beyond Chunuk Bair, using McCay's 2nd Brigade. Landing just below Hell Spit, the 5th Battalion would follow the 11th's route and push through it to occupy the southern slopes of Hills Q and 971. The 8th Battalion would follow the 5th and occupy the northern slopes of Hill Q and Chunuk Bair at the head of the spurs running up from the Fisherman's Hut. The 7th would land at Anzac Cove and, making its way via Russell's Top and the main range, would occupy the head of the spurs running into the Anafarta Valley from Hill 971. The 6th would be in reserve behind the 11th Battalion's line. MacLaurin's 1st Brigade was the divisional reserve. Considering the barbed wire entanglements along the southern stretch of Brighton Beach, he assigned three engineer sections (50 men in each) of the 1st Field Company (New South Wales) to the covering force, placing them in the leading boats with grappling hooks and ropes to help

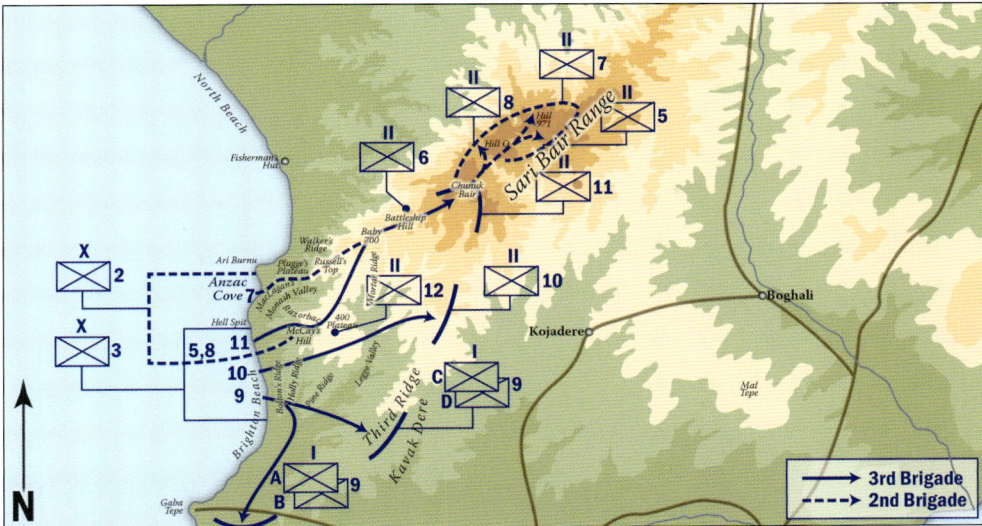

The 1st Australian Division Plan. Landing immediately south of Anzac Cove the 3rd Brigade will capture a covering position with the 11th Battalion taking Chunuk Bair and the head of Third Ridge, the 10th taking the central portion of Third Ridge, and the 9th in two groups taking the lower end of the ridge and Gaba Tepe. The 12th Battalion will form the brigade reserve. Following on, and echeloned slightly north to include Anzac Cove, the 2nd Brigade will push up the main range through the left flank of the covering force and take Hill Q and Hill 971 with 5th, 7th and 8th battalions, while the 6th will be in reserve on Battleship Hill.

clear the obstacles for the infantry. They would also accompany the infantry inland with the task of destroying the Ottoman artillery pieces with guncotton charges.

Bridges' plan was heavily weighted on the vital ground. Five battalions would be clustered on a two-kilometre frontage between Battleship Hill and Hill 971, leaving three battalions, including MacLagan's reserve, to hold five kilometres of Third Ridge until the 1st Brigade could get ashore. This was not an impossible task for well-trained troops. It was not necessary to have troops lined all along the ridge — troops are not positioned on ground that can be covered by fire. Third Ridge dominated the ground to the south and east and, properly deployed and supported by six Maxim guns, the battalions and companies could cover the gaps between them with interlocking fire. Furthermore, working on the rule that an attacker requires a minimum force ratio of three to one, three battalions were capable of

Holly Ridge and the southern end of Bolton's Ridge looking south from Lone Pine. Gaba Tepe is in the distance. The intended landing site for the 3rd Brigade was behind these ridges on the right side of the photo (John Lafferty image).

holding Sefik's two battalions until reinforced, or at least forcing him to deploy before he reached Third Ridge. Formations have succeeded in holding a position in the face of worse odds. In front of Hazebrouck in April 1918, four Australian battalions successfully defended a frontage of around nine and a half kilometres against several attacks by three German divisions. If, however, Sefik concentrated his force against the 9th Battalion companies at the southern end of the ridge, he might well overwhelm them, but he would have to fight for the position from inferior ground, the 9th's companies buying time for reinforcements from the 12th Battalion or 1st Brigade to move up.

Hill Q (nearest) and Hill 971 from the inland shoulder of Chunuk Bair. This was the 2nd Brigade's objective with the 5th Battalion taking the southern slopes (right) of Hill Q and Hill 971, and the 7th Battalion securing the eastern (beyond the crest) and northern edge (left) of Hill 971. The 8th Battalion would secure the northern slopes of Hill Q (author's image).

Nonetheless, this was a difficult task in difficult terrain, particularly for a raw and inexperienced force. First the troops had to land and break through the coastal defences. Having done this, speed in reaching the covering position was paramount, and this was emphasised to the commanders and troops all the way down the line. Lieutenant Noel Loutit of the 10th Battalion recalled being told they had to move quickly, and that if the covering position was not taken the operation would fail. Even if they quickly broke through the coastal defences, it would be a race to reach Third Ridge ahead of the Ottoman reinforcements. Once ashore, Sinclair-MacLagan would have little direct control over his force given the distances and the means of communication available to him. Much would devolve on his inexperienced battalion and company commanders. While it was a logical plan, it reflected a highly optimistic assessment of ANZAC's operational capabilities and little regard for those of the Ottoman Army.

Sinclair-MacLagan was deeply impressed by these difficulties, and rightly so. Catching sight of Gaba Tepe during the naval reconnaissance he remarked, 'If that place is strongly held with guns it will be almost impregnable to my fellows.' As he departed for his destroyer on the eve of the landing, he lugubriously told Bridges, 'If we find the Turks holding these ridges in strength, I honestly don't think you'll ever see the 3rd Brigade again.' His message to the troops was hardly inspirational: 'You may get orders to do something which appears in your positin [sic] as, [sic] to be the wrong thing to do and perhaps a mad enterprise. Do not cavil at it but carry it out wholeheartedly and with absolute faith in your leaders, because we are after all only a very small piece on the board. Some pieces have to be sacrificed to win the game ...' He was right not to underestimate the difficulty of the task, but war is as much a psychological contest as it is a physical one. Napoleon reportedly declared that, 'In war, the moral is to the physical as three is to one.' Sinclair-MacLagan's pessimism was hardly conducive to the firm, confident leadership and flexibility in battlefield command required to accept calculated risks, overcome adversity and manoeuvre a force despite the difficulties. It was to have a fateful influence on the coming battle.

The northern end of Brighton Beach looking south towards Gaba Tepe, with McCays' Hill on the left. The Kilid Bahr plateau is on the horizon, and Hell Spit is behind the camera. This was the intended site of the landing, with the 11th Battalion expected to come ashore in the immediate foreground. In the event C Company of the 9th Battalion and C Company of the 12th landed at the foot of McCay's Hill immediately in front of the camera (author's image).

Mal Tepe, the conical feature middle distance, taken while crossing the Dardanelles from Chanakkle to Eceabat (Maidos) with the Sari Bair Range on the horizon to the left. This area was the southern end of ANZAC's final objective (author's image).

CHAPTER 6
A MISPLACED LANDING

Men of the first wave of the 11th Battalion transferring from a destroyer onto HMS *London* in Mudros Harbour at around 12.00 pm on 24 April. These men would be some of the first ashore, landing north of Anzac Cove in the pre-dawn darkness the following morning (AWM P02034_019).

At 11.30 am on Saturday 24 April, two companies each of the 9th, 10th and 11th battalions, comprising the first wave of the assault, accompanied by three sections (150 men) of the 1st Field Company began transferring to HM battleships *Queen*, *Prince of Wales* and *London* respectively. The rest of the 3rd Brigade remained on their transports. Two and a half hours later, with the sun shining and amid a crescendo of cheering, the battleships slowly steamed through the throng of shipping in Mudros Harbour and turned to port for the 96-kilometre journey to the peninsula. By 11.00 pm the armada was off Imbros, the hulking island whose eastern shores lie 29 kilometres from Gaba Tepe. Under a glorious moon, seven destroyers sidled up to the 3rd Brigade's transports and began embarking the second and third waves, together with the 3rd Field Ambulance, taking in tow the lifeboats and cutters that would eventually carry them ashore. On the peninsula the *27th Regiment* was conducting a night exercise near Gaba Tepe.

The battleships stopped at 1.00 am. Boats were swung out onto a calm sea and formed into tows of three boats each. Quietly scrambling down rope ladders, the men of the first wave, with their assigned engineers, began disembarking into the boats half an hour later. From each battleship four tows were formed carrying 500 men. At the head of each tow was a steamboat or pinnace, armed with a Maxim machine-gun in the bow, to pull the boats on their final leg to shore. By 2.35 am they were ready. Slowly and noiselessly the armada crept on.

Captain Faik was woken at around 2.00 am and told of ships seen offshore. Grasping his binoculars he peered out over a moonlit, glassy Aegean Sea. There, directly in front of him, was a large group of ships. He peered hard through his binoculars hoping to ascertain the size of the ships and whether or not they were moving. Grabbing the telephone, he reported the news to Major Ismet, then dashed off a written report. Ismet advised him not to be alarmed: 'at worst, the landing will be at Gaba Tepe'. Moving to a new observation point, Faik continued watching. Deciding that the great mass was moving towards him, he rang *9th Division* headquarters at around 2.30 am and spoke to the Chief of Staff; then, having reported the presence of a large number of vessels, he was left to remain nervously at his post. At the same time, Second Lieutenant Muharrem's *2nd Platoon*, positioned around Anzac Cove and having also seen the ships, manned its posts ready for action. Alerting his reserve platoon to stand by, Faik waited. At 2.53 am, as the moon sank behind Imbros clothing the invasion force in darkness, the battleships, with two tows tethered on each side, inched towards a silent shore.

Men of the first wave of the 11th Battalion assembled at the stern of HMS *London* in Mudros Harbour at about 1.30 pm on 24 April. They steamed out of Mudros Harbour shortly afterwards to the thunderous cheers of sailors manning other warships in the harbour (AWM A01829).

THE RUN TO THE SHORE

At 3.30 am the ships stopped and the order was given: 'Go ahead and land.' The steamboats cast off and moved ahead some 140 metres apart to set the frontage for the landing of the covering force. They had just over three kilometres to go. Almost immediately Clausewitz's friction, that ever-present irritant on every battlefield and the military version of Murphy's Law, took effect. Lieutenant Commander John Waterlow, RN, leading the southernmost tow (No. 1), was to set the direction. Waiting for him to get underway, Midshipman Savill Metcalf in No. 2 tow was angrily ordered by HMS *Queen* to get moving, and he set off, leaving Waterlow to follow. It was almost impossible to see the tows on either side, and keeping station was difficult. Midshipman Eric Bush, leading No. 8, the northernmost tow of the 10th Battalion, closed in to his left for fear of losing touch; other tows followed suit reducing the frontage of the assault. After 15 minutes, fearing that he was too close to Gaba Tepe, Metcalf altered course two points to port, forcing some boats north of and behind him to shift left. Another 15 minutes later he again altered course one and a half points to port, further narrowing the frontage. Waterlow found the whole line, other than No. 3 tow, which had crossed behind Metcalfe, heading for a different part of the shore. Realising his course would leave him and his neighbour isolated on Brighton Beach, he swung his steamboat to port to join the rest. As the tows ran for the shore there was some intermingling of the 9th and 10th battalions' tows, reducing the frontage even further.

Men of the first wave of the 11th Battalion on HMS *London* en route to Gallipoli late on the afternoon of 24 April. Immediately ahead is the cruiser HMS *Bacchante* which follows the battleship HMS *Prince of Wales* carrying the first wave of the 10th Battalion (AWM A02468).

In the open boats the men were exposed to a 'keen biting breeze' and Private George Combs of the 11th Battalion remembered 'not a man whispered or coughed or stirred, all that could be heard by those close to the pinnace was the very gentle tick-tick-tick of the engine ...' A 9th Battalion soldier '... was shaking all over with nervousness and excitement' while Lieutenant Aubrey Darnell of the 11th Battalion felt the run into the beach seemed 'to go on forever'. When the steam pinnaces had cast off from the battleships, men of the second wave had disembarked into the tows beside the destroyers. At 4.10 am they were signalled to go on, and the destroyers increased speed to follow the first wave. A few minutes after 4.20 am, Leading Seaman Worsely in Bush's steamboat indicated that he could touch the bottom with his boathook; the engines were cut and the boats cast off. The weigh of the boats carried them past Bush as muffled oars were lowered to haul them the last 70 to 80 metres to the shore. By now the intended 1500-metre frontage had narrowed to 450 metres centred around Ari Burnu, missing Brighton Beach altogether.

The northern half of Anzac Cove showing Ari Burnu to the left, on which was located a section post of the *2nd Platoon*, and the spur leading up to Plugge's Plateau, the high ground on the right. This is the area where the leading waves of the 9th and 10th battalions struck the beach and climbed to the plateau. The road did not exist on 25 April 1915 (Glenn Wahlert image).

GETTING ASHORE

In the dark silence, Metcalf saw 'No 3 tow ... ghosting in close on my port side. There was the sound of feet crunching on the shingle as the first wave of those brave AIF troops marched on the beach from the leading boat in my tow.' As his boat grounded in Anzac Cove Lieutenant Duncan Chapman of the 9th Battalion leapt ashore, followed by Sergeant Fred Coe. Private Alex Wilson was helping Coe remove his pack when a shot rang out above them. There was a pause and then several more shots cracked in the darkness. In a boat nearing the shore Sapper John Moore of the 1st Field Company remembered, 'Then CRACK, every man's heart gave a jump. I know mine did. Then crack, crack, crack, a few seconds, then a continuous volley. This in turn was added to by the vicious spilling crackling of machine-guns.' Offshore, No. 3 pinnace had opened fire with its Maxim machine-gun and other steamboats followed suit as the fusillade and noise increased in weight and volume. Lance Corporal Mitchell recorded in his diary, 'The pinnace on our right opened with the maxim mounted in her bow. Woof-woof-woof came her throaty bellow making a great contrast to the tapping sound of the foe's small arms ... the long flame which flickered from her muzzle lit up the scene like an arc lamp..' Several of the 10th Battalion's boats grounded either side of Ari Burnu, while others glided into the cove. Further north, those of the 11th Battalion ran past Ari Burnu with the northernmost tow, No. 12, reaching the beach about 200 metres north of the point. The misplaced landing had thrown the 1500 men of the first wave smack into the 80 or so riflemen of the *2nd Platoon* above the cove, and Ibrahim's nine-man rifle squad of the *1st Platoon* at the southern end of North Beach.

Above the cove, Muharrem's men had been peering through the darkness for the past two hours. Offshore a trail of flame suddenly shot out of one steamboat's funnel for around 30 seconds. Seeing shapes moving towards the beach, first one man, and then others opened a ragged rifle fire, only to be met with return fire from the steamboats' machine-guns, wounding Muharrem in both shoulders. As he was being evacuated, the *2nd Platoon* put up a spirited fusillade, engaging the destroyers and the boats emerging through the darkness further out to sea, inflicting casualties on the men in the second wave and those still on the decks of the destroyers.

Fortunately, the first wave landing in the cove was largely sheltered from the Turks above and it was still sufficiently dark to make accurate shooting impossible. Corporal Percy Harrison of the 9th Battalion recalled, 'we formed up under the protection of the cliffs, and awaited instructions to advance. The Turks on the cliff above us opened fire on the torpedo boats [destroyers], and other craft which could be just discerned in the water. They had heard the noise of our men in the boats rowing for the shore.' Clustered around the foot of Plugge's Plateau, the men threw off their packs and started hauling themselves up the steep slopes. Lieutenant Eric Talbot-Smith shouted to his scouts of the 10th Battalion, 'Come on, boys, they can't hit you!' and led them straight up the hill. Near the northern end of the cove, Major James Robertson, second-in-command of the 9th, was confronted by a steep bank that foiled all attempts to climb it. Finding a rough track around it, he led his men up the hill. As they reached the crest of Ari Burnu, the Turkish squad there fled back up the slope, although one man was captured. Further south, Weir ordered a mixed group of the 9th and 10th up the hill. Pushing and scrambling through the waist-high scrub, and using it to haul themselves up, they set off up the steep slope.

A steam pinnace takes a tow of four boats to the beach early on the morning of 25 April. This image shows how the first wave of the 3rd Brigade was taken from the battleships for the final run to the beach in total darkness, although their tows consisted of three boats drawn by a steam pinnace, rather than the four in the photograph. A Maxim gun was mounted in the bow of each pinnace and opened fire on the Turks on the top of Plugge's Plateau after the first rifle shots rang out (AWM P1287.11.01).

North of the cove, Private Murray Aitken of the 11th Battalion recalled that 'everything went smoothly until the keels were just grating on the beach when bang! went the enemy's signal, followed closely by two more shots, and then a whole fusillade.' Ibrahim's detached rifle squad of the *1st Platoon* had a clear field of fire and, joining in the firing, they inflicted casualties among the first wave of the 11th Battalion and accompanying engineers. Sergeant Thomas Newson of the 1st Field Company later wrote home that 'a terrific fire opened on us and the beach was ablaze with rifle fire ... Our boat was the first to land. There was [sic] not many of our men in the boat hit. Those hit got it about the legs, bullets going right through the boat.' While the heavier boats grounded in deeper water, others ran to the shore. Captain Edward Brennan, the 11th Battalion's medical officer, in the northernmost tow wrote, 'I was in the second boat of the tow, and being a fairly light boat we ran well into the beach. The first boat of the tow was a big pinnace, and having 50 men on board she grounded a fair distance out, and when the troops got out they were up to their shoulders in water; we were only up to our waists. There were only a few casualties in our boat ...' Sapper Sedgwick Mansfield remembered, '[the fire] got a bit hot so we jumped into the water and we waded ashore. It wasn't very deep here ... There was one of our chaps, as soon as he got off the beach he got it right through the forehead. He went down like a log. Didn't even twitch.'

North Beach from Ari Burnu Point showing the area where the 11th Battalion and A Company of the 12th landed. The perpendicular face of The Sphinx juts out from Russell's Top in the centre. Walker's Ridge, up which Captain Tulloch's party climbed, runs up from the right to Russell's Top behind The Sphinx. Lieutenant Colonel Clarke's party climbed the spur to the right of The Sphinx (author's image).

Reaching the beach many threw themselves behind the low embankment skirting the shore. Under the leadership of Major Edmund Drake-Brockman and Captains Raymond Leane and William Annear, the men nearest Plugge's Plateau dumped their packs, swung right and started climbing its steep northern slopes. Brennan heard an officer shout: 'Fix bayonets, lads and up we go!' and with a yell they started up the hill, which was so steep in places that they had to crawl on their hands and knees. More men were coming behind them, following the others up the slope. Those further along the beach, together with the engineers, fixed bayonets and took on Ibrahim's detached rifle squad who were blazing away at the troops pouring ashore. Newson wrote: 'with a yell we charged with bayonets to get the Turks on the go.' With overwhelming numbers confronting them, the rifle squad took off, fleeing inland and up the steep ridge behind them.

High up on Second Ridge, Captain Faik heard the gunfire and immediately sent two sections under Sergeant Ahmed to reinforce Muharrem. He ordered the remainder of his reserve platoon forward onto Russell's Top to occupy trenches near The Sphinx, overlooking North Beach. Faik then requested fire support from Captain Sadik's mountain battery on the 400 Plateau. Sadik replied that his priority target was Brighton Beach, and he could only fire or change his target on Ismet's orders. The support was not forthcoming. After sending a further report to Ismet, Faik set out to follow the bulk of the *3rd Platoon*.

Sunrise over the Sari Bair Range, 25 April. HMAT *Galeka* on the right of the photograph is disembarking the 7th and 6th battalions while, in the centre, HMAT *Novian*, carrying the 2nd Brigade headquarters and the 5th Battalion, is making her way to her allotted berth. To the rear of *Novian* are tows taking the 8th Battalion ashore (AWM G00894-1).

The destroyers, still maintaining the intended 1500-metre frontage, had dashed in, pulling the tows of the second wave. Although it was still 'too dark to see a man at 50 metres', men in these boats, and those still on the decks of the destroyers, were sustaining casualties from the Ottoman defenders. Aboard HMS *Chelmer* Private Arthur Williams of the 11th Battalion was mortally wounded, as was Corporal Alexander McDonald from the 1st Field Company, aboard HMS *Scourge*. The 'shots sounded like hailstones on a tin roof as they rattled against the destroyer', recalled Corporal Elmer Laing of the 12th Battalion, while on HMS *Colne* Captain John Whitham, commanding C Company of the 12th, remarked that

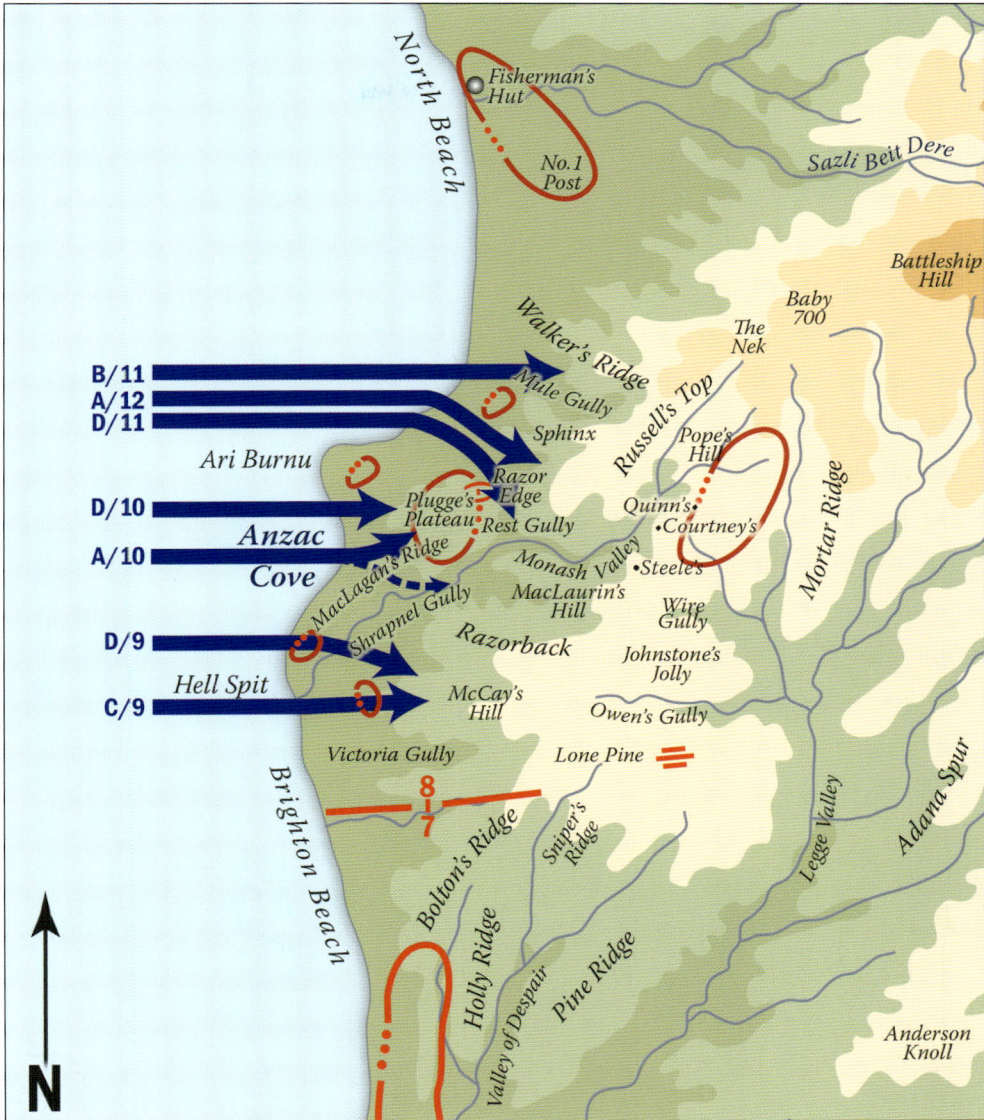

The landing of the first wave of the 3rd Brigade. The battleship tows landed astride Ari Burnu, with A and C companies of the 11th Battalion landing on North Beach below Plugge's Plateau, while B and C companies of the 10th, and A and B companies of the 9th land around Ari Burnu and in Anzac Cove.

'the flashes of rifles were quite visible against the dark background … Several men [were] hit by rifle bullets as the boats left the destroyers, and one or two were struck when standing on the destroyer's decks.' Casting off the tows, the destroyers sent the second wave ashore astride Anzac Cove. On the right, C Company of the 9th under Captain John Milne missed the cove altogether and landed in the area originally intended for the 11th Battalion. Dropping their packs, the Queenslanders set off up McCay's Hill, heading for the 400 Plateau. Captain Isaac Jackson's D Company came ashore around Hell Spit. Confronted by overwhelming

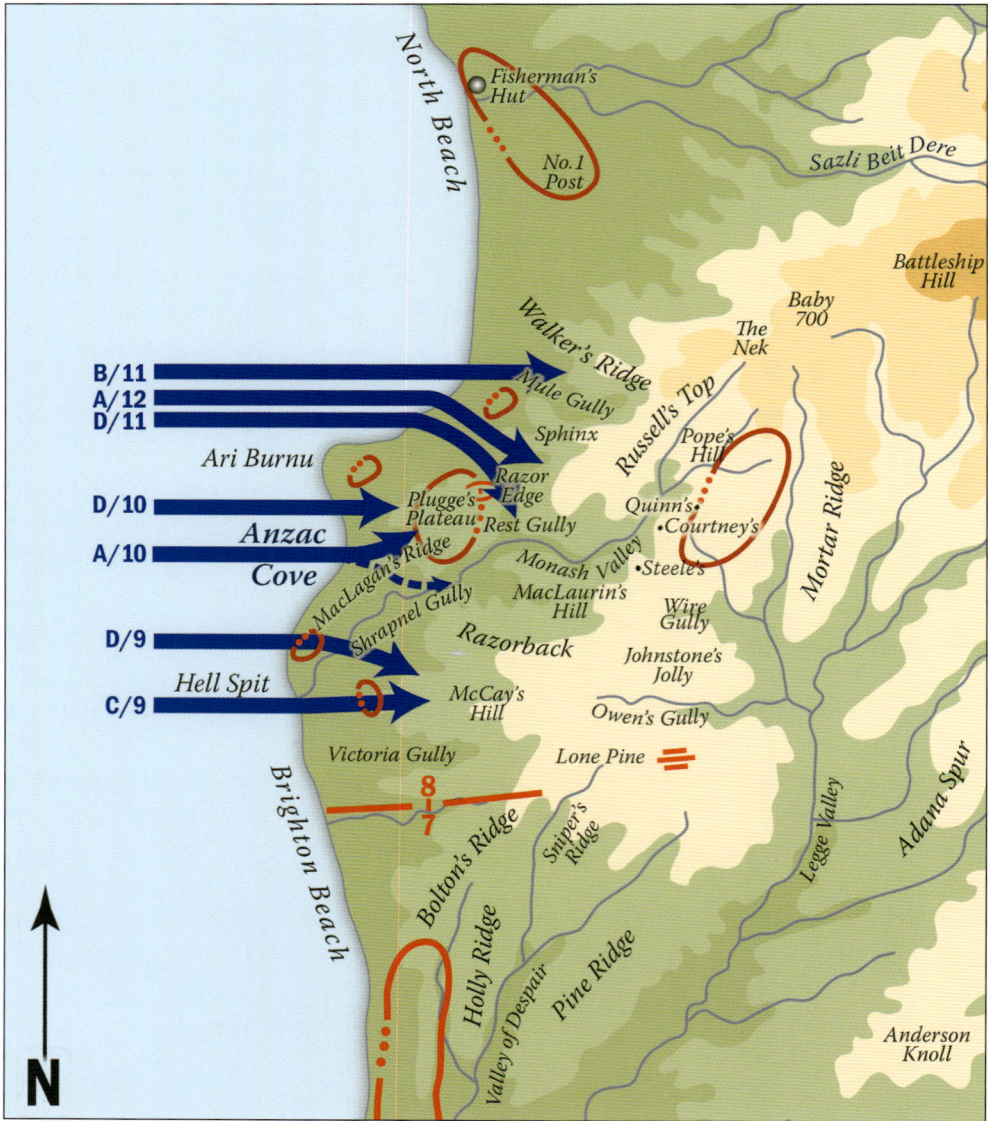

The landing of the second wave of the 3rd Brigade. B and D companies of the 11th Battalion and A Company of the 12th land on North Beach, A and D companies of the 10th come ashore in Anzac Cove, while D Company of the 9th Battalion lands astride Hell Spit. Further south C Company of the 9th lands at the northern end of Brighton Beach and ascends McCay's Hill.

forces, the Turkish squad there took to its heels. Private Adil recalled many years later that they headed up Shrapnel Gully, over Second Ridge and eventually stopped on Third Ridge near Scrubby Knoll. As D Company crested the end of MacLagan's Ridge, Jackson was hit and Captain John Dougall took command, leading them across Shrapnel Gully and up the slope of McCay's Hill, where they joined Milne's company. The 10th Battalion's companies landed in the cove. While most of them climbed towards Plugge's Plateau to join the first wave some, including Loutit's platoon, scaled MacLagan's Ridge, crossed over and chased the retreating Turks up Shrapnel Gully.

Bugler Fred Ashton, with D Company of the 11th, recalled that his boat, which had slipped past Ari Burnu, was approaching the beach in pitch darkness when, some 120 metres from shore, the first shot rang out, followed by a scattered volley which then settled down to a 'steady rifle fire'. Reaching the beach, they threw themselves on the ground north of the point in the same area where the first wave companies had landed. 'With our officer lying on the beach with a gaping wound in his chest ... we were rather at a loss to know what our next move should be. So we fired at the rifle flashes.' This fire, and that of others in the second wave, had unfortunate consequences, hitting some of the men nearing the crest of Plugge's Plateau. Mortally wounded, Sergeant Herbert Fowles muttered as he lay dying, 'I told them again and again not to open their magazines.' Further north, Lieutenant Colonel Clarke, with Major Charles Elliott's A Company of the 12th Battalion, came ashore with the second wave opposite The Sphinx. Hearing firing from the north, and believing it was a machine-gun, he despatched Lieutenant Rupert Rafferty's platoon with instructions to deal with it. On the left of the assault, part of B Company of the 11th under Captain Eric Tulloch, and some of the 12th under Lieutenant Edward Butler grounded around 300 to 400 metres north of Ari Burnu under fire from Ibrahim's *1st Platoon* to their far left. Once ashore, Tulloch set out for Walker's Ridge, and began the long climb to Russell's Top.

As the leading Australians reached the top of Plugge's Plateau, Captain Annear was killed in a short sharp skirmish before the survivors of the *2nd Platoon* fell back to the inland edge, putting up a brief fight before dropping off the feature and bolting inland, with Talbot-Smith and his scouts in pursuit. By 5.00 am most of the first wave was congregating on the plateau in high spirits, a few lining the edge blazing away at the dim forms of Turks running inland. Major Alfred Salisbury of the 9th told Charles Bean, 'We did not get much disorganised going from the beach to Plugge's, except a platoon of B Company got into our centre and a few men of the 10th Bn intermingled with our left.' Of the three leading battalion commanders, only Weir was in control of his unit. Johnston of the 11th had sprained an ankle on the beach, and the first shock of battle had unnerved Lee of the 9th; three hours later Bridges found him on the beach huddled under the bank. The senior officers present sorted out whatever intermingling had occurred, sending those of the 11th to the left, the 10th to the centre, and the 9th to the right of the small, triangular, flat-top plateau.

ASSESSING THE SITUATION

By 5.00 am dawn had broken and the main features of the topography were becoming visible to the Australians. Over their right shoulder was the low, black promontory of Gaba Tepe, some three and a half kilometres away; to their front, Second Ridge and the 400 Plateau obscured all view of the country beyond; and to their left front was the steadily rising Russell's Top, behind which the inland shoulder of Baby 700 was discernible. In the left far distance was Suvla Bay. Consulting their maps, the officers determined their location and the general direction of their objectives. Weir of the 10th realised that his was behind the 400 Plateau roughly to his right front. Major Edmund Drake-Brockman, now senior officer of the 11th, reckoned his was beyond Russell's Top, some three kilometres along the main range, while the 9th's officers knew their objectives were some distance to the right. Moltke the Elder's dictum that no plan survives first contact with the enemy was holding true, although in this instance it was due to an error in navigation rather than the impact of the enemy. The mark of good battlefield commanders is the ability to quickly adapt to the unfolding situation, make adjustments and fight and manoeuvre to achieve their objective and their commander's intent. History records numerous battles won from disadvantageous positions by bold commanders and resolute troops. Much has been made of the misplaced landing, many regarding it as the major reason for the ANZAC failure that day. In *Anzac to Amiens*, Bean wrote that it 'tore the plan to shreds'; yet he also wrote in Volume I of the *Official History* that, once on Plugge's, the officers knew where their objectives were and set out to take them.

Looking along the Razor Edge towards Russell's Top from Plugge's Plateau. Some men from the 11th Battalion climbed its steep side from the left and dropped over into Rest Gully on the right. This narrow knife-edge ridge had a significant effect on the battle as it prevented movement directly from the plateau to Russell's Top and the ground of tactical importance. Consequently the reinforcements destined for Baby 700 were forced to drop down into the congested Monash Valley, where many were unnecessarily diverted to positions along Second Ridge (Glenn Wahlert image).

The situation confronting the Australians around 5.15 am was not irretrievable. Fortuitously, the misplaced landing had avoided the strongest Ottoman defences and negated any direct interference from Gaba Tepe and the platoon on Bolton's Ridge. The Australians were ashore with minimal casualties and had punched a gaping hole in the light coastal screen. Apart from the Gaba Tepe defences on the promontory, the only Ottoman forces between them and their objectives were Captain Faik's *3rd Platoon* near The Sphinx, and the scattered remains of the *2nd Platoon* retreating inland. Only the *2/27th's 5th Company*, two and a half kilometres east of Gaba Tepe, was available to offer Faik immediate support. Sefik's *1/27th*, *3/27th* and machine-gun company, having completed their night exercise around midnight, had returned to Maidos, some eight kilometres beyond the centre of Third Ridge. The *19th Division* was closer, some three and a half kilometres from Hill 971 but, as the *Fifth Army* reserve, it required Liman von Sanders' authority before being committed to the battle.

EFFECT OF THE MISPLACED LANDING

The misplaced landing disrupted the 3rd Australian Brigade no more than might have been expected had it landed on Brighton Beach as intended. While it was placed ashore in more difficult terrain, the climb from Brighton Beach would have been much the same as that up Plugge's Plateau. To what extent, however, were the battalions disorganised and unable to fulfil their missions? Intermixing of some platoons had occurred, and each battalion contained misplaced men from other units, while individual parties had pushed inland independently. Nonetheless, with the exception of the 12th Battalion, most of the brigade was in good shape.

On the right, the 9th Battalion was split into the two basic groups originally intended. On Plugge's Plateau, Salisbury managed to keep most of his company and a portion of Major Sydney Robertson's together, while Robertson gathered the remainder of his men. They had two objectives: clearing the trenches on Bolton's Ridge, and then swinging south to seize the gun battery behind Gaba Tepe. Originally, this would have entailed fighting to secure Bolton's Ridge and a long fight through the remainder of the defences around Gaba Tepe. Now, over three and half kilometres from the promontory, their objective was considerably further away, although instead of attacking the Turks on Bolton's Ridge head-on as planned, an advance south would now throw them on the *7th Company*'s flank and rear. Moreover, after an initial engagement with Dougall's men of the 9th, Hakki's platoon of *7th Company* on Bolton's Ridge had withdrawn to Third Ridge leaving an even larger gap in the Ottoman defences, and they would have had a clear run to the defences on the promontory itself. Salisbury set off for the 400 Plateau while, inexplicably, Robertson headed up Monash Valley. The 9th's second wave companies were probably more intact than they would have been on Brighton Beach. Having joined up, they were making their way towards the 400 Plateau. Originally, they probably would have been drawn into the first wave's fight through the trenches on Bolton's Ridge. Once through the defences, they then had a 1400-metre advance due east to their objective in the area around Anderson Knoll. From the 400 Plateau, they now had to swing south-south-east and make a two-kilometre advance which would take them behind the Ottoman defences rather than through them.

In the centre, Weir's 10th Battalion was largely intact on Plugge's Plateau. He had control of the first wave companies, and most of the second were making their way up the slope to join him, although Talbot-Smith's and Loutit's men were heading up Shrapnel Gully. Originally the 10th would have struck the northern edge of the Ottoman defences on Bolton's, concentrated on the crest, and then advanced across a series of spurs for two kilometres to

Third Ridge. Now they were almost the same distance from their objective with only an additional 200 metres to travel. Swinging south-east, they would have to plunge into the deep Monash Valley, climb the steep slopes of the 400 Plateau, and strike out across Legge Valley. Undaunted, Weir set off for his objective.

Looking from the edge of Johnston's Jolly across Monash Valley to First Ridge. From the left MacLagan's Ridge runs up to Plugge's Plateau which was taken by the leading wave of the 3rd Brigade within 20 minutes of the initial landing. From the right-hand edge of Plugge's the ground drops suddenly to the extremely narrow Razor Edge, which prevented movement from the plateau along First Ridge to the vital ground, forcing the troops down into Shrapnel Gully and along Monash Valley. The second wave of the 11th Battalion came over the Razor Edge and dropped down into Rest Gully, which sits between Plugge's and Russell's Top. To the right is Russell's Top, the continuation of First Ridge to The Nek and Baby 700. The Sphinx can be seen peeping over the crest of Russell's Top. Lieutenant Colonel Clarke and members of A Company of the 12th Battalion reached the Top in the area below the Sphinx and advanced to the right of the photo, driving elements of the *3rd Platoon* ahead of them (Glenn Wahlert image).

On the left, the 11th Battalion was split, and although small parties became separated as they struck inland, most were in three basic groups. Drake-Brockman was gathering most of the first wave on the plateau, although a number of men were still on North Beach where they were joined by D Company of the second wave. Together, under Captain John Peck, this group climbed the steep slopes of the Razor Edge and dropped down into Rest Gully between Plugge's Plateau and Russell's Top, where Drake-Brockman soon joined them. B Company was spread further along North Beach but, with many of them in tow, Tulloch was already making for Walker's Ridge; ascending it would bring him to Russell's Top. The landing had placed the battalion 800 metres closer to its objective, but in more broken country. Originally, the 11th was to make its way across the 400 Plateau, along Second Ridge to Baby 700 and up the main range. Now those in Rest Gully had to climb to Russell's Top and head along the crest, while those on North Beach faced a scramble up steep cliffs or the haul up Walker's Ridge. Once on Russell's Top, however, it was relatively easy going along the crest to Battleship Hill and Chunuk Bair, albeit against a fighting withdrawal by the *3rd Platoon*.

Originally tasked to concentrate in Victoria Gully between McCay's Hill and Bolton's Ridge, the 12th Battalion was now scattered across the whole front. This had more to do with the landing arrangement and command decisions than it did with the misplaced landing or any intermingling of the tows. The battalion had been spread across all seven destroyers and brought ashore on the 1500-metre frontage straddling Anzac Cove. A Company, with Clarke, had been aboard HMS *Ribble* in the far north and came ashore among the second wave of the 11th Battalion. The rest of the battalion was shipped in half-company groups across the other six destroyers and ferried ashore in the third wave. Clarke had initially waited for the rest of his battalion to come ashore, but soon felt that this was taking too long. With some of Faik's *3rd Platoon* firing on the Australians along North Beach, Clarke struck out with those of his men at hand to climb the precipitous slopes near The Sphinx. While his courage and decisiveness is indisputable, his decision to become involved in the advance rather than trying to consolidate his battalion as the brigade reserve is questionable. Whether he could have gathered them is uncertain. When Whitham arrived on the beach, he reported to Sinclair-MacLagan in the cove, and was told to occupy the ridges to the right. A little later, Major Ernest Smith's B Company climbed Plugge's Plateau where Sinclair-MacLagan committed them to the battle, sending them forward to Second Ridge. D Company landed on the northern end of Brighton Beach and, instead of making its way to the Victoria Gully rendezvous, or around into Anzac Cove, the men headed straight up McCay's Hill after Milne's company of the 9th. The 12th was no longer an effective fighting entity and Sinclair-MacLagan had lost his reserve, largely through his own actions, and Clarke's and D Company's decisions to join the advance.

The misplaced landing was not as disastrous as is often portrayed. Other than the badly scattered 12th Battalion, the rest of the 3rd Brigade was relatively intact. The 9th Battalion was still in the two basic groups it would have formed on Brighton Beach, most of the 10th was under the control of its commanding officer and, although the 11th was separated, three-quarters of the battalion were soon together in Rest Gully, while many of its B Company were converging on the main range. Nor was the brigade incapable of completing its task. Certainly the leading companies of the 9th Battalion had a tougher job, but its second wave companies and the 10th Battalion were still within striking distance of their objectives. The 11th was considerably closer to Battleship Hill and Chunuk Bair than originally intended. The Turkish opposition was far from overwhelming; instead, in the immediate area of the landing, they were vastly outnumbered at around 28:1. With a force ashore now numbering almost 4000 men, and about to be reinforced by another 4000, the 3rd Brigade was opposed by Captain Faik's two scattered platoons of no more than 140 men retreating up First Ridge and Monash Valley. Further afield were another 500 Turks: the *7th Company* in the defences around Gaba Tepe and the *5th Company* positioned a kilometre from the southern end of Third Ridge. To the north, Second Lieutenant Ibrahim's *1st Platoon* was still at the Fisherman's Hut and could only help resist the advance if it withdrew to Battleship Hill or Chunuk Bair. In many ways the 3rd Brigade was in a better position than it would have been had the landing proceeded as intended. Indeed the brigade had successfully avoided the emplacements around Gaba Tepe and breached the Ottoman defences with few casualties. Birdwood believed the misplaced landing was fortunate, while the 12th Battalion historian felt it was an act of providence for which the battalion was profoundly grateful.

The earliest photo of troops landing in Anzac Cove. It is captioned as the 2nd Brigade landing, although the dark shadow indicates the photo was taken at a very early hour, and is probably the leading elements of the 7th Battalion around 5.30 am. HMS *Bacchante* is offshore, and the steam pinnace on the right shows how close some of them were able to get before releasing the first wave tows (AWM P10140_004).

Taken a couple of minutes after photo P10140_004, this image shows men, probably of the 7th Battalion, landing in Anzac Cove at a very early hour, possibly as early as 5.30 am, an hour after the initial landing. The transports carrying the 1st and 2nd brigades are offshore (AWM P10140_007).

Anzac Cove looking north towards Ari Burnu. The shadow on the beach on the right indicates an early hour, probably after 6.00 am, and shows men of the 2nd Brigade on the beach. On magnification, the items around the man bending over appear to be packs probably dropped by the initial waves of the 3rd Brigade (AWM H00197_1).

The centre of Anzac Cove looking south, with Hell Spit in the background. The photo appears to have been printed in reverse as shown by the B on the boat in the foreground, and the terrain is the same as other photos taken of Hell Spit. Ari Burnu rises more steeply. Taken between 6.30 and 7.00 am it shows men of possibly the 1st, 3rd or 5th battalions disembarking (AWM P02148-005).

CASUALTIES ON THE BEACH: MYTH AND REALITY

Visual depictions of the landing show the Australians storming ashore suffering heavy casualties. *The Hero of the Dardanelles*, shot on Sydney's Tamarama Beach in June 1915 and which depicts bodies strewn in large numbers from the water's edge to the rocks, set the scene for later interpretations. *Tell England* (1931) shows slouch-hatted Australians shot down as they leave the boats, with Turkish machine-guns causing much of the carnage. Charles Dixon's painting *The Landing at Anzac* portrays a similar image. In the television series *Anzacs* (1985), the episode on the landing has the 8th Battalion coming ashore in broad daylight amid a hail of fire, bodies strewn across the beach, soldiers falling wounded or killed, and stretcher-bearers scurrying back to the boats laden with casualties, all adding to the high drama of a very bloody landing and reinforcing the image popular in Australian minds. Yet several accounts speak of negligible casualties sustained on the beach, and the photographic evidence of Anzac Cove taken within an hour and a half to three hours of the initial assault bears this out. Only one photograph, taken around 8.00 am, clearly shows a corpse.

With the cove largely in dead ground to the Turks and the landing taking place under cover of darkness — which made accurate shooting nigh on impossible — the lack of corpses in the early photos of Anzac Cove is not surprising. Several casualties occurred ashore on North Beach, and the accounts of men landing there reflect this, in contrast to those written by men who landed in the cove. Other casualties occurred among the men in the boats bringing the second wave ashore and on the destroyers which were targeted by Muharrem's men on the heights above the cove and Ibrahim's platoon to the north. But these were not heavy, as accounts refer to between one and four men hit in some boats while others record no casualties at all. More were sustained climbing the heights, but these also appear to have been negligible due to the fall of the ground and the enshrouding darkness. In response to the exaggeration of the popular image, Bean wrote in 1946: 'Neither then nor at any time later was that beach the inferno of bursting shells, barbed wire, and falling men that has sometimes been described or painted.'

The precise number of casualties sustained in effecting the landing remains uncertain, but what is clear is that they were not as heavy as generally believed. The ANZAC Administrative War Diary estimates casualties from the 'landing first party' at 'about 100', but this is a guess, as accurate reports were not available, even after the battalion roll calls on 29–30 April. If this estimate is reasonably correct, however, it would mean that the 3rd Brigade's casualty rate in getting ashore was just 2.5%.

Troops of the 2nd Brigade landing between 5.30 and 6.00 am. Taken from MacLagan's Ridge near Hell Spit looking north along Anzac Cove to Ari Burnu, the image shows where the first wave companies of the 9th Battalion, the whole of the 10th Battalion, and a company of the 12th came ashore. The length of the shadow across the near half of the beach testifies to the very early hour it was taken, and shows the 6th and 7th battalions coming ashore. Magnification of the photo shows packs dropped by the leading waves on the beach, and probably two corpses, one lying near the soldier stooping over at the shoreline, and the other beside the soldier walking in the sunlight. Other than these, the beach is remarkably clear of corpses, which disproves the view that the 3rd Brigade stormed ashore under machine-gun fire suffering heavy casualties (AWM P10140_008).

CHAPTER 7

THE PLAN UNRAVELS

Colonel Ewan Sinclair-MacLagan came ashore with the destroyer tows of the second wave. After conferring with Major Charles Brand, his brigade major, and directing him to take charge of operations at the front, he set off for the heights above while Brand headed for the 400 Plateau. By the time Sinclair-MacLagan arrived on Plugge's Plateau, both the 10th Battalion and the 9th's leading companies had departed. To his left, Drake-Brockman was preparing to descend into Rest Gully. Considering his position in the early morning light, the brigade commander decided to put the brakes on the advance. Ignoring Bridges' instructions and his own to push on quickly 'at all costs' to seize the objectives, Sinclair-MacLagan decided to halt and dig in along Second Ridge and Baby 700. Orders were sent for the 9th and 10th battalions to dig in on Second Ridge. Salisbury recalled that he had crossed Shrapnel Gully and was nearing the crest of the 400 Plateau when the order reached him. Pointing out the various landmarks at the northern end of Second Ridge, Sinclair-MacLagan gave directions for the 11th to occupy these. Soon after, Smith's company of the 12th arrived and the brigade commander directed him to Second Ridge to occupy a position to the right of the 11th, effectively committing all that remained of the brigade reserve. Sinclair-MacLagan then returned to the beach, where he was to make the second fateful decision that altered the course of the battle.

A ship's boat loaded with 35 men of either the 6th or 7th Battalion about to depart for the shore early on the morning of 25 April. Note the crammed state of the boat and the easy target it presented as Jackson's men rowed through the fire from Ibrahim's *1st Platoon* during the last three to four minutes before reaching the shore. On average, 57% of the men in Jackson's boats were killed or wounded (AWM C01420).

Major Ismet had reported the landing to the *9th Division* at 4.45 am but could provide little detail. His regimental commander, Lieutenant Colonel Sefik, ordered the *1/27th*, *3/27th*, the machine-gun company and the regimental 'A' echelon to fall in, and awaited orders to move. As dawn revealed the size of the British invasion fleet, Ismet realised its significance and, at 5.20 am, 50 minutes after the initial firing, he reported 'landing is serious'. Impatient to get moving, Sefik again rang the *9th Division* for orders to move, but there were concerns that the landing might be a diversion, and he was told to wait until the situation could be clarified.

ACTION AT THE FISHERMAN'S HUT

Offshore, the transports carrying the 2nd Australian Brigade (Victoria) had already anchored. On the far left, HMAT *Galeka*, carrying Lieutenant Colonel Walter McNicoll's 6th Battalion and 'Pompey' Elliott's 7th, was stationed off the Fisherman's Hut. With none of the returning tows and steamboats nearby, the *Galeka*'s captain began disembarking the 7th Battalion in the ship's boats at 5.00 am. The first four, with 140 men of B Company under Major Alfred Jackson, set out directly for the bulk of Ibrahim's *1st Platoon* around the Fisherman's Hut. In the growing daylight they made an easy and concentrated target. Ibrahim's 60-odd riflemen were capable of delivering between 900 and 1200 rounds a minute into the packed boats. As Jackson's men slowly rowed to shore the Turks opened fire from 200 metres out with telling effect. By the time they grounded three or four minutes later, 80 of Jackson's men had been killed or wounded. Toppling over the sides, the survivors sheltered under the sand hummocks near the water's edge. Captain Herbert Layh told the men around him to fix bayonets and show them above the sheltering sand hummocks. The firing ceased.

To their south, two platoons of Australians were coming to their aid. Having been ordered by Clarke to deal with the fire from the left flank, Rafferty's platoon had been joined by Lieutenant Fred Strickland's of the 11th Battalion. In extended order they had advanced north along the coastal flat until they reached the mouth of a deep gully where they came under fire from Ibrahim's men at No. 1 Outpost. To his left front Rafferty saw Jackson's boats rowing directly for the Fisherman's Hut and decided to assist their landing. Scurrying out of the creek, they doubled across a flat under fire, losing several men killed or wounded, until they reached shelter in dead ground below the knoll of No. 1 Outpost. Breasting a spur, Rafferty saw that the boats had landed, and that a line of men now lay motionless in front of them. By now the firing had ceased and Private Arthur Stubbings volunteered to investigate. Sprinting to the southernmost boat he found most of the men dead or grievously wounded, and ran back to Rafferty with the news. Rafferty, who had received orders to retire, now withdrew to the south to rejoin the remainder of his battalion.

The firing had ceased because most of Ibrahim's men had exhausted their ammunition and he had ordered them to withdraw. Leaving the squad near the Aghyl Dere to observe the Australians, Ibrahim moved up the Sazli Beit Dere with the bulk of his platoon towards Battleship Hill and Chunuk Bair. Sensing that the Turks were no longer there, Layh took his small party forward and occupied the Turkish trenches on the knoll above the Fisherman's

COLONEL EWAN SINCLAIR-MACLAGAN, DSO

Commander 3rd Australian Infantry Brigade

A British regular soldier born in Scotland in 1868, Sinclair-MacLagan served in the militia before gaining a commission in the Border Regiment in 1889. He saw active service on the North West Frontier of India during the Waziristan expedition in 1894–95 and in the South African War where, as a company commander, he was wounded, Mentioned in Despatches and awarded the Distinguished Service Order. Posted to Australia in 1901, he was appointed Adjutant of the New South Wales Scottish Rifles and Deputy Assistant Adjutant-General, New South Wales. Here he met Lieutenant Colonel William Bridges, who was to exert a significant influence on his career. He returned to England in 1904, was promoted major and transferred to the Yorkshire Regiment (The Green Howards). When Bridges was recruiting staff for the new Royal Military College of Australia, Sinclair-MacLagan was chosen as Director of Drill and promoted temporary lieutenant colonel. He was serving at the college when the Great War broke out. When raising the AIF, Bridges chose Sinclair-MacLagan to command the 3rd Infantry Brigade, promoting him colonel. Other than Bridges, he was the only senior commander who was a regular soldier and, while he had a strong regimental background, like Bridges he had no senior command experience.

Bridges chose Sinclair-MacLagan's 3rd Brigade as the covering force at Anzac. Assessing the magnitude and difficulties of the task as beyond the ability of his brigade, Sinclair-MacLagan expressed doubts over its chances of success. A naturally pessimistic man, this state of mind was evident in his comments and the message to his troops prior to the landing. Acting hastily without any firm information on the situation, and with a preconceived view that the Turks would attack from Gaba Tepe, his two fateful decisions to halt his 3rd Brigade and divert the 2nd, completely changed the nature of the ANZAC operation from offensive to defensive.

Following the landing his brigade held the southern sector of the line. Evacuated sick in August 1915, he did not return to the 3rd Brigade until January 1916 and led it in France until December. Between January and July 1917 he commanded the AIF depots in Britain, but when Major General William Holmes was killed at Messines, Sinclair-MacLagan was appointed GOC 4th Australian Division and promoted major general. A conservative and considerate commander, Sinclair-MacLagan performed competently in the set-piece battles fought by his division under corps control during the remainder of the war and in the defence of Dernancourt in March 1918. At the war's end he returned to the British Army to command the 51st Highland Division. Retiring to Scotland in 1925, he died there in 1948.

Hut, while Jackson headed south to the 3rd Field Ambulance, which had landed with the 12th Battalion, to seek succour for his wounded. In the meantime, Pompey Elliott had embarked in the fifth boat but, instead of following Jackson, he led the remainder of his battalion to the right where steamboats picked them up and took them into Anzac Cove.

This photograph was taken around 7.00 to 7.30 am from the southern end of Anzac Cove looking towards Ari Burnu with Plugge's Plateau top right. This, together with other photographs taken during the morning, disproves the view that the Australians suffered heavy casualties on the beach or that it was heavily shelled by the gun at Gaba Tepe (AWM A03785-1).

Men of the 2nd Field Company landing in the centre of Anzac Cove around 7.20 am. Infantry are assembling on the beach and in the gully in the background (AWM P02226_014_2).

GALLIPOLI PENINSULA
3rd Brigade Landing and Move Inland

Legend:
- 12th Battalion
- Rafferty
- 10th Battalion
- Loutit
- 9th Battalion
- Plant
- 11th Battalion
- Tulloch

The landing and movements of the 3rd Brigade. The 10th Battalion and the bulk of the 3rd Brigade. The 10th Battalion and the bulk of the 9th and 12th occupied the 400 Plateau by 6.30 am while, after a delayed start, most of the 11th reached the area of Quinn's, Courtney's and Steele's Posts by around 7.30 am. Some two and a half companies from the 9th, 11th and 12th battalions occupied Baby 700 at around 8.00 am, and Tulloch pushed on to Battleship Hill arriving at 9.00 am. To the right, Loutit and Haig reached Adana Spur at around 6.45 am, and Loutit walked up to Hill 165. Plant headed for the 9th Battalion objective south of Anderson's Knoll (out of picture) reaching it after 7.00 am.

THE ADVANCE TO SECOND RIDGE AND BABY 700

On Russell's Top the *3rd Platoon* was also retreating. In a remarkable feat, 57-year-old Clarke and his men clawed their way up the precipitous spurs and reached Russell's Top south-west of The Sphinx. Ahead of them were some of Sergeant Major Suleyman's *3rd Platoon*, whom they charged. The Turks fled back along the Top. With Captain Tulloch's party moving up Walker's Ridge to his right rear and threatening to cut him off, Captain Faik ordered the remainder of the platoon to withdraw. Clarke shook out the 50 or so men with him and advanced, clearing the ridge as they went and, nearing The Nek, they saw Faik deploy his men on Baby 700. Clarke stopped to write a message and was immediately killed. The remaining men, under Lieutenants Ivor Margetts and Penistan Patterson, went to ground and a firefight ensued. Presently the firing ceased and Margetts sent two of his scouts, Privates Arthur Tilley and George Vaughan, forward to determine whether the enemy had withdrawn. The two men advanced cautiously up the broad slope through knee-high scrub to the crest, where they signalled back that the way was clear. Corporal Laing recalled that the time was now around 6.45 am. By now, Margetts and Patterson had been joined by Tulloch and Captain Joseph Lalor with more of the 12th. Recalling his battalion's reserve function, Lalor ordered the 12th to entrench on Russell's Top short of The Nek while Tulloch, realising that his objective was beyond Baby 700, set off along the inland slope with some 60 men. Soon after, two platoons of the 11th under Lieutenants Clement Buttle and Mordaunt Reid, sent forward by Drake-Brockman, reached Lalor, who sent them off after Tulloch. Crossing Baby 700 they were joined by Lieutenant Samuel Jackson's platoon of the 11th, and together they pushed on, eventually joining Tulloch's party.

Boats returning to the transports during the transfer of the 1st Brigade to the shore, with North Beach in the background and the top of the Sphinx jutting above the skyline of Russell's Top. The ridge immediately above the boat on the left is Walker's Ridge up which Captain Tulloch took his group from the 11th Battalion (AWM G00900).

In the centre, remnants of the *2nd Platoon* fell back across Shrapnel Gully and reached the 400 Plateau, warning Captain Sadik of the Australians' approach. The 400 Plateau is a two-lobed feature joined on its seaward edge, and cleft to the east by Owen's Gully running into Legge Valley. At the time of the battle the northern lobe, Johnston's Jolly, was a flat, bare feature 150 metres wide which thrust east for 400 metres. The southern lobe, Lone Pine to the Anzacs and Kanli Sirt to the Ottomans, runs south-east for 600 metres, punching out beyond Johnston's Jolly. At its seaward edge it is barely 150 metres wide and remains so for much of its length until broadening out to 350 metres at its eastern face, overlooking what was then the grass-covered Legge Valley. There, from its southern flank, Pine Ridge drops slowly away to the south-west. Lone Pine was covered with knee to waist-high scrub, while its eastern face and Pine Ridge were covered with firs.

Sadik's guns were on Lone Pine. He immediately ordered them dismantled and packed on mules. Before they could escape, however, Loutit and his platoon of the 10th arrived on Johnston's Jolly with Major Brand, who ordered him to take the battery. Loutit decided to outflank the Turks and moved across the Jolly to take the guns from the rear. Talbot-Smith and his scouts also reached the plateau and found the Turks hastening to move the guns away. At the same time Lieutenant George Thomas's platoon of the 9th Battalion arrived from McCay's Hill. In the ensuing skirmish three of the guns were captured, while the fourth took off down Legge Valley. By now the *2nd Platoon* was scattered, the survivors striking out for the crest of Third Ridge. Pushing around Owen's Gully, Loutit was joined by a small party of the 9th and 10th battalions under Lieutenant James Haig. Together they headed across Legge Valley towards the 10th Battalion's objective on Third Ridge. According to Loutit, they 'had trouble keeping up with [the Turks]. They were in scattered groups which when dispersed did not hold us up.'

Troops of the 2nd Brigade landing on the northern end of Anzac Cove probably between 6.30 and 7.00 am. Ari Burnu is on the left of the picture (AWM A02462_1).

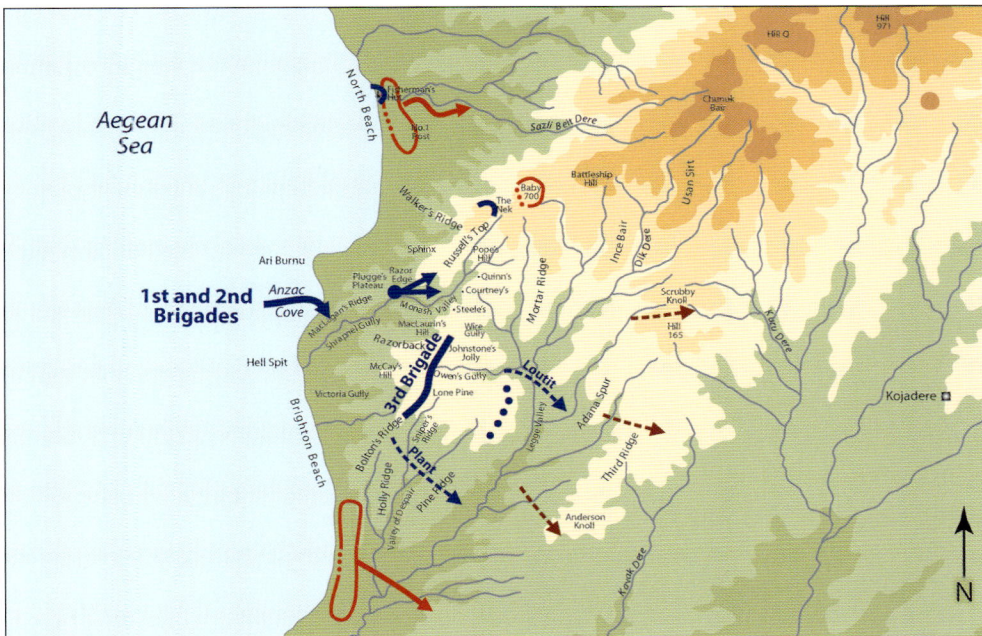

Situation around 6.30 am, 25 April. The 3rd Brigade has punched a gaping hole in the Ottoman defences, scattering Muharrem's *2nd Platoon*, but is now digging in on Second Ridge, while Loutit and Plant are moving towards Third Ridge. Ibrahim's *1st Platoon* is withdrawing up the Sazli Beit Dere, and to the south Hakki's platoon of the *7th Company* is withdrawing to Third Ridge. Only the *3rd Platoon* of Faik's company is offering resistance on Baby 700 against the Australians at The Nek. The remainder of Sefik's *27th Regiment* is an hour away from reaching the southern end of Third Ridge, while Kemal and the *19th Division* are waiting at Boghali.

Slipping and sliding down the steep inland slopes of Plugge's Plateau, Major Salisbury's company of the 9th Battalion had struck out across the valley where he recalled 'There was practically no opposition beyond a few snipers while we were crossing Shrapnel Gully', while Corporal Harrison recounted, 'We were met with some rifle fire from a few snipers who had remained behind, but we soon dispersed them'. On climbing the steep, scrub-covered slopes of the 400 Plateau, Salisbury remembered 'there was a great deal of rifle fire from the east and south-east …' which was probably the firefight in which Thomas's platoon captured Sadik's three guns. Having received orders from Sinclair-MacLagan to halt the advance and dig in, on cresting the plateau Salisbury pushed Fortescue's platoon forward overlooking Owen's Gully to act as a screen, and instructed his own men to entrench along the western edge of Lone Pine. Leaving Plugge's Plateau, Lieutenant Colonel Weir and most of the 10th Battalion slid into Monash Valley intent on reaching their objective. Before arriving at the 400 Plateau he also received the order to halt and dig in, and consequently deployed his battalion along the seaward edge of Johnston's Jolly, extending his line to the left towards MacLaurin's Hill, a small bump on Second Ridge which would soon be occupied by the 3rd Brigade headquarters.

On the right, the second wave companies of the 9th Battalion had topped McCay's Hill before 5.30 am. Both were still intent on reaching their objectives. While Thomas's platoon went east onto Lone Pine and encountered Sadik's battery, a group under Lieutenant Eric Plant swung south-east and headed for Anderson Knoll some two kilometres away. Milne's company came under fire from a trench at the head of Bolton's Ridge which they captured, while Dougall's D Company began to break up. Two platoons headed across Lone Pine where, after the skirmish which captured the mountain guns, Major Brand told them to occupy its eastern edge. The other two under Dougall's direction were drawn into Milne's fight, and swung down Bolton's Ridge until they reached an empty trench which they occupied. After this initial engagement, Hakki's platoon of the *7th Company*, which had been opposing Milne's and Dougall's men of the 9th, received fire from its right rear and withdrew heading for Third Ridge to avoid being taken from the rear. This was probably after Plant's group had passed behind them, as Plant pushed down Legge Valley unopposed. The two companies of the 12th Battalion (D and C) which had climbed McCay's Hill behind Milne's and Dougall's of the 9th respectively, came in on the right of Salisbury. Smith's B Company of the 12th, sent forward by Sinclair-MacLagan, arrived and slipped in between Salisbury and Weir rather than extending the 11th Battalion's right as originally intended. Thus a firing line comprising the best part of six intermixed companies of the 9th and 12th battalions on the right, and the bulk of the 10th Battalion on the left was established from the head of Bolton's Ridge and along the seaward edge of the 400 Plateau. Forward of them on Lone Pine were at least three platoons of the 9th Battalion providing an outpost line.

Back on Plugge's Plateau, Drake-Brockman had been directing the bulk of the 11th Battalion to implement Sinclair-MacLagan's instructions. Major James Denton's and Captain Charles Barnes' companies were to move up Monash Valley and occupy the northern half of Second Ridge, while Drake-Brockman's and Captain Raymond Leane's companies would occupy Baby 700. At that moment Major Stephen Roberts, the 11th's second-in-command, arrived and inexplicably directed Leane's company to remain with him on Plugge's Plateau as a reserve. Drake-Brockman then decided to reconnoitre the ground by climbing Russell's Top. There he met Lalor of the 12th and Robertson of the 9th who had gone left rather than right. They agreed that the combined party should occupy Baby 700 where Drake-Brockman would join them. Eventually only half of Drake-Brockman's company arrived on Baby 700. The remaining companies of the 11th, plus a composite group of men from all four battalions under Captain Reginald Everett, occupied positions along Second Ridge at what would later become Quinn's, Courtney's and Steele's Posts, extending the firing line to the north of the 400 Plateau.

By 6.30 am a lull had fallen over the battlefield with the 3rd Brigade digging in along Second Ridge. Some 1600 metres ahead of them the crest of Third Ridge lay unoccupied, save for a few scattered remnants of the *2nd Platoon*. Only the small parties under Tulloch, Loutit and Plant were moving toward their battalions' original objectives, unaware of the change in plan.

Judging from their colour patch, these are men from either the 8th or 4th Battalion and are disembarking from their transport to the ship's boats early on the morning of 25 April (AWM J05589-1).

DIVERSION OF THE 2ND BRIGADE

Further changes to the plan had already been implemented. 'Pompey' Elliott arrived at Anzac Cove at 5.30 am and met Sinclair-MacLagan, who directed him to take the 7th Battalion to the right, in preparation for going into action alongside the 3rd Brigade, rather than moving left to secure the vital ground. Gathering his companies as they landed under shrapnel fire from the gun at Gaba Tepe, Elliott sent them over Hell Spit to a brigade rendezvous in Shrapnel Gully close under the Razorback, the last group arriving there after 6.00 am. Two platoons were immediately despatched to support the 9th Battalion. The leading companies of the 6th Battalion were also coming ashore under bursts of shrapnel, although with only one old, 'slow firing Mantelli', it could not have been heavy. When McNicoll landed, Sinclair-MacLagan directed him to also support the 3rd Brigade to the right. As each boatload arrived, the men formed up and moved to the rendezvous Elliott had selected.

At Maidos, Sefik finally received orders at 5.55 am to move to Gaba Tepe and take the mountain battery located at Camburu on the Maidos–Kilid Bahr road with him. The battery was half an hour away. Rather than waiting, he detached a company to escort it and, just after 6.00 am, set out for the battlefield eight kilometres away, hoping to reach the centre of Third Ridge before the enemy. At the same time Ismet sent Second Lieutenant Mustafa's platoon of the *5th Company* north to support the *8th Company*. Moving behind Third Ridge and to the west of Kojadere village, Mustafa met Faik, who had been wounded, and after being briefed on the situation, took his platoon up onto Third Ridge. Elsewhere, Mustafa Kemal's *19th Division* had been preparing for a field exercise when news of the landing arrived. Cancelling the exercise, Kemal awaited orders from the *5th Army*.

A steam pinnace towing ships' boats loaded with men of the 2nd Brigade, heading for Anzac Cove around 5.30 am on 25 April (AWM C01890).

HMAT *Novian*, carrying Colonel James McCay, his headquarters and Lieutenant Colonel David Wanliss's 5th Battalion, had experienced some difficulty getting to her berth and now had to wait for the tows to arrive. Consequently, in another case of friction, McCay and the 5th, which was to be the first battalion of the 2nd Brigade ashore, did not land until after 6.00 am, by which time Elliot's 7th Battalion and McNicoll's 6th, the intended brigade reserve, were already ashore, and being committed to the right flank. By the time McCay reached the beach, the 7th Battalion had departed, as had the leading companies of the 6th, and the 8th was already landing. There, according to Major Walter Cass, the brigade major, he was greeted by Sinclair-MacLagan who told him: 'Well McCay, the position is this. I've gone to the left following the enemy instead of to the right. If you can change your plans and go to the right then it will settle the difficulty and things will be all right ...' McCay remonstrated that he was being asked to disobey orders and suggested going forward to assess the situation for himself. Sinclair-MacLagan retorted, 'There isn't time. I assure you my right will be turned if you do not do this.' McCay asked for assurance that the left was secure and, on being told that it was, he agreed to divert his brigade to the right flank. Sinclair-MacLagan then set off for the firing line and established his headquarters on MacLaurin's Hill, just north of Johnston's Jolly.

In taking these decisions, Sinclair-MacLagan completely changed the focus of the operation, and it was his actions, rather than the misplaced landing, which 'tore the plan to shreds'. While it was acceptable for a subordinate commander to take contrary action

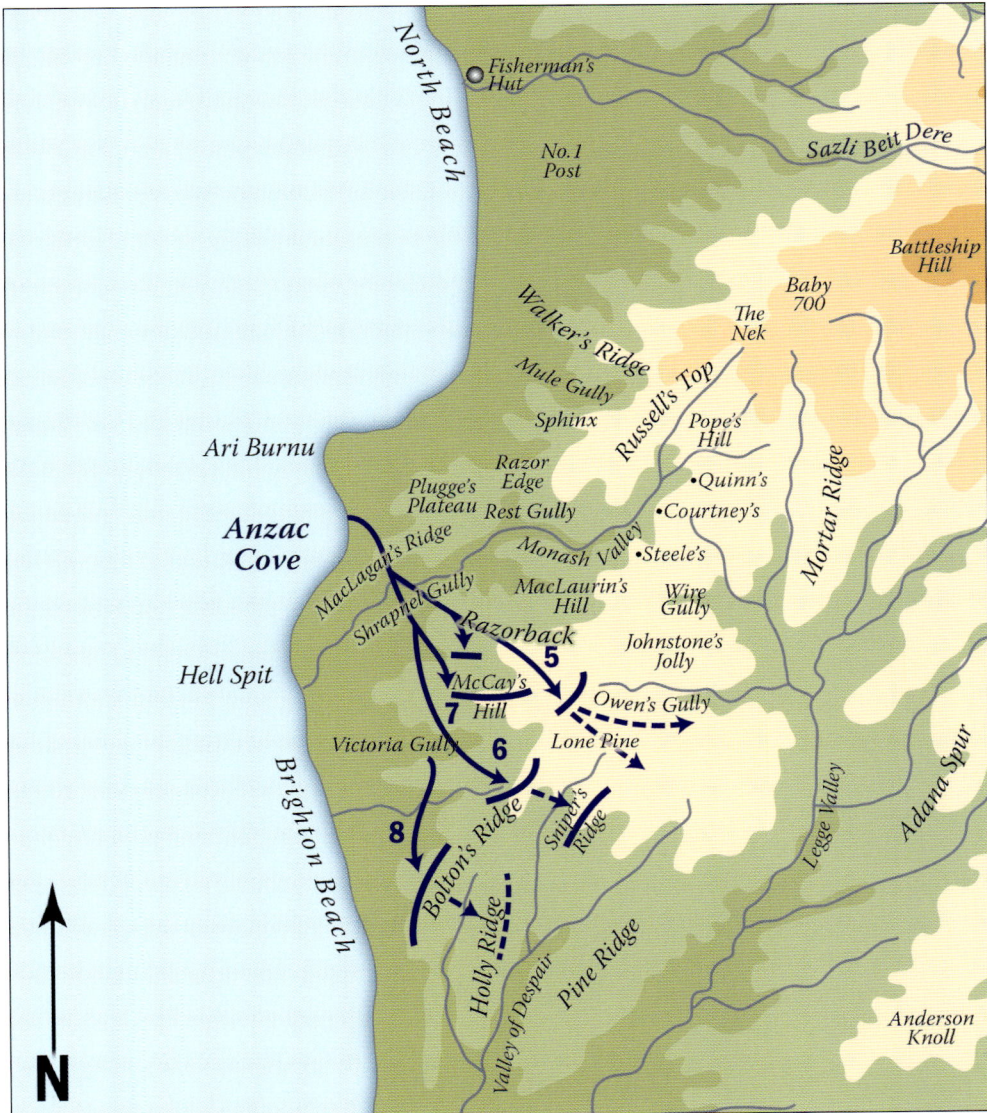

The diversion of the 2nd Brigade. Rather than pushing up the main range to secure the heights of the Sari Bair Range, the brigade is diverted to the right flank, with the 5th Battalion drawn into the 3rd Brigade on Lone Pine, the 7th holding McCay's Hill, and the 6th and 8th along Bolton's Ridge and pushing forward over the spurs running south off Lone Pine.

if the circumstances demanded, there was no evidence that such a drastic change was required at this point. The Turkish defenders at Anzac Cove were in full retreat, and Sinclair-MacLagan had no indication of any immediate threat from the right. It would seem that his earlier concerns about the Ottoman defences around Gaba Tepe, and an assumption they would counter-attack his flank, bore heavily on his thinking. He was right to consider that possibility, but had he gone to the 400 Plateau or McCay's Hill, he would have gained a more accurate battle picture before making such drastic alterations. Indeed, he was in a better position to resist a counter-attack now than had he been engaged on Brighton Beach. Three companies of the 9th Battalion, together with two of the 12th, were on the right flank, and the plateau and the head of Bolton's Ridge offered a suitable defensive position which dominated the ground over which such an attack would have come. Sinclair-MacLagan's fear for his right may have been justified, but he had the equivalent of more than a battalion to protect it, and the Navy could fire across his front enfilading any Ottoman attack from the south. Moreover, by attacking down and behind Bolton's Ridge himself, he could have retained the initiative and countered a threat from that quarter. Unbeknown to him, Hakki's platoon on Bolton's Ridge had withdrawn leaving the way open to Gaba Tepe, and a more resolute approach would have exposed the huge gap in the Turkish defences, and the relative lack of opposition across the entire front.

Furthermore, swapping the two brigades would not 'settle the difficulty' and set things 'right'. The 3rd Brigade's mission was to provide a dispersed covering screen to delay and disorganise any enemy reinforcements approaching Third Ridge. The 2nd Brigade was to pass through the northern corner of the screen and secure the vital ground. If these tasks were still to be achieved, it was not simply a matter of reversing the missions with the 3rd Brigade going to the left and the 2nd going to the right. They had two quite different roles. Tasks would have to be reallocated to battalions and leaders briefed on their new missions if chaos and confusion were not to prevail. A reversal of roles, however, was never intended. The 3rd Brigade had not gone to the left following the enemy. It had been ordered to dig in along Second Ridge, reflecting a decision not to push on and take either the covering position or the vital ground. In diverting the 2nd Brigade, Sinclair-MacLagan had supplanted his divisional commander and taken it on himself to abort the 1st Division's mission without any battlefield information justifying such a decision. Given the information available at the time, it was not his decision to make. A more prudent commander would have moved forward and ascertained the situation rather than acting hastily on assumptions. A bolder one would have told the 10th and 11th battalions to seize their objectives, and pushed the 9th out to secure the right flank, or ordered it to flank the Turkish defences and attack along Bolton's Ridge.

These two decisions changed the whole complexion of the battle. For ANZAC they negated the purpose of the landing and converted an offensive operation to a defensive one, largely on unfavourable ground of little tactical value. They also handed the initiative to the Ottoman commanders and bought them time to use it.

Part of the 1st Brigade being taken ashore early on the morning of 25 April. The flat-topped Plugge's Plateau, which the first wave of the 3rd Brigade assaulted in the dark, looms above Anzac Cove. Immediately on the left of the plateau is the Razor Edge, which prevented the Anzacs from progressing from the plateau up along Russell's Top to the vital ground. Further left is the end of Russell's Top and, to the right of the plateau, the upper reaches of MacLagan's Ridge slope down towards Hell Spit (AWM G00901).

CHAPTER 8

SEIZING THIRD RIDGE

On receiving the order to move, Lieutenant Colonel Sefik despatched three small cavalry patrols to obtain information on the unfolding situation. Two headed for Ari Burnu and Third Ridge, while the third went to Gaba Tepe to seek an update from Major Ismet. By 6.15 am Sefik's infantry were moving out. Concerned about naval gunfire and reconnaissance aircraft, he directed Major Malatyali Ibrahim's *1/27th* to avoid the main Maidos–Gaba Tepe road and take a newly opened track some 300 metres north, while Captain Halis's *3/27th* and Senior Captain Hamdi's machine-gun company took another route further north. 'A' echelon, carrying additional ammunition, brought up the rear. Sefik's fears were well founded. The British had hoisted an observation balloon tethered to HMS *Manica* lying off Gaba Tepe, which Sefik could see in the distance as he crossed the plain. Reconnaissance aircraft deployed aloft from HMS *Ark Royal* and flew along the main road, forcing the columns to take cover along the side of the tracks. However, the position of the sun, which shone directly in the airmen's eyes, and the presence of a low mist, made observation difficult and, to Sefik's relief, his troops passed over the plain without incident.

Men of the 1st Australian Brigade landing between 7.00 and 8.00 am on 25 April. The colour patch on the arm of the man in the foreground, and the boat numbered A8 suggests they are from the 4th Battalion and Headquarters 1st Brigade, which disembarked from the transport *Lake Michigan* (A8). The body lying on the water's edge is the only one shown in photographs taken in Anzac Cove on the morning of 25 April, disproving the myth of the Australians suffering heavy casualties as they came ashore. Bean records him as a dead Australian engineer (AWM P00035-001).

THE AUSTRALIAN ADVANCED PARTIES

Ahead of Sefik, the small parties of the 9th and 10th battalions under Lieutenants Plant, Loutit and Haig had reached Third Ridge. Breasting it well to the south of Anderson Knoll, Plant could look out across the plain. Behind him the two companies that were originally tasked to seize this area of Third Ridge were nowhere to be seen. When Sefik's force approached his isolated post, Plant ordered his vastly outnumbered group to retire to avoid being cut off, and headed back across Legge Valley towards the main firing line on Second Ridge.

Taken in 1985, this photograph shows Private Adil Sahin who was in the *2nd Platoon* squad post on Hell Spit when the 9th Battalion's second wave landed on the point. His squad withdrew up Shrapnel Valley and over the 400 Plateau to Scrubby Knoll. He and the survivors of his squad may have been the group that fired on Lieutenant Noel Loutit when he reached the crest of Third Ridge at about 7.40 am on 25 April (Harvey Broadbent image).

Further north Loutit and Haig reached Adana Spur to the south-west of Scrubby Knoll. While Bean records that they halted in the face of enemy resistance from Third Ridge, Loutit later hotly denied this, claiming that he stopped because he realised that he was outrunning the main body and decided to wait for them to arrive. Private Robert Rayney, who was invalided to Australia in August 1915, told Loutit's father that 'they halted and waited for their flanks to come up, which had not advanced so rapidly'. Taking two men, he then made his way up the spur to the crest of Third Ridge, reaching it close to Hill 165, and looked out towards the Narrows. The party was then fired on, possibly by the remnants of Private Adil's squad of the *2nd Platoon* or Mustafa's platoon of the *5th Company*. Loutit recalled that the 'fire was pretty hot' and one of his men was wounded in the stomach. Although he attempted to carry him back, Loutit was eventually forced to leave the man behind. Returning down the spur he discovered that his platoon had been engaged by a small Turkish force to its front. 'If you want my honest opinion,' Loutit said later, 'I think the

Turks came back when they realised we had stopped chasing them.' However, the Turkish force to his front was possibly Hakki's platoon of the *7th Company* which had withdrawn from Bolton's Ridge, as Hakki later claimed to have halted the Australian advance on Third Ridge. If not it was the advance guard of the *27th Regiment*. Seeing Australians on the forward edge of the 400 Plateau, Loutit sent a man back for reinforcements, and eventually a party of the 9th Battalion under Captain John Ryder joined him.

By this time a third party had reached the ridge. While the 10th Battalion was digging in at around 6.30 am, Captain Mervyn Herbert instructed two scouts, Lance Corporal Phillip Robin and Private Arthur Blackburn, to reconnoitre forward of Second Ridge. They reached Third Ridge north of Scrubby Knoll, finding no sign of the enemy. Moving south along the far slope they had passed Scrubby Knoll when they observed Turks approaching up the Kavak Dere, the valley behind the southern portion of Third Ridge. Slipping back over the ridge they saw Loutit's force engaged with a party of Turks and returned to Johnston's Jolly. Strangely, they did not encounter the Turks who had fired on Loutit during his reconnaissance of the crest.

THE *27TH REGIMENT* ARRIVES

Having crossed the plain unmolested, Sefik's battalions now converged. As they reached the mouth of the Kavak Dere, 1100 metres south-east of Anderson Knoll, the column halted while Sefik questioned a wounded *7th Company* man who informed him that the enemy was nearby, possibly referring to Plant's group. While the advance guard headed for Anderson Knoll, the remainder moved up the Kavak Dere, using Third Ridge to shield their movement from the Australians, and dropping off three-man security parties along the crest as flank guards. Initially the advance was slow until Sefik ordered them to push on. Reaching Anderson Knoll, he heard sporadic firing and saw Australians moving about on the 400 Plateau. With the plateau higher than the knoll, and being in enfilade to naval gunfire, Sefik pushed on up the Kavak Dere, looking for a more favourable position. Reaching Hill 165, just south of Scrubby Knoll and overlooking the 400 Plateau, he decided that this was a suitable position from which to mount and support an attack. He had taken two hours to cover the eight kilometres, although it was another hour before the tail of the column arrived. Despite starting with a disadvantage of around six and half kilometres to the Australians' 1600 metres from Second Ridge, Sefik had won the race to take Third Ridge.

As each company arrived the battalions shook out into their assembly areas behind Hill 165, while Sefik surveyed the scene and received reconnaissance reports from his cavalry patrols. Security elements were pushed forward and, according to Sefik, exchanged shots with Loutit's party sometime between 8.30 and 9.00 am — which accords with Loutit's version of events. Soon after the 'A' echelon arrived, Sefik sent a pack train north to the main range to replenish the *1st* and *3rd platoons* of the *8th Company* with small arms ammunition, while stockpiling the rest behind his position and sending the mules back to the ammunition dump at Boghali for more.

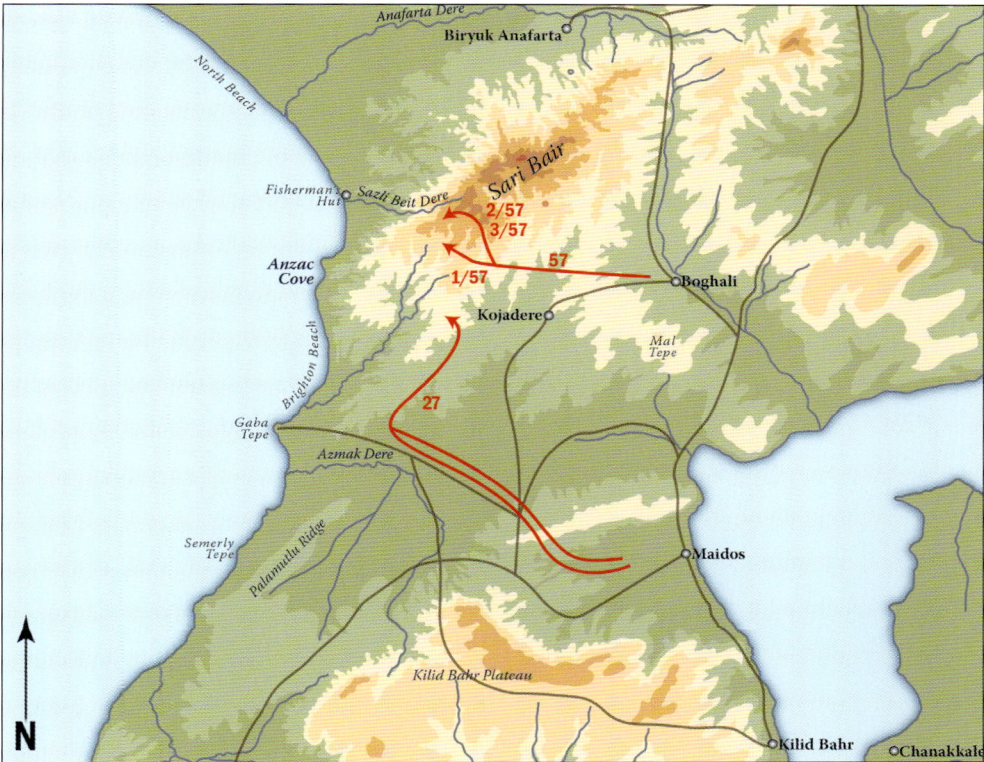

The routes taken by the *27th* and *57th regiments*. Departing Maidos just after 6.00 am, the *27th* crossed the Gaba Tepe–Maidos valley to the southern end of Third Ridge and then advanced north behind it to Hill 165 reaching that feature around 8.00 am. Departing at 8.10 am, the *57th* headed west over the spurs and ridges running off the Sari Bair Range. The head of the column reached Third Ridge around 10.00 am. The *1/57th* then pushed over Third Ridge and engaged Tulloch's group on Battleship Hill, while the *2nd* and *3rd battalions*, with the machine-gun company, deployed north to Chunuk Bair.

Assessing that the ANZAC flanks rested on Baby 700 and the 400 Plateau, Sefik decided to use his men as a covering force to disrupt and delay the enemy from seizing the dominating ground, and buying time for reinforcements to arrive. To achieve this he planned to engage his adversary on a broad front: the *1/27th*, less one company as his reserve, would attack the Australians on Lone Pine, while the *3/27th* would attack further north driving towards the Sari Bair Range. Both would be covered by the machine-gun company under Sefik's direct control from Hill 165. The mountain battery, which had yet to arrive, would support the attack from the same location. Sending a message to Halil Sami, he outlined the situation and his proposed attack, and requested that reinforcements be sent to secure the Sari Bair Range.

By now Sefik was facing almost 11 Australian battalions, a numerical disadvantage of over 5:1. Opposite him, more than six battalions from the 2nd and 3rd brigades were clustered around Bolton's Ridge and the 400 Plateau. Further north, four companies primarily from the 11th and 12th battalions occupied posts along Second Ridge. Baby 700, the ground of tactical importance dominating the flank of the Australian line, was occupied by a total of two and a half companies drawn from the 9th, 11th and 12th battalions, and forward of them

Tulloch's group was approaching Battleship Hill. Behind this line, the 1st Australian Brigade had begun disembarking between 5.30 and 6.45 am. By 8.00 am, the 1st and 3rd battalions, and half of the 2nd and 4th battalions, were ashore, and at 7.55 am two companies of the 3rd Battalion had been sent to reinforce the 3rd Brigade along Second Ridge.

Tulloch had been joined by Buttle's, Reid's and Jackson's platoons, bringing his numbers up to around 180 men. Using fire and movement in section rushes they had pushed the *3rd Platoon, 8th Company*, back up the range, driving it from two successive spurs. At around 9.00 am they halted on Battleship Hill, which formed part of the battalion objective. Tulloch deployed his men along the south-eastern shoulder of the feature, the head of Ince Bair, looking out over Dik Dere to the upper reaches of Third Ridge, while Jackson was sent to hold the crest on the left facing Chunuk Bair. Soon after, having made the long climb up the Sazli Beit Dere, Ibrahim's *1st Platoon* arrived on the seaward slopes of Chunuk Bair and, replenishing their ammunition, joined in the fight. More help was on the way.

Captain Ahmet Zeki, Commanding Officer of the *1st Battalion, 57th Regiment*, who travelled with Mustafa Kemal at the head of the *57th*'s column and went into action against Captain Tulloch's party on Ince Bair between 10.30 and 11.00 am on 25 April. He was wounded during the fighting for Baby 700 and was evacuated at around 4.00 pm (AWM ART02868).

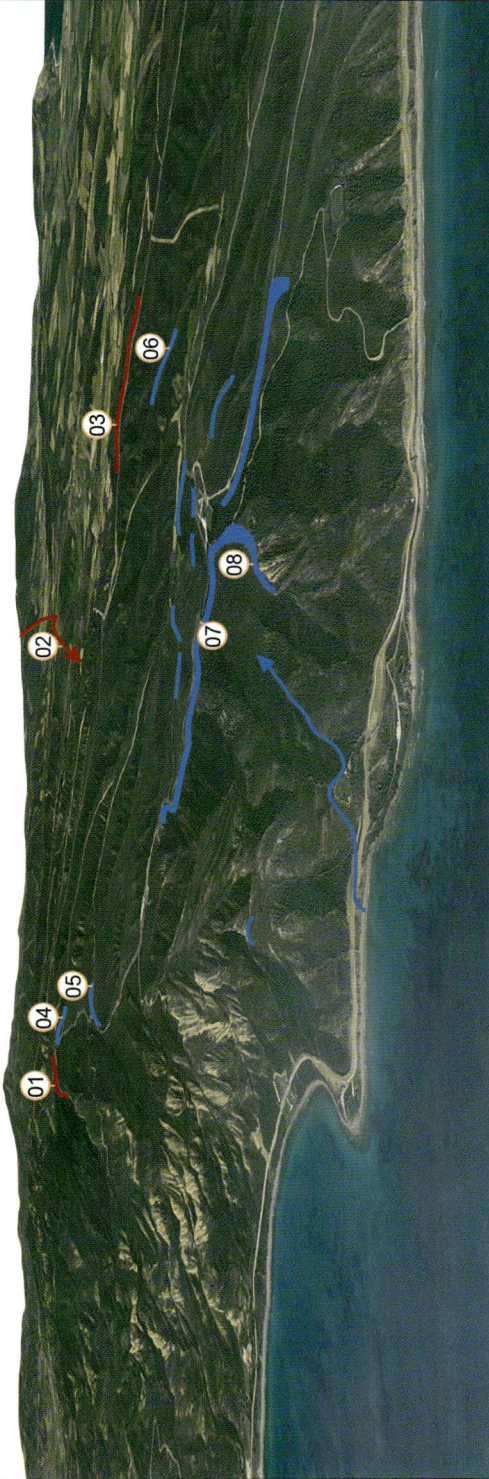

GALLIPOLI PENINSULA
Situation 9.30 am

01. 8th Company (-)
02. 57th Regiment
03. 27th Regiment (-)
04. Tulloch
05. Elms 9th, 11th & 12th Battalions
06. Loutit, Haig & Ryder
07. 3rd Brigade
08. 2nd Brigade

The situation around 9.30 am. While the bulk of the 2nd and 3rd brigades are entrenching along the lower reaches of Second Ridge, on the vital ground Tulloch's party is engaged with the *1st* and *3rd platoons* of the *8th Company, 2/27th Regiment*. Behind him on Baby 700 are some two and a half companies of the 9th, 11th and 12th battalions. Loutit and Haig are at Adana Spur engaged in a firefight with either Hakki's platoon of the *7th Company* or the advanced guard of the *27th Regiment*, while its *1st* and *3rd battalions* are assembling behind Hill 165. In the distance the head of the *57th Regiment* is marching cross-country towards Third Ridge.

THE *57TH REGIMENT*

The greatest contradictions in the Turkish accounts refer to the actions of Mustafa Kemal and the movement of the *57th Regiment*, discussed in Appendix 6. Ottoman messages sent on the day show that, far from moving as soon as news of the landing was received, as claimed by Kemal, he appeared to be slow to move, and the messages reveal his initial reluctance to move without orders from his superiors. They indicate that Kemal received the order to despatch one battalion to Ari Burnu at 7.45 am, and that he departed Boghali just after 8.00 am. What is not in dispute is that, realising the importance of the vital ground around Koja Chemin Tepe (Hill 971) and Chunuk Bair, Kemal took all three battalions of the *57th Regiment*, its machine-gun company and a mountain battery, and set off for these crucial features. Kemal wrote that he struck out cross-country directly to Koja Chemin Tepe (Hill 971), but Captain Ahmet Zeki, commanding the *1/57th*, told Bean, while escorting him around the battlefield in 1919, that the column's route took them south of Hill 971 towards Chunuk Bair to intercept the 'English' before they could reach the high ground, and pointed out where they reached Third Ridge — just north of Scrubby Knoll. On reaching the Kuru Dere to the north-east of Scrubby Knoll — not on Chunuk Bair as claimed by Kemal — Zeki claims they met men of the *8th Company*

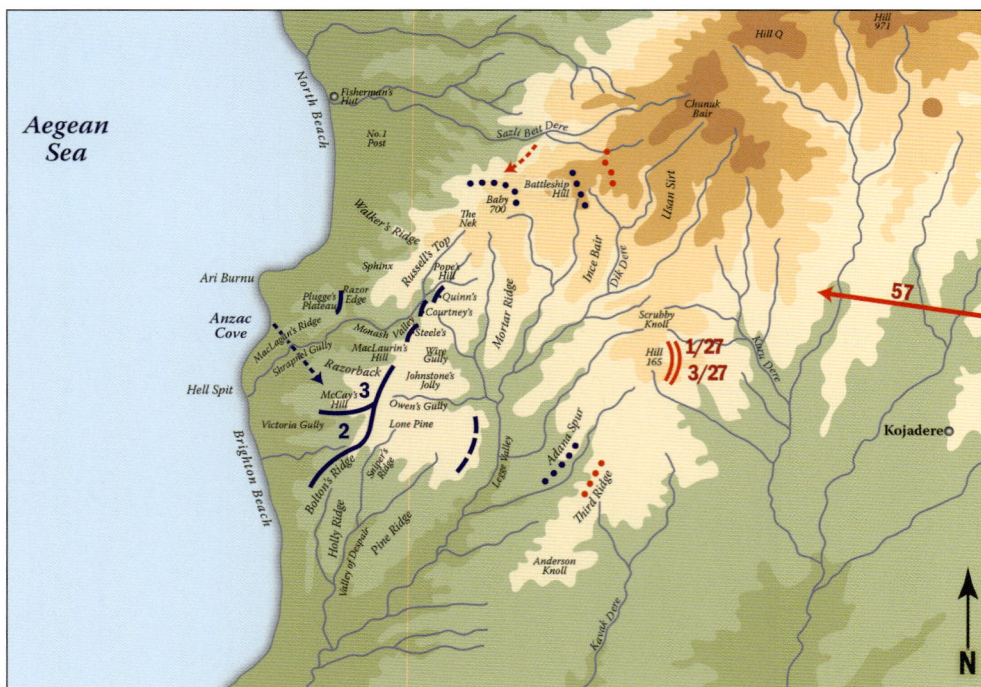

The situation at 9.30 am. The 3rd Brigade is digging in along the 400 Plateau and the 2nd Brigade is deploying to McCay's Hill and along Bolton's Ridge. Loutit, Haig and Ryder are on Adana Spur in contact with either Hakki's Platoon, or the *27th Regiment*. Elements of the 9th, 11th and 12th battalions have occupied Baby 700 and Tulloch's party of the 11th is on Battleship Hill. The *1st* and *3rd battalions* of the *27th Regiment* are assembling behind Hill 165, while on Chunuk Bair the *1st* and *3rd platoons* of the *8th Company*, *2/27th*, are in contact with Tulloch. The *57th Regiment* is marching cross-country to join the battle.

retreating with news that they were out of ammunition and the enemy was advancing. Turning to Zeki, Kemal directed his battalion to attack immediately, advising him that the *2/57th* would assault on his right, and gave instructions for the mountain battery to take post on Third Ridge to the north of Scrubby Knoll when it arrived. It was now after 10.00 am. However, the cross-country march had badly strung out the column, scattering it along the route. Zeki gathered those with him, primarily the advance guard company and, pushing onto Third Ridge, he saw Australians on the slopes of Battleship Hill. Moving over Dik Dere, Zeki closely engaged Tulloch's force on the upper reaches of Ince Bair from the south-east. Although outnumbered, the Ottomans now controlled Third Ridge. However, with the column strung out, it would take time to mount a coordinated regimental attack and to bring the mountain battery into action to support it. While the head of the column engaged Tulloch's men on Battleship Hill, Kemal, who believed these initial actions had halted the Australian advance up the main range, began organising a proper counter-attack to drive the enemy back towards the beach.

Esat Pasha, Commander *III Corps*, on the left visiting a mountain gun position later in the campaign. He moved from the northern end of the peninsula during the morning of 25 April, established a tactical headquarters on Mal Tepe around midday and took control of the battle, coordinating the actions of the *9th* and *19th divisions* (Turkish General Staff archives, courtesy Harvey Broadbent).

LIEUTENANT COLONEL MEHMET SEFIK

Commander *27th Regiment*

Mehmet Sefik was an energetic Ottoman commander born in Kastoria in northern Greece in 1877 who graduated from the Ottoman Military Academy in 1896. As a junior officer he fought in the Greco–Turkish War of 1897, later saw active service in the Italian–Turkish War in 1912 and, as a major, commanded a reserve infantry regiment during the fighting in Salonika in the First Balkan War. Appointed to command the *27th Regiment* in 1914 and assigned the Gaba Tepe area to defend, he trained his unit hard on the ground they would later fight over on 25 April. Under General Otto Liman von Sanders' defence posture, Sefik's *2nd Battalion* guarded the 12 kilometres of coastline from the Fisherman's Hut to Semerly Tepe, while his *1st* and *3rd battalions* and machine-gun company were held in reserve just west of Maidos.

By 5.00 am on 25 April he was ready to advance on Gaba Tepe but was told to wait for further information. Chafing at the bit, he finally departed Maidos just after 6.00 am and marched his men hard to Third Ridge, selecting Hill 165 as his command post at 8.00 am. There he accurately assessed the extent of the ANZAC position before committing his troops. Determined to act as a covering force until reinforcements arrived, and to seize the initiative, he drove off the small Australian force on Adana Spur and prepared to attack the main Australian position on Lone Pine with his *1st Battalion*, and the main range with his *3rd Battalion*. On learning that he had been placed under command of Lieutenant Colonel Mustafa Kemal commanding the *19th Division*, Sefik apprised Kemal of the situation and coordinated his attack with that of the *57th*. He launched the assault at 12.30 pm and his men fought fiercely for possession of Lone Pine, slowly driving the Australian outposts back across the plateau and recapturing the three mountain guns lost earlier that morning. Reinforced by the *77th Regiment* that evening, he directed it to attack south of Lone Pine, driving the Australians off Pine Ridge. On 27 April his regiment again attacked Lone Pine but with little success.

In August 1915 Sefik assumed command of the *19th Division* from Mustafa Kemal, who had been appointed to lead *XVI Corps*. Sefik later commanded the *59th* and *49th divisions*, ending the war as Deputy Commander *XXI Corps*. During the Turkish War of Independence he led the *57th Division*. A competent and frank officer who freely spoke his mind, Sefik was not always on good terms with his superiors, who regarded him as overly critical. He retired in 1931 and died in Istanbul in 1964.

A Turkish machine-gun company on the march showing the gun broken down into its loads, including ammunition. This company has the wheeled mount and, while the photo is not of either the *27th* or *57th regiments* machine-gun companies, it shows how the Maxim was carried when deploying forward to the battlefield (AWM P04411_095).

THE POSSIBILITY OF REACHING THIRD RIDGE

Historians have generally accepted Bean's argument that Sinclair-MacLagan stopped on Second Ridge to reorganise his force before pushing on, but before this could be done the Ottomans seized Third Ridge in force. This ignores several issues. According to Bean's account, which is supported by Salisbury's statement, the leading companies had largely sorted themselves out on Plugge's Plateau, and the 9th and 10th battalions had departed and were heading towards their objectives before Sinclair-MacLagan arrived on the plateau. Most of the 11th were regrouping and simply needed to push along Russell's Top to reach their objective. Thus the need to reorganise was spurious. Further, Sinclair-MacLagan's early order for his brigade to dig in along Second Ridge was not the action of a commander intending to push on, aware that time was crucial if the objective was to be seized. Nor does his subsequent action in diverting the 2nd Brigade to take post on the right flank indicate a desire to push forward. Moreover, Sefik's battalions did not arrive at Hill 165 until after 8.00 am, which means the 3rd Brigade had sat unmolested on Second Ridge for almost two hours. Bean's argument appears to be seeking to justify Sinclair-MacLagan's actions, and contradicts his earlier comments.

Members of Headquarters 1st Australian Division coming ashore at Anzac Cove at around 10.15 am on 25 April. The transports offshore indicate the distance covered in ferrying the NZ&A Division battalions to the shore by mid to late morning. The destroyer HMS *Ribble*, which carried Clarke and A Company, 12th Battalion, lies close offshore to the right (AWM G00903).

Could the 3rd Brigade have reached Third Ridge and Chunuk Bair ahead of the *27th* and *57th regiments*? Noel Loutit thought so, but commented, 'They didn't seem to want to come.' That Lieutenant Plant was able to reach the ridge somewhere south of Anderson Knoll before the *27th* arrived would indicate that some of the 9th Battalion could have done so. Whether they would have been able to hold their position is unclear. Nonetheless, had they arrived to support Plant, they could have forced Sefik to deploy early and made him fight for possession of the southern end of the ridge, which was what the covering force was expected to do. Indeed, had Plant opened fire as Sefik approached, he would have forced the Turks to deploy on the plain, slowing them down before he withdrew. Further north, given Robin's and Blackburn's reconnaissance, there is little doubt that had they not been ordered to halt, the 10th Battalion could have seized the central portion of the ridge ahead of the *27th*. The 10th Battalion reached Johnston's Jolly just after 6.00 am, the same time Sefik was departing his camp near Maidos. Their objective was 1600 metres away with only the scattered remnants of the *2nd Platoon* ahead of them, although Robin and Blackburn reported no sign of the enemy on Third Ridge when they were there. By comparison, the *27th* was eight kilometres away. While Tulloch had to fight his way along the main range, he reached Battleship Hill an hour before the head of the *1/57th*'s column reached Third Ridge. Had the rest of the 11th Battalion moved up in support, they could have at least held Battleship Hill in force, and probably driven the two platoons of the *8th Company* off Chunuk Bair to reach their objective. The bulk of the battalion was ready to climb out of Rest Gully onto Russell's Top before 5.45 am, had Sinclair-MacLagan not intervened. Thus, in the two and a quarter hours before Kemal departed Boghali, or the four and a quarter hours before the head of the column reached Third Ridge, the 11th had to travel about two and a half kilometres along the relatively easy crest of the main range to reach its objective.

Departing just after 8.00 am, the *57th Regiment* had to travel four kilometres over projecting ridges, spurs and gullies which slowed its rate of advance, before arriving at Third Ridge. The *57th* then had to march another 1000 metres to reach Chunuk Bair. Bold Ottoman and cautious Australian action handed both the initiative and the ANZAC covering force position to the defenders.

Members of Headquarters 1st Australian Division at the northern end of Anzac Cove at around 10.00 am, 25 April (AWM AO1000).

The northern end of Third Ridge taken from the north-eastern edge of Lone Pine looking across Legge Valley. Chunuk Bair (11th Battalion's objective) is on the left horizon, and Scrubby Knoll on the right. In 1915 Legge Valley was grass covered. The lower end of Mortar Ridge is in the left near distance of the photo (immediately left of the red flag and behind the bush in the fore ground), while between it and Chunuk Bair is the lower reaches of Ince Bair (with the long scar running up it). Dik Dere runs between Ince Bair and Third Ridge. Robin and Blackburn passed Third Ridge between Chunuk Bair and Scrubby Knoll in the early morning and moved to the right beyond Scrubby Knoll. Later, Zeki's men of the *1/57th* crossed the ridge roughly centre of the photo and into Dik Dere, before climbing Ince Bair and engaging Tulloch's men on Battleship Hill (out of the photo to the left) (author's image).

CHAPTER 9

SQUARING OFF

Friction and the fog of war increasingly affected the battle fought by the Anzacs. Their problems were many and varied: the tortured terrain; unfamiliarity with the ground; rudimentary communications; inadequate reconnaissance compounded by vague and incorrect information; hasty decisions; imprecise orders; and the inexperience of raw troops and commanders, all of which contributed to the fragmentation of units. This was to be an issue that bedevilled the Australians and New Zealanders throughout the day.

Looking across Brown's Dip and Victoria Gully to McCay's Hill from the seaward edge of Lone Pine. Landing on Brighton Beach and Hell Spit, the second wave companies of the 9th Battalion, together with D Company of the 12th, climbed the feature in the early hours of 25 April. At about 7.00 am, 'Pompey' Elliott's 7th Battalion occupied it and remained there throughout the day (Glenn Wahlert image).

THE 2ND BRIGADE DEPLOYS

While the advanced parties were pushing forward and the *27th Regiment* was marching towards Third Ridge, the 2nd Brigade deployed to the right of the 3rd Brigade's line. Taking Elliot and the 7th Battalion with him, McCay climbed to the crest of McCay's Hill where he told Elliot to establish a firing line abutting the 400 Plateau. The 8th would extend his line towards the sea, the 6th Battalion would be in support of him, and the 5th in support of the 8th. Returning to the rendezvous, McCay instructed the 6th to move up, but the battalion became fragmented, a problem that was to afflict many other units throughout the day. The 6th was unclear of what was expected of it and, rather than supporting Elliot, when the two leading companies reached McCay's Hill, they passed over the crest into the broken country beyond. McNicoll established his headquarters on Bolton's Ridge and promptly lost contact with them. Major Henry Bennett, his second-in-command, went forward, found the leading companies and, rather than bringing them back, organised them into a defensive line along Sniper's Ridge. Whitham saw the new line being established and took his company of the 12th Battalion forward to join them. A third company of the 6th, under Major Richard Wells, had been diverted to Lone Pine and eventually established a line north of Bennett, but his company was out of contact with both Bennett and McNicoll. Lieutenant Ralph Prisk's platoon had been told to move along the seaward slope of Bolton's Ridge as a flank guard. Picking up some men of the 9th Battalion, they advanced south for over half a mile down Bolton's Ridge. Finding no Turks in the area, Prisk despatched half the platoon to reconnoitre towards Gaba Tepe while he took the rest eastwards, passing over the southern end of Holly Ridge. Reaching the lower end of Pine Ridge, he halted at the edge of Legge Valley. Again, there were no Turks in sight. Later Prisk and his men were fired on by Australians to his rear, so they withdrew and returned to McNicoll's headquarters.

The 8th Battalion followed the 6th, and again it appears the orders were unclear. On reaching Bolton's Ridge, Major Robert Gartside, the second-in-command, sent two companies and the machine-gun section forward into the broken ground south of the plateau, some of the men reaching the northern end of Pine Ridge. The remainder established a defensive line along Bolton's Ridge to around 750 metres from its junction with Lone Pine.

Staff of Headquarters 1st Australian Division coming ashore at Ari Burnu at around 10.00 am on 25 April. The packs in the right foreground may have been dropped by men from the first wave of the 3rd Brigade before they scaled the heights of Plugge's Plateau (AWM G00904-1).

BRIDGES TAKES CHARGE

Major General Bridges came ashore at 7.20 am and, on being told of the changes, strode out to McCay's Hill with his Chief of Staff, Colonel Brudenell White. Arriving there sometime around 8.00 am he surveyed the scene. Apart from distant sporadic shots, the battlefield was quiet. Ahead of him Bolton's Ridge was lined with Australians. To his left, Third Ridge appeared free of enemy troops. Unaware that the *27th Regiment* was moving behind the ridgeline, Bridges considered that there was nothing to prevent the advance from continuing in that area. White agreed, remarking that 'the precious hour in which an advance might still be made [was] being allowed to slip away.' Precious time had already been lost. The 3rd Brigade had been on Second Ridge for two hours, the time it had taken the *27th Regiment* to march the eight kilometres from Maidos to the centre of Third Ridge. Inclined to order the men on Bolton's Ridge to advance, but lacking a grasp of the entire situation, Bridges told the line to hold fast. Concerned with his left, he then set off, intending to walk along Second Ridge. Instead he became caught up with the troops digging in and decided to return to Anzac Cove.

As Bridges arrived at the cove, he met Wanliss and the two leading companies of the 5th Battalion. Striding down MacLagan's Ridge waving his cane, Bridges told Wanliss to reinforce the firing line immediately. He was not to wait for the rest of his battalion but instead to push on. They formed fours and set off but, as they climbed the Razorback, the company commanders, Major Erle Fethers and Captain Robert Flockart, realised that, other than Bridges' vague instructions, they had no clear idea where to go. By this time Wanliss had left them, having taken a different track. While they halted to clarify the situation, Major Richard Saker's company joined them, and they decided to continue up the Razorback towards Johnston's Jolly, drawing them into the 3rd Brigade rather than the 2nd. Only the last company ashore actually reached McCay on McCay's Hill.

Discovering that he could see little of the battlefield from Ari Burnu and that Plugge's Plateau was too steep for him to climb, Bridges returned to the beach. With telephone communications now established with the 2nd and 3rd Brigade headquarters, he gave permission for the 1st Division headquarters to be established in the gully above the cove. There he remained for the rest of what was turning into a sunny and pleasant spring day.

At this stage Bridges' force was heavily weighted to the right, while the left, his ground of tactical importance, was dangerously short of troops — dangerous because Baby 700 dominated much of Sinclair-MacLagan's line. The equivalent of seven battalions was deploying on Bolton's Ridge and the 400 Plateau, four companies held the centre of Second Ridge, and only two and a half companies were sited on the left. Command and control was also skewed to the Australian right, where two brigade headquarters were located within 500 metres of each other, while the ground of tactical importance was controlled by three company commanders out of contact with Sinclair-MacLagan and Bridges. If the left was to be secured, Bridges would need to send the 1st Brigade to Baby 700 — and soon.

MAJOR GENERAL WILLIAM BRIDGES, CMG

General Officer Commanding 1st Australian Division

Born in Scotland in 1861, Bridges entered the Royal Military College of Canada in 1877. However, when his parents emigrated to New South Wales, Bridges followed them, failing his studies as a means to secure his release from the college. Appointed a lieutenant in the New South Wales Permanent Artillery in 1885, he qualified as an instructor in gunnery and, having attended a series of courses in Great Britain, returned to Australia as the Chief Instructor at the School of Gunnery. During the South African War he was attached to a British cavalry division until May 1900 when he was evacuated with enteric fever. From 1901 he was heavily involved in the creation of the Australian Army, strongly supporting the imperialist approach of raising an army to augment the British Army while opposing the nationalist concept of maintaining the force purely for the defence of Australia.

A competent administrator and organiser, Bridges was an able staff officer and was widely considered Australia's 'best soldier' despite having no regimental or field experience. He founded the Australian Intelligence Corps and in 1909 became Chief of the Australian General Staff. Appointed to found the Royal Military College of Australia in 1910, he was Duntroon's first commandant until May 1914 when he became Inspector-General. In August he raised the AIF and was promoted to major general, holding the twin posts of Commander of the AIF and GOC 1st Australian Division.

The 1st Division was Bridges' first field command, an appointment for which he had received no training and possessed no prior experience. Though personally courageous, his dour, brusque and often rude manner discouraged initiative and frank advice from his subordinates. Some of his officers considered him 'an academic soldier', while Colonel Talbot Hobbs, the 1st Division's chief gunner, regarded him as 'an uncouth, ignorant boor'.

At the landing, his lack of practical field command experience told, and he was found wanting as a formation commander. Presented with a stalled offensive, while believing there was nothing to stop the advance continuing, he returned to Anzac Cove, accepted the situation and failed to take a grip on the battle and impose his will on its progress. Establishing his headquarters in the cove, he simply responded to calls for reinforcements from the front. That night, accepting impending defeat, he urged Birdwood to consider an immediate evacuation which, had it gone ahead, would have been catastrophic. His only personal intervention in the battle resulted in the ill-fated advance by the 4th Battalion on 26 April.

Following the landing he took charge of the right-hand sector of the ANZAC line and recklessly exposed himself to enemy fire as he made his rounds of the line. On 15 May he was mortally wounded and died aboard the hospital ship *Gascon* on 18 May, having been knighted (KCB) the day before by King George V. His greatest achievements were the establishment of the Royal Military College of Australia and the raising of the AIF.

A Company, 3rd Battalion, on the firing line on the north side of Wire Gully at around 10.00 am, 25 April. MacLaurin's Hill is behind them. The three men in the foreground appear to be observing and sniping at Ottoman troops on Third Ridge. Others are resting in their shell scrapes (AWM AO1854).

DRIVING IN THE ADVANCED PARTIES

As Sefik's battalions were deploying, the company detailed to escort the mountain battery arrived without the guns, having been sent on ahead by a senior artillery officer. Deciding to delay the attack until the battery arrived, Sefik eventually spotted an artillery convoy approaching from Kojadere. It was Sadik with the single gun that had escaped capture on Lone Pine. Once in position, Sefik directed Sadik to shell the Australians around the lost guns. But, while the few shells scattered the Australians, Sefik considered the effect minimal. His machine-guns and riflemen then opened an intermittent fire, the Australians replied, and a firefight erupted at long range. Sefik's riflemen moved slowly forward engaging the nearest Australians — Loutit's, Haig's and Ryder's force along Adana Spur. By 10.00 am these forces were 'locked in battle'. Sinclair-MacLagan interpreted the engagement as an Ottoman counter-attack and ordered Salisbury's and Milne's companies to the eastern edge of Lone Pine to meet it, while appealing to Bridges for more reinforcements. The weakness of the Australian position on the right now became evident. From the heights of Battleship Hill to Hill 165, the 400 Plateau 'stood out like a Greek amphitheatre' and any men moving onto and over it could be clearly seen.

Sefik certainly observed the movement. Interpreting it as the arrival of reinforcements for Loutit, Haig and Ryder, he engaged Lone Pine with his machine-guns. At the same time the three companies of the 5th Battalion reached the 400 Plateau and were immediately drawn into the conflict. Lieutenant Alfred Derham took his platoon across the plateau in section rushes under shrapnel and machine-gun fire, although he recalled that the machine-guns were 'firing too high and the shrapnel was poor stuff'. By the time he reached the forward slope he had 'only my NCOs and few of the more reliable men'. The rest were scattered in the brush behind him. There he could see Sadik's gun some 1600 metres away and some Ottoman infantry moving down the slope in skirmishing order. He fired on these men, forcing them to duck for cover.

How long Ryder, Haig and Loutit remained on Adana Spur is unclear, but eventually Ryder decided to withdraw to Lone Pine. Loutit was quite critical of Ryder and thought his decision premature 'as we were not being pressed heavily'. However, Ryder's decision may have been correct as the Turks, higher up the spur, would have been moving onto the Australians' left flank and, once Ryder fell back, Loutit and Haig did the same, moving north over the spurs running off Third Ridge. 'It was late morning, closer to 10.30 or 11' Loutit later recalled. Pursued by elements of the *3/27th*, he eventually slipped across Legge Valley and, around midday, established a post in Wire Gully between Johnston's Jolly and MacLaurin's Hill. Third Ridge was now cleared of Australians. The *3/27th* had pushed up along Third Ridge, picking up Mustafa's platoon of the *5th Company, 2/27th*, until they reached Ince Bair where they encountered Tulloch's party and Ahmet Zeki's advanced force from the *1/57th*.

Members of the 3rd Battalion in Wire Gully on 25 April. The advanced nature of their trenches suggests the position was taken at around 10.30 am or later. The group in the centre appears to be observing Turkish troops on Third Ridge, while the man in the foreground is deepening his trench (AWM AO3226).

FRAGMENTATION OF THE 1ST BRIGADE

Back at the beach at 9.15 am, Bridges responded to urgent requests to reinforce the 3rd Brigade by sending Lieutenant Colonel Leonard Dobbin's 1st Battalion forward. In a process that was to be repeated throughout the day, the battalion became fragmented and entered the battle as individual companies thrust into separate parts of the firing line, rather than retaining its identity as a formed fighting battalion. Major Ross Dawson's A Company scaled the Razorback and reinforced the mixture of companies already at Lone Pine. Major Albert McGuire's B Company wandered into White's Valley behind McCay's Hill where McCay promptly employed it as his brigade reserve in lieu of the missing 5th Battalion companies. Captain Philip Hill's C Company headed up Monash Valley and, responding to calls from the heights above, platoons splintered off and reinforced the 11th Battalion posts north of MacLaurin's Hill. As the tail of the battalion was passing over Plugge's Plateau, Lieutenant Colonel Robert Owen, commanding the 3rd Battalion, informed Major Frederick Kindon, the 1st Battalion's second-in-command, that Sinclair-MacLagan had asked for reinforcements to go to Baby 700. Kindon detached Major Blair Swannell's D Company from the column and headed along Russell's Top, over The Nek and onto Baby 700. Dobbin now had nothing left to command.

Captain Halis, Commanding Officer, *3rd Battalion*, *27th Regiment*, who drove Loutit's party from Third Ridge and fought against Captain Leer's 3rd Battalion group on Mortar Ridge from late morning on 25 April. Halis was a brave and fearless leader who, when wounded, refused to be evacuated for much of the day until forced out of the battle through loss of blood. A very modest man, when exhorted by his officers to get down during the fighting on Mortar Ridge, he admonished them saying that he was too fat to keep getting up and down, and preferred to stand to observe the Australians (Serdar Ataksor image).

Similarly, the 3rd Battalion was also frittered away in penny packets. Two companies had been committed at 7.55 am. With vague instructions to reinforce the left flank, they wound their way along Monash Valley and enthusiastically responded to calls from troops on the ridge high to their right. Two platoons of Major Malcolm Lamb's B Company scrambled up the steep sides of the valley and went into the firing line on MacLaurin's Hill opposite Wire Gully, while the rest reinforced the 11th Battalion's position at Steele's Post. Major Ernest Brown's company failed to make it that far. Again responding to calls from the ridge above, the company occupied a position to the south of 3rd Brigade headquarters on MacLaurin's Hill. At 9.30 am Owen received orders to commit his remaining two companies. They moved up the valley but fared no better. With instructions to reinforce the left and secure Baby 700, Captain Charles Leer reached the fork of the valley at the foot of Pope's Hill. Swinging right, his C Company climbed the almost sheer sides of Second Ridge north of Quinn's Post, crossed over into the next gully and climbed towards the crest of Mortar

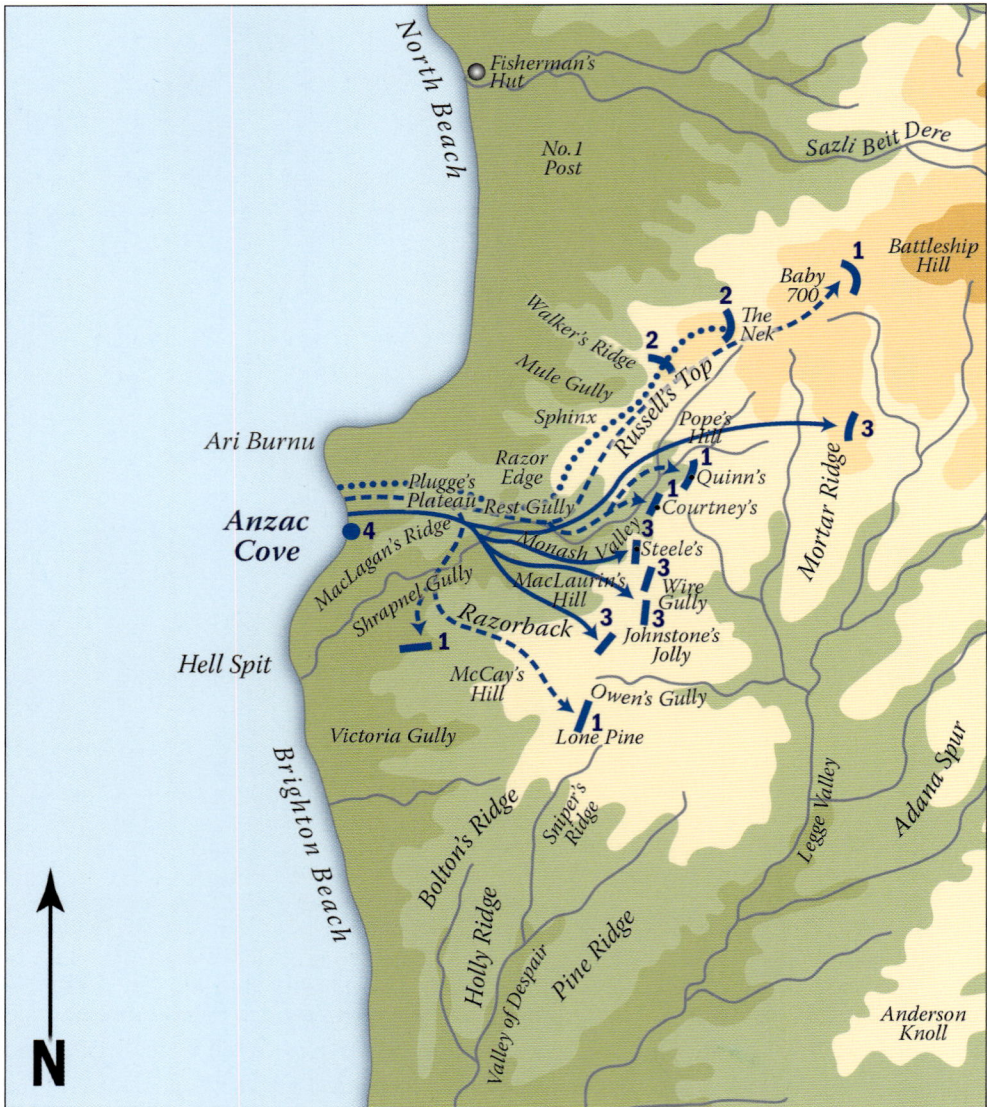

The fragmentation of the 1st Brigade. Three companies of Dobbin's 1st Battalion are drawn into the firing line between McCay's Hill and Quinn's Post, while D Company ends up on Baby 700. Two companies of the 2nd Battalion reach The Nek around midday, while the other two arrive at the junction of Walker's Ridge and Russell's Top early afternoon. Owen's 3rd Battalion is scattered along Second Ridge from Johnston's Jolly to Steele's Post, and Leer's company pushes onto Mortar Ridge. The 4th Battalion remains in Anzac Cove, the last companies landing between 12.00 and 1.00 pm.

Ridge, where they encountered Turks moving forward. On reaching Ince Bair, Captain Halis, commanding the *3/27th*, had decided to leave two platoons there to cover the right flank against Tulloch's party on Battleship Hill. Then, taking the rest of the battalion, he struck west to Mortar Ridge, where the *10th* and *12th companies* ran into Leer's company ascending the western spurs. Both sides stood firm and a bloody firefight ensued. Where Captain Charles Coulter's D Company went is not recorded but, like the others, it entered the maul that was forming along Second Ridge.

At 10.45 am the fragmentation of the 1st Brigade continued when Lieutenant Colonel George Braund, commanding the 2nd Battalion, was told to hive off two companies to occupy The Nek. Fifteen minutes later Major Robert Scobie, the battalion second-in-command, led Major Charles Gordon's A Company and Captain Clifford Richardson's D Company forward and occupied ground at The Nek and Second Ridge north of Quinn's Post around midday. Bridges was left with four companies as his reserve, two each from the 2nd and 4th battalions, with two companies of the 4th yet to land. He also had a spare brigade headquarters with nothing to command.

Looking south from Russell's Top across Monash Valley to the 400 Plateau and McCay's Hill where the bulk of the 2nd and 3rd brigades began digging in at around 6.30am. Monash Valley was the route taken by most of the 1st Brigade and the Auckland Battalion as they moved to either support the 3rd Brigade or reinforce the Australians on Baby 700 (out of picture left). The first spur is Braund's Hill leading onto the northern edge of Johnston's Jolly, which was occupied by the 10th Battalion from around 6.00 am. The monument on the skyline marks Lone Pine, which was occupied by much of the 9th Battalion and some of the 12th Battalion, and was the scene of the bitter struggle between the *1/27th* and the Australians from 12.30 pm until late on the night of 25 April. To the right of the photo, the first spur beyond the foot of Braund's Hill is the Razorback, up which three companies of the 5th Battalion climbed to Lone Pine. The spur behind the Razorback is McCay's Hill, which runs up to Lone Pine where the 2nd Brigade was diverted as it came ashore. The 7th Battalion held the top of the hill throughout 25 April (Glenn Wahlert image).

GAINING THE UPPER HAND

Between 10.00 and 10.30 am, Sefik received news from Halil Sami that the GOC *19th Division* and the *57th Regiment* were marching to the Sari Bair Range, and that he was now under Mustafa Kemal's command, thereby unifying control of the forces facing ANZAC. He was also instructed not to incur unnecessary casualties, and to hold one battalion in reserve in case the enemy landed south of Gaba Tepe. Having seen the head of the *57th Regiment* arriving to his north sometime after 10.00 am, Sefik immediately sent a message to Kemal describing the situation and advising him of his proposed attack.

By 11.30 am the Ottoman situation had begun to improve. On the main range two platoons of the *8th Company*, *2/27th*, were engaged with Tulloch, while to their south and south-west two platoons (one each from the *2/27th* and *3/27th*) and the leading elements of the *1/57th* had also joined the firefight. The remainder of Kemal's force was slowly arriving and deploying to the main range. On the northern end of Mortar Ridge two companies of the *3/27th* were engaged with Leer and other Australians on the southern slope of Baby 700. The other two companies of the *3/27th* were along the southern end of Mortar Ridge exchanging shots with the Australians on Second Ridge. The *1/27th* was on the western slopes of Third Ridge opposite the 400 Plateau. Sefik's machine-gun company was deployed in two platoons (each of two guns) on Hill 165, one supporting the *3/27th* and the other engaging the Australians on Lone Pine. At Gaba Tepe, the *7th Company*, less Hakki's platoon, and part

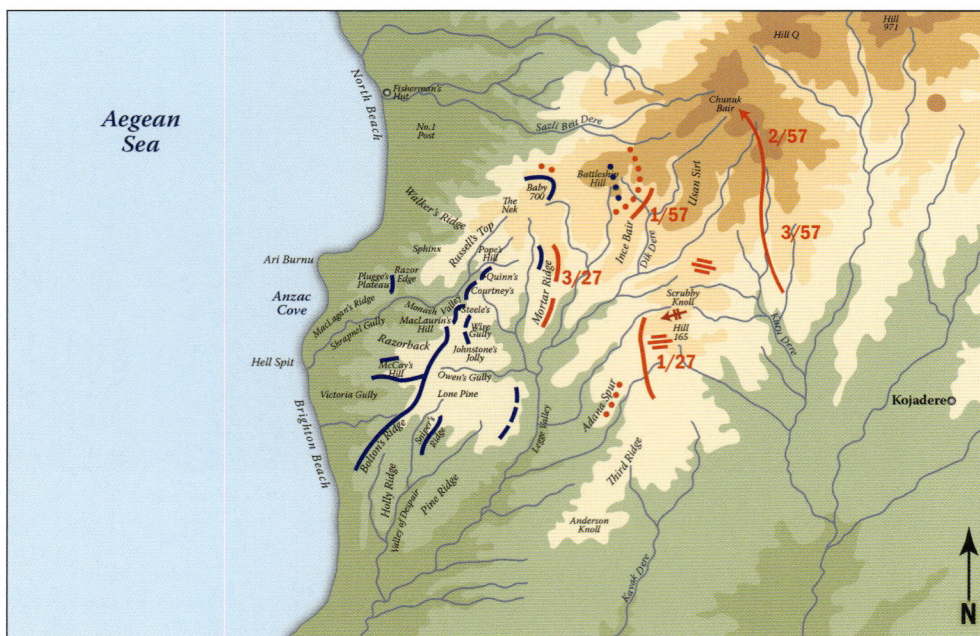

The situation at 11.30 am. The *1st* and *3rd platoons* of the *8th Company*, *2/27th*, the leading elements of the *1/57th*, and a platoon each from the *2/27th* and the *3/27th* are engaged with Tulloch on Battleship Hill. The *3/27th* is fighting Captain Leer's group on Mortar Ridge and Australians on Second Ridge. The *1/27th* around Hill 165 is engaged in a long-range firefight with the Australians on the 400 Plateau. Kemal is organising his counter-attack against both Australian flanks.

of the *5th Company, 2/27th*, confronted the Australians to the south. The missing mountain battery had arrived at around 10.30 am and was in position alongside Sadik's lone gun by 11.00 am. The invasion had not only been contained, it had been confined to a narrow and shallow beachhead that provided no room for manoeuvre. Moreover, the ANZAC position was of little tactical value other than as a defensive line covering the beach. With five and a half battalions, however, the Ottomans were still outnumbered roughly 2:1. By 11.00 am, 11 and a half Australian battalions were ashore, while the Auckland Battalion had begun landing at around 10.30 am.

A portion of the 26th (Jacob's) Mountain Battery on the beach at around 10.30 am. The 10-pounder guns have been assembled and the mules appear to be carrying boxes of ammunition. This battery went into action on the edge of the 400 Plateau a little before 12.00 pm. Judging by the colour patches on the men in the foreground, they are possibly Australian engineers (Alexander Turnbull Library).

The 1st Australian Division was not in a good position to exploit this superiority. The force's disposition was unbalanced, and its command and control was a shambles. On the left flank, Tulloch's party remained unsupported on Battleship Hill, and a mixed force of the 1st, 9th, 11th and 12th battalions — roughly four companies — was behind him on Baby 700, and another two from the 2nd Battalion were moving up to The Nek. Immediately to the south, the upper end of Second Ridge was unoccupied, although Leer's company of the 3rd Battalion, plus others, were forward of it on the northern end of Mortar Ridge. Further south, a mixture of companies and platoons of the 1st, 3rd and 11th battalions occupied the line from Quinn's Post to MacLaurin's Hill. Along Johnston's Jolly was Weir's largely intact 10th Battalion, together with companies of the 5th and 12th battalions. Lone Pine was an organisational mess. Scattered across and around the lobe were sections, platoons and companies of the 1st, 5th, 6th, 9th and 12th battalions badly intermingled and under no central control. They were also congested, presenting an ideal artillery target. Elliott's 7th Battalion occupied McCay's Hill and a company of the 6th was at the head of Bolton's Ridge. Immediately south of the plateau, two companies of the 6th Battalion and Whitham's company of the 12th occupied Sniper's Ridge, extending back towards Lone Pine. Among the other spurs thrusting south of Lone Pine was a group of the 8th Battalion and, well to its rear, the rest of the battalion extended down Bolton's Ridge.

The southern end of Anzac Cove, possibly mid-morning 25 April, judging by the shadows. Congestion is increasing as stores, mules, horses and carts are brought ashore. The colour patches on the men in the left foreground suggest that they may be from the 2nd Battalion. A sunken boat lies offshore, while behind it other boats are clustered around Hell Spit (AWM NZ PADL-000398).

Both forces were heavily weighted on their right flank. The difference was that the Ottoman weight was on the vital high ground and their units still retained a reasonable degree of autonomy, most under their regimental and battalion commanders. They also had the advantage of holding ground overlooking the ANZAC position and, consequently, their artillery and machine-guns were in a superior position for observation and fire. On the vital ground three Ottoman battalions and a machine-gun company were swinging into action against Tulloch's company, and behind him on Baby 700 the equivalent of one Australian battalion, although another two Australian companies were moving up in support. On the Australian right the equivalent of seven battalions opposed Sefik's defenders at Gaba Tepe and the *1/27th*.

The Australian command and control arrangements were far from satisfactory. No brigade commander was controlling the ground of tactical importance other than Sinclair-MacLagan, who was 1000 metres away and out of sight of the firing line on the inland slopes of Baby 700. Although Kindon might have nominally taken control once he arrived on Baby 700, it was largely held by companies from different units under their own officers. Nor did they have telephone communications with Sinclair-MacLagan or Bridges, relying instead on runners to get information back to them, if indeed any were sent. MacLaurin was available to take charge of the left but, while his brigade was being committed piecemeal, no-one thought to send him there to take control and establish a telephone link back to the 1st Division in order to provide Bridges a clear understanding of the situation on his vital left flank. Meanwhile the other two brigade commanders oversaw the action either side of the 400 Plateau within 500 metres of each other. The situation was worse at battalion level where control had fragmented and devolved largely to independent company and platoon commanders. Only Weir had good control of his battalion and, while the 7th was relatively compact, Elliott had been wounded and forced out of the battle. The 1st, 2nd, 3rd, 5th, 6th, 8th, 9th, 11th and 12th battalions were dispersed and their commanding officers were either dead (Clarke), controlled a company or two (Braund, McNicoll and Bolton) or, like Dobbin, Owen and Wanliss, controlled nothing but the men around them. Two — Harry Lee and James Lyon Johnston — were still on the beach.

The mast of the corps radio providing communications from Headquarters 1st Division to ANZAC is established on the beach at the foot of Ari Burnu. The shadows indicate that this photograph was taken at around 10.30 am, not long after it was erected. The Cressy class cruiser HMS *Bacchante* lies offshore (AWM G00905).

The Ottomans also enjoyed an advantage in terms of fire support. While the 26th (Jacob's) Indian Mountain Battery had come ashore at 10.30 am to provide much-needed artillery support, by around 11.30 am Ottoman artillery slightly outnumbered that of ANZAC by nine mountain guns to six, and occupied superior ground. In contrast, the 26th Battery held an inferior position on the eastern edge of the 400 Plateau overlooked by the Ottoman guns. Each force's machine-guns were deployed quite differently. The two Ottoman machine-gun companies were concentrated on each flank under the control of their respective regimental commanders providing a concentrated and powerful auxiliary. Some of the Australian machine-guns were deployed across the front providing close support on the firing line, operating independently under their young section commanders, while others were held in reserve under battalion control.

The good news was that an attempt was being made to rectify the imbalance on the Australian left. The headquarters of the NZ&A Division, less Godley, began landing at around 10.00 am. In a conference with Bridges, Colonel William Braithwaite, the NZ&A Chief of Staff, agreed that, when it landed, the New Zealand Brigade would extend to the left of the 3rd Australian Brigade. Once the Auckland Battalion was complete on the ground it would be sent to Baby 700, followed by Lieutenant Colonel Douglas Stewart's Canterbury Battalion. It was now a question of whether they would arrive in time.

Men of the Auckland Battalion in boats ready to go ashore from HMAT *Lutzon* between 10.00 and 11.00 am on 25 April (Alexander Turnbull Library).

MOUNTAIN GUN, BL 10-POUNDER

Calibre: 2.75 inches (69.9mm)

Barrel Length: 1.9m

Gun Weight: 396.36kg

Action: Single motion wedge breech mechanism with hydro-spring recoil system

Range: 3380m with time fuze; 5486m with percussion fuze

Ammunition: 10 pounds (4.53kg) shrapnel and high explosive

Fuze: Time and percussion

The British breech-loading 10-pounder mountain gun was introduced in 1901 to replace the 2.5-inch mountain gun which was outranged during the South African War. The barrel came in two pieces which were screwed together when coming into action. It had no recoil absorber or recuperator mechanism like those on the quick-firing field guns and the Krupp 75mm mountain gun. Carried on pack animals, the gun was broken down into four loads: two for the two-piece barrel, one for the trail, and one for the wheels. On coming into action the gun had to be unloaded and assembled, either on the gun line or in dead ground just to the rear. It was normally used in the direct fire role. These guns were organised into six-gun batteries.

This was the gun that supported the Anzacs briefly on 25 April when the 26th (Jacob's) Battery came into action on the edge of the 400 Plateau around noon, but was forced out of action at about 2.30 pm. The 21st (Kohat) Battery landed at around 5.30 pm but did not come into action on 25 April.

CHAPTER 10
COUNTER-ATTACK

Anzac Cove between 10.30 and 11.30 am taken from a boat bringing men of the Auckland Battalion to shore. On the shore are men who appear to be Indian troops of the 26th (Jacob's) Battery which landed at 10.30 am (Alexander Turnbull Library).

OTTOMAN PREPARATIONS

Kemal was issuing instructions to Major Huseyin Avni, the *57th Regiment*'s commander, when Sefik's message reached him at around 10.45 am. He decided to coordinate a two-pronged attack: the *57th Regiment* against the Australians' left flank on the main range, while Sefik would attack the right flank resting on Lone Pine. He replied to Sefik's message asking him to hold his attack until the *57th* was ready and advising that, after the *27th* went forward, the *57th* would then launch its attack. By staggering the timings he may have been hoping to use the *27th*'s attack to draw the Australian reserves to the threatened point before committing the *57th*, thereby giving his men an easier run down the main range.

Zeki's *1/57th* was to attack on the inland side of the range, while Captain Ata's *2/57th* would attack along the seaward side. Captain Hayri's *3/57th* would be held in reserve. They would be supported by the attached mountain battery from north of Scrubby Knoll and the *57th*'s machine-gun company higher up Third Ridge. Kemal departed after midday having received an erroneous message that the British were landing at Kum Tepe, six kilometres south of Gaba Tepe, prompting him to take his remaining regiments, the *72nd* and *77th*, south to counter the threat. He would not return to the Sari Bair battlefield until later that afternoon.

Sefik issued his orders at noon. While the two northern companies of the *3/27th* (*10th* and *12th*) would continue engaging the enemy on Battleship Hill, Mortar and Second ridges from their current positions, the remainder would be directed against Lone Pine, avoiding Johnston's Jolly as it was flat and devoid of any cover. Three companies of the *1/27th* and the *11th* of the *3/27th* would conduct the attack, with two companies held in reserve. Should the Australians attack from the southern spurs of Lone Pine, the *7th Company, 2/27th*, was directed to intervene on the Australian flank, otherwise it would remain in position defending Gaba Tepe. Two of his mountain guns were redeployed to Anderson Knoll to support the attack and engage any Australian move south of the plateau; the remaining three and the machine-gun company would support the attack from Hill 165. In essence, the artillery would hit the Australians with a crossfire of shrapnel.

Preparing the way for the infantry, the guns opened up on the congestion around Lone Pine, each shrapnel shell showering the unprotected troops with 230 balls in swathes roughly 20 metres wide and 200 metres long, while the massed machine-guns added their contribution with bursts of fire across the plateau. The 26th Battery replied, but the Turkish guns occupied a superior position, and the Indian battery, concentrated on the edge of the 400 Plateau, was in plain view of the Turkish artillery observers. Once the Ottoman artillery and machine-guns found their range they eventually forced the battery out of action at around 2.30 pm, leaving the Australians and New Zealanders without artillery support for the remainder of the afternoon.

Members of the Auckland Battalion landing in Anzac Cove at around 11.00 am on 25 April (Alexander Turnbull Library).

ENTER THE NEW ZEALANDERS

By noon the Auckland Battalion and two companies of the Canterbury Battalion were ashore. However, Colonel Johnston had been taken ill and his brigade headquarters was still offshore. Stepping into the breach, Brigadier General 'Hooky' Walker, who had arrived around 8.00 am to gain first-hand knowledge of the unfolding events and to keep Birdwood informed, assumed command of the New Zealand Brigade. He directed the Aucklanders to move to Baby 700 via Walker's Ridge. As they wound their way up the steep spur near the mouth of Mule Gully, Walker became increasingly concerned that, on reaching the crest, they would be exposed to fire from the Turks further inland and suffer unnecessary casualties. At 12.30 pm he recalled them, instructing them to take the less exposed route over Plugge's Plateau and up Monash Valley. While commendable for his concern, the decision was fateful in that it added considerable time to their approach march and seriously affected their eventual deployment. Whereas Walker's Ridge would have taken them directly to Russell's Top and onto Baby 700, a distance of 1600 metres from North Beach, the new route doubled the distance and fed them into the congested Monash Valley.

The battalion about-turned. With Major Walter Alderman's 16th (Waikato) Company now leading and vague orders from Lieutenant Colonel Plugge to 'Reinforce the first Australians on the left', they made their way back down the spur, along North Beach, around Ari Burnu, and up onto Plugge's Plateau, where they halted to wait for the rear of the column to catch up. Shrapnel began to take its toll, and from this point the battalion ceased to operate as a fighting entity. The 16th Company slipped down into the aptly named Shrapnel Gully, taking two platoons of the Canterbury Battalion with it. There the congestion delayed the column: ammunition parties moved up, stretcher-bearers and walking wounded struggled against the flow, while an Australian company crossed their path to reinforce the right flank. Westmacott remembered that 'we kept halting frequently to let the rear come up'. Slowly they pushed up Monash Valley looking for the Australian left flank, uncertain of its exact location.

Looking onto the Turkish section post on Ari Burnu at around 1.00 pm on 25 April. This photograph is taken from the spur leading from the post up to Plugge's Plateau. According to Bean, who took the photo, the men filing along the beach are from the Auckland Battalion and are returning from Walker's Ridge. They are making their way around Ari Burnu point before climbing to Plugge's Plateau (AWM G00906).

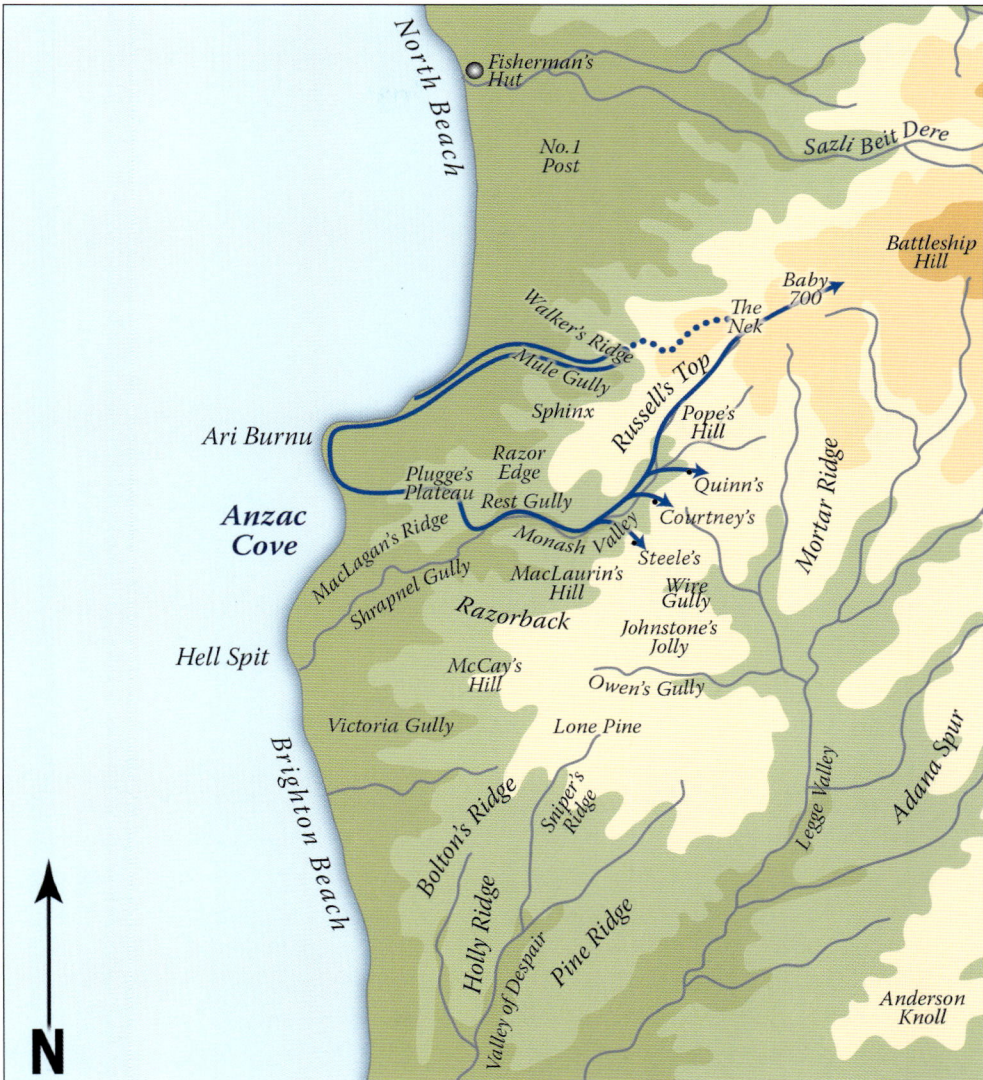

Route taken by the Auckland Battalion. After beginning the climb up Walker's Ridge and the shortest route to Baby 700 (dotted line), the battalion was recalled at 12.30 pm. Heading around Ari Burnu, over Plugge's Plateau and up the congested Monash Valley, only the 16th (Waikato) and 6th (Hauraki) companies reached Baby 700 at around 2.30 pm. The other two companies were drawn into the firing line along Second Ridge.

Sometime around noon, Bennett, Whitham and others advanced to Pine Ridge. The forward Australian line confronting Sefik now comprised an assortment of platoons and companies from six battalions holding the inland edge of Lone Pine, and down along Pine Ridge for around 750 metres. They were intermixed, the waist-high vegetation and pine trees made control over the whole line difficult, and most groups worked independently of the others. Behind them much of the 2nd and 3rd brigades were along the seaward edge of the 400 Plateau and Bolton's Ridge, while between these two lines small parties occupied positions in the scrub across Lone Pine and some of the spurs running south off the plateau.

Australian infantry passing over Plugge's Plateau on 25 April. Taken by Bean as the next in sequence after the photo of the Aucklanders filing around the foot of Ari Burnu, these are possibly men from Braund's 2nd Battalion on their way to the junction of Russell's Top and Walker's Ridge at around 1.30 pm (AWM G00907).

FIRST COUNTER-ATTACK

Sefik's attack commenced at 12.30 pm. Covered by artillery and machine-gun fire, his infantry crossed Legge Valley unscathed and climbed the fir-covered slopes of Lone Pine. Nearing the edge of the plateau, they were confronted by the Australian forward platoons among the brushwood 30 to 50 paces away. A ferocious and prolonged fight broke out at close range. The Turks moved forward with the bayonet, and the Australians slowly gave way, regrouped and counter-attacked in turn with the bayonet. On the western end of Lone Pine individual skirmishes swayed back and forth in which, according to Sefik, 'both sides fought fiercely'. Sitting off to the flank Captain Whitham observed 'Several times during the afternoon portions of the line on our left about 224.N.9 [the south-east corner of Lone Pine] broke and fell back but reformed whenever reinforcements arrived or when an officer was able to rally them.' The mountain guns now pounded the middle and seaward edge of the plateau as the battle swayed to and fro. A platoon of the *2nd Company* tried to advance along the southern slope of Johnston's Jolly but was swept away by heavy small arms fire, the survivors falling back to the shelter of Legge Valley. To the south the Australians down along Pine Ridge were largely unaffected by the attack, as the Turkish frontage did not extend that far. However, they were lashed by bursting shrapnel from the guns at Anderson Knoll. Messages sent by Bennett supplying the guns' location brought no response from the Indian battery which was having its own problems coping with the Turkish shrapnel. On Lone Pine, with grievous losses mounting on both sides, the stubborn Australians slowed the equally determined Turks in a grinding, bitter fight that was often hand-to-hand and always at close range. From his command post high on Third Ridge, Sefik observed a line of Australians

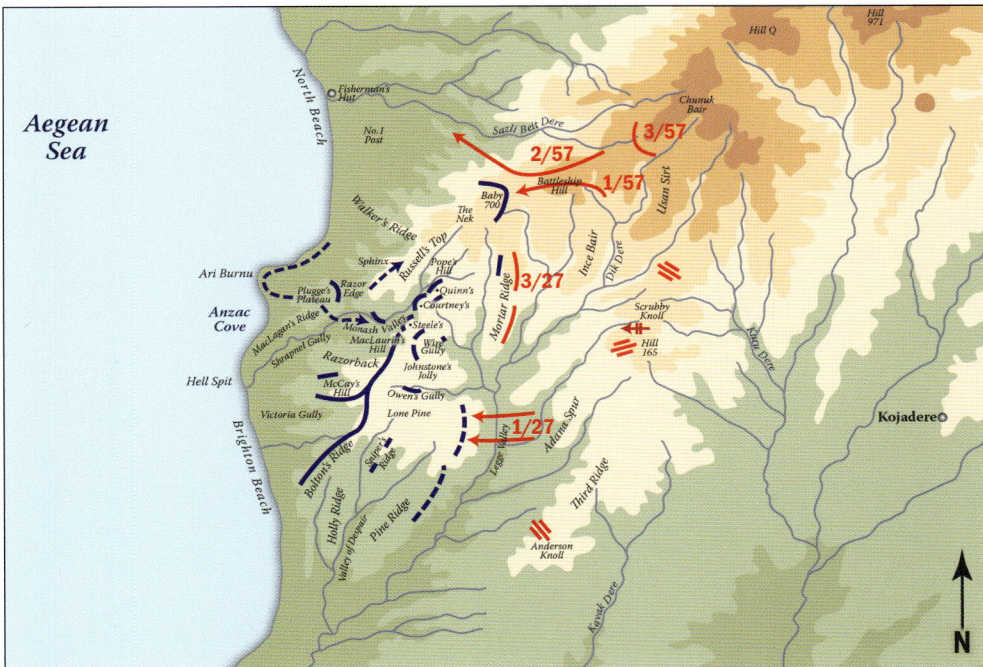

The Turkish counter-attacks. At 12.30 pm the *1/27th* attacks Lone Pine and is engaged in a fierce struggle with the Australian outposts. On the other flank, sometime after 1.00 pm, the *1/57th* and *2/57th* drive Tulloch's party off Battleship Hill and are then stalled in front of Baby 700. Many of the *2/57th* slide off the range and head for the Fisherman's Hut and the spurs north of Baby 700.

rise from the scrub and rush forward in a bayonet charge. His Turkish riflemen sprang to their feet and charged, and in a melee of bayonet fighting they pushed the Australians back. In turn the Australians counter-attacked and pushed his own men back. Recognising that the attack was stalling, Sefik committed his two reserve companies and, after further bitter fighting, by around 4.00 pm, the Turks had slowly fought their way to the three mountain guns that had been lost in the centre of the plateau earlier that morning.

After Sefik's men had crossed Legge Valley and engaged the Australian right, the *57th* prepared the way for its attack down the main range. Up on Battleship Hill, Tulloch's party was hit with salvos from the supporting mountain battery sweeping the ground. Private Herbert Hitch recalled that 'the pellets flew past and they sounded like a flight of parrots and puffs of dust rose here and there where [they] struck the ground.' The *57th*'s machine-gun company added to the deadly mix. Directing his men on the far right flank, Lieutenant Reid was hit in the thigh, seriously wounding him. Refusing all offers of assistance he slowly crawled to the rear, never to be seen again. Half an hour later, heavily outnumbered, with mounting pressure on his flanks and two battalions of Ottoman infantry advancing against him, Tulloch ordered a withdrawal by sections sometime after 1.00 pm. 'As I jumped up to run,' recalled Hitch, 'the air was alive with bullets, most of them going overhead ... We ran back about 200 yards ... [and] opened fire, about 6 or 7 rounds each just to keep the enemy from coming on too quickly, and then we all ran back together for another 150 yards, and the order was passed along reform left.' There they encountered 'a fine looking body of men ... They weren't running but were walking very quickly, but as they came under our fire they ran back.' The Turks came on again, and Tulloch's party abandoned Battleship Hill, falling back to join the Australian line on Baby 700. Despite being under fire from their front and flanks, they had held Battleship Hill for four hours. As the *1/57th* and *2/57th* swept down and around the slopes of Battleship Hill, the Australians on Baby 700 opened fire, and a bloody fight for the feature ensued.

Taken in 1919 from the line occupied by Tulloch's party on Battleship Hill, looking west towards Baby 700 in the background. In the foreground are the remains and equipment of men who fought there. It was over the intervening ground to Baby 700 that the bitter fighting on the afternoon of 25 April took place, with the ANZAC line on the forward slopes of Baby 700, and the *57th Regiment* attacking from the camera towards the Anzacs (AWM G01875).

The initial Australian firing line across the hill, and on the upper reaches of Mortar Ridge, now comprised almost six companies from the 1st, 3rd, 9th, 11th and 12th battalions, and was capable of delivering a devastating fire of at least 12,000 rounds a minute. As the leading companies of Turks advanced down the broad, open slopes of Battleship Hill, the Australians poured a withering fire into them, cutting down enemy troops in droves and forcing the remainder to ground. Reflecting the tendency to overestimate the enemy opposition, Sergeant Coe wrote home '... it was at 2 o'clock when we got it heavy. We were on the extreme left flank and at 2:30 the Turks put six battalions on us. We, on the left, got a good share of them, as it was the key of the position, for if they beat us back they could have enfiladed the centre and the right, so there was no retiring where we were.' In a desperate firefight, the Ottoman rear companies moved up and began working around the seaward and inland slopes of Battleship Hill where the gullies either side of the main range provided some protection from the Australian rifle fire. In doing so, many of the *2/57th* slipped off the range and moved down the ridges and gullies towards the Fisherman's Hut, while others engaged the Australians on the seaward slope of Baby 700. The fighting turned into a slugfest as each side poured heavy small arms fire into the other. The Ottoman artillery joined in, flaying Baby 700 with shrapnel. Coe wrote: 'the shrapnel was so thick that a certain regiment was unable to come to our aid.' One Turkish officer described it as 'a bitter struggle' and losses on both sides mounted as the Australians fought hard to retain the hill amid a hail of Turkish bullets. Private Reginald Donkin of the 1st Battalion was hit in the thigh, and other bullets pierced the top of his cap, ripped through his left sleeve, and his webbing. He was fortunate to survive to be evacuated. Officers directing their men were exposed to fire and casualties rose steadily. Already thrice wounded, Major Robertson raised his head to get a better view and was hit again. Turning to Lieutenant William Rigby beside him, he groaned, 'Carry on Rigby', slumped forward and died. Rigby carried on until he too was killed. Over on the left flank Captain Lalor died, while on the forward slope Major Swannell was killed, and Tulloch seriously wounded. Gordon's A Company of the 2nd Battalion was drawn into the fight, and Richardson's D Company moved across The Nek in support. Heading across to the seaward slopes of Baby 700 to join the fighting on the left of the line, Richardson saw Gordon's men doubling up to the summit to his right.

Anzac Cove, early afternoon on 25 April. As troops file up the Ari Burnu spur on the skyline at the top left of the photo, boxes of ammunition are being stockpiled on the beach to the right. At this stage the 1st Australian Division, the Auckland Battalion and half of the Canterbury Battalion of the New Zealand Brigade were ashore, and the leading elements of the Otago Regiment were about to land (Alexander Turnbull Library).

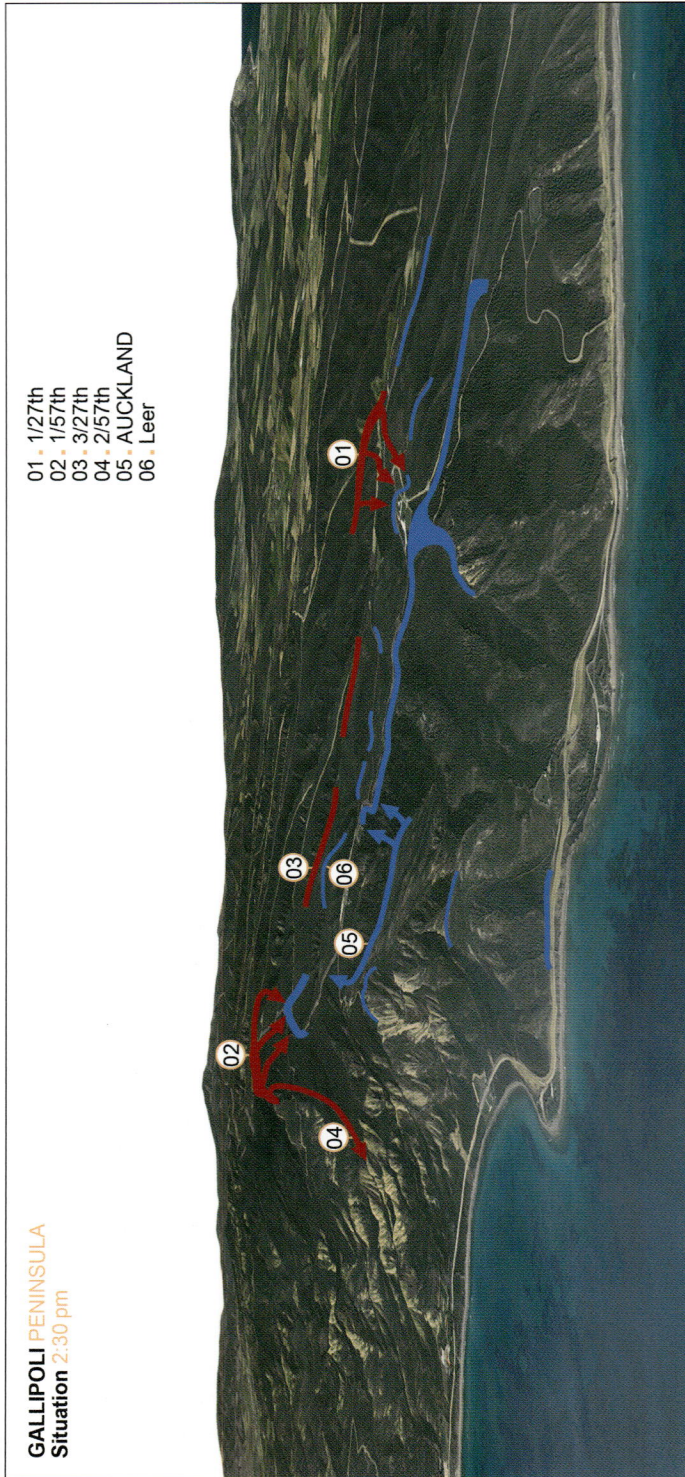

GALLIPOLI PENINSULA
Situation 2.30 pm

01 · 1/27th
02 · 1/57th
03 · 3/27th
04 · 2/57th
05 · AUCKLAND
06 · Leer

Situation around 2.30 pm. On the main range, the *1/57th* and *2/57th* have driven Tulloch off Battleship Hill but their advance has stalled under withering fire from almost six Australian companies. The *2/57th* has dropped off the main range towards the Fisherman's Hut. Two companies of the Auckland Battalion are reaching Baby 700 to reinforce the Australians, while the other two have been diverted to the firing line along Second Ridge. The *3/27th* and Leer's group on Mortar Ridge are slugging it out, while the *1/27th* is in a fierce fight with the Australians on Lone Pine.

REINFORCEMENTS

Given the distance they had travelled, and the frequent halts along the way, the first troops of the Auckland Battalion could not have reached the head of Monash Valley until around 2.00 pm at the earliest. Unsure of the situation to the front, a patrol under Lance Corporal Jack Petersen was sent ahead, and on returning reported that the Australian line was over the next ridge 200 to 300 metres ahead. Alderman sent Westmacott's and Second Lieutenant Herman Baddeley's platoons forward, and waited for the rest of his company to arrive. Climbing onto The Nek and shaking their men out into extended line, they strode through the scrub up the broad slope of Baby 700 with Westmacott heading towards the right flank. According to Kindon, the Aucklanders arrived at around 2.30 pm. On the way a returning Australian officer briefed Westmacott on the situation: the Australian firing line was beyond the crest and 'they're getting Hell' before he headed downhill. As Westmacott crossed the crest and moved down the slope: 'the fire was very heavy, terrific it seemed to me ... I doubled less than twenty yards jumping over dead men ... [the Australian] firing line had ceased to exist ... Every man there had been killed or wounded. They had fought on there unsupported, rather than retire', he recalled.

Following behind the 16th Company, Major Frederick Stuckey's 6th (Hauraki) Company eventually climbed out of Monash Valley and headed to the left flank on the seaward slopes of Baby 700 where the fighting was equally bitter. The remainder of the battalion, however, had hived off to join the firing line before reaching The Nek, much the same as had occurred to the Australian battalions earlier in the day. '... we found it rather tough going', recalled Sergeant Harris. 'We passed streams of Australian wounded going down hill and they were all urging us to go to this place, or that, as reinforcements were wanted.' Eagerly responding to calls for reinforcements as they wound their way up the valley floor, the 3rd (Auckland) Company had been drawn into the fight at Quinn's Post, and the 15th (North Auckland) Company into Courtney's Post. The Australians and New Zealanders on Baby 700 fought on, and the butcher's bill rose. On the right flank, Privates Albert Cowdrey and Arthur West of the 16th (Waikato) died instantly, shot through the head, while Private Anthony Fagan recalled that the bullets flew through 'the scrub over my head and I thought I'd better get out of this and get to a bit of cover.' Jumping up to run forward, he was hit in the chest.

The 1st (Canterbury) and 2nd (South Canterbury) companies of Lieutenant Colonel Stewart's battalion had been instructed to follow the Aucklanders, but in the congestion and confusion on Plugge's Plateau they had become separated. Two platoons of Major Robert Row's 1st Company slipped into Shrapnel Gully becoming entangled with the Auckland Battalion and eventually joined the firing line at Quinn's and Courtney's Posts, while the other two remained on Plugge's Plateau as a reserve. Stewart took Major David Grant's 2nd Company up onto Russell's Top and established a support position short of The Nek. At about 1.30 pm, Braund took his remaining two companies of the 2nd Battalion to Walker's Ridge and established a defensive position at the junction with Russell's Top, overlooking the ridges and spurs dropping down from the seaward flank of Baby 700, where they could counter any Turkish attempt to slip around the feature and seize the upper reaches of

Walker's Ridge. The right of his line joined Stewart's Cantabrians. At around 2.00 pm, in response to a message that the Turks were working around the ANZAC left flank, Captain Arthur Critchley-Salmonson of the Canterbury Battalion took a mixed group of Australians and New Zealanders across to Walker's Ridge, occupying the lower end with his left flank resting on the beach. A significant gap existed between him and Braund's companies at the top of the ridge.

General Birdwood and Major General Godley arrived at 3.00 pm and, in the gully above the beach, were briefed on the situation by Bridges. What was said is not known, but with the noise of battle raging in the distance and Bridges having little real idea of what was actually occurring across the ANZAC battlefront, except that a firing line had been established well short of the intended covering position, Birdwood's reaction was surprising. As Godley's division was still in the process of landing, Bridges would retain command of the battle. Birdwood then returned to his transport offshore, leaving the inexperienced Bridges in charge of what was turning into a desperate fight and a dangerous situation. The NZ&A Division's war diary records that, once the Aucklanders and half the Cantabrians had landed, the rest of the disembarkation suffered a 'complete hiatus', stretching out until the next morning. Lieutenant Colonel Athelstan Moore's Otago Battalion began landing at 2.30 pm, his last companies reaching the beach at 4.00 pm. Only then did the remainder of the Canterbury Battalion come ashore, while offshore Malone fumed that his beloved Wellington Battalion had not yet disembarked.

On 'the other side of the hill', Ottoman reinforcements were arriving more rapidly. Esat had arrived at Maidos at around 11.30 am and later established a rudimentary *III Corps* headquarters at Mal Tepe. There he conferred with Halil Sami and Kemal, and rearranged the southern peninsula into two discrete battle zones. Kemal, with the *19th Division* and the *27th Regiment*, was given charge of the Ari Burnu front, while Halil Sami, with the *25th* and *26th regiments*, retained control of the Cape Helles front where the British were stalled on the beaches having encountered far heavier opposition on the toe of the peninsula and suffered terrible casualties. Having ascertained that the British were not landing at Kum Tepe, Kemal now directed his *72nd* and *77th regiments* to move to Sari Bair at around 2.00 to 2.30 pm. Arriving back at Scrubby Knoll mid-afternoon, Kemal realised that the *57th Regiment's* attack down the main range had stalled in front of Baby 700, and the *1/27th's* attack on Lone Pine was meeting strong resistance. To regain the momentum he reinforced both the *27th* and *57th regiments*: the two battalions of Captain Saip's *77th* were directed to support Sefik, while Major Mehmet Munir's *72nd Regiment* and another mountain battery from the *3/39th Arty* was ordered to the Sari Bair Range. However, these reinforcements would not reach the battlefield until late afternoon, the *72nd* around 4.00 pm and the *77th* an hour later.

Less the losses on both sides incurred during the first attack, the Ottoman odds continued to improve: ten battalions would now face the equivalent of 14 ANZAC battalions. On the ground of tactical importance however, the odds would favour Kemal. There he had two battalions of the *57th*, one of which (the *3/57th*) was fresh (most of the

2/57th was moving on the Fisherman's Hut or to the spurs opposite Walker's Ridge), with another three fresh battalions of the *72nd* coming up in support. Opposing him were the equivalent of two weakened ANZAC battalions in a jumble of eight depleted rifle companies from six different units. In artillery terms the advantage was swinging further in favour of Kemal, who was bringing up the three field batteries from the *39th Arty* to support the two mountain batteries already deployed, although most of them would not reach the battlefield until after dusk. The Anzacs had naval gunfire support with inadequate communications and an inability to provide close support to the infantry. The 26th (Jacob's) Battery had been forced out of action mid-afternoon and, while one gun of the 4th Australian Field Artillery (AFA) Battery came ashore late in the afternoon, it did not swing into action until 6.00 pm. The 21st (Kohat) Battery would not land until after 5.30 pm. Other field guns brought to the beach during the day were ordered to return to the transports; Bridges had requested that the divisional artillery not be landed, largely due to the difficulty of finding suitable gun positions in the confined beachhead, and partly out of concern that it might be captured.

Indian mountain gunners from either the 21st (Kohat) or 26th (Jacob's) Battery cleaning a 10-pounder mountain gun. Six of these guns from the 26th Battery, posted on the edge of the 400 Plateau, provided the only ANZAC artillery support on 25 April, firing between 12.00 and 2.30 pm, before being forced out of action (AWM C02192).

COMMANDERS' SITUATIONAL AWARENESS

The Ottoman situational awareness was good and both Kemal and Sefik had observation over the ANZAC position. They had defined the limits of the ANZAC frontage, ascertained that the enemy was making no attempt to break out of the confined beachhead, and assessed that they had contained the invasion for the moment. Further, Kemal had recognised the importance of the key terrain on the main range, and was concentrating his strength there. At the same time he was maintaining pressure on the ANZAC right flank with Sefik's smaller

LIEUTENANT COLONEL MUSTAFA KEMAL

Commander *19th Division*

Born in 1881 in Salonika, Kemal graduated from the Ottoman Military Academy in January 1902, the Ottoman General Staff College in 1905 and served in staff positions in the *Fifth Army* and later in the *Third Army*. In 1911 he fought in Libya during the Italian–Turkish War, successfully defending Derna until war's end in October 1912. Returning to Turkey in December, he was appointed Chief of Operations of the *Gallipoli Provisional Army* and fought in Thrace during the First Balkan War. During the Second Balkan War he participated in the fighting that recovered most of eastern Thrace from the Bulgarians, and was subsequently promoted to lieutenant colonel and appointed Ottoman Military Attaché to all the Balkan states. In January 1915 Kemal was tasked with raising and training the *19th Division* at Maidos. Although a part of *III Corps*, his division was assigned as the *Fifth Army* central reserve for the defence of the Dardanelles.

On the morning of 25 April, when news of the ANZAC landing arrived, he cancelled his divisional exercise and awaited orders from the *Fifth Army*. At around 8.00 am he was directed to send a battalion to Ari Burnu. Appreciating the importance of the Sari Bair Range, he set off with the complete *57th Regiment* and a mountain battery and coordinated the attacks of the *27th* and *57th regiments* against the ANZAC line before returning to Boghali in response to a reported British landing at Kum Tepe. Esat Pasha then assigned him command of the Sari Bair front. Arriving back at Scrubby Knoll that afternoon, he found the Ottoman counter-attacks stalled, and assigned the *72nd* and *77th regiments* in a renewed effort to drive the Anzacs into the sea. Determined to crush the invading forces, he organised a massive counter-attack by all the forces assigned to him on 27 April, but a breakdown in coordination led to piecemeal attacks that were shot to pieces by the withering ANZAC fire.

During the August Offensive his aggressive and firm leadership proved decisive when he defeated Allied attempts to seize the heights of the Sari Bair Range and gain the high ground inland of Suvla Bay. Kemal then assumed command of *XVI Corps* and later commanded the *Seventh Army* in Palestine, which was destroyed on its retreat from Nablus in September 1918. During the Turkish War of Independence, as Commander-in-Chief of the Turkish Army, he inflicted crushing defeats on the Greek forces in 1921 and 1922 that eventually secured the new Turkish Republic. As President of the new state he reformed the country and is regarded with reverence as the father of modern Turkey. He died in Istanbul in 1938.

force, which would limit ANZAC's ability to reinforce its left. What he didn't know was the ANZAC's strength, other than the beachhead was being reinforced which was evident from the transports which continued to arrive offshore.

ANZAC's situational awareness was poor. After being briefed by Bridges at 3.00 pm, Birdwood returned to his ship, having made no effort to view the battle front for himself and relying entirely on the information provided by Bridges. Yet Bridges was not in control of the battle. Sequestered in Anzac Cove since his reconnaissance that morning, he had made no further effort to see the situation on the ground for himself, relying purely on messages and telephone conversations with Sinclair-MacLagan and McCay. He had little or no idea what was occurring on his ground of tactical importance, or that several companies of the battalions he had sent there had been diverted onto Second Ridge. His only communication with his left flank was through runners, if any were sent, who would have taken considerable time to reach the beach if they were not killed or wounded on the way. Although MacLaurin was without a command, no attempt was made to send him forward to take control of the vital left flank and run a telephone cable back to divisional headquarters to provide Bridges with a picture of what was occurring there. Further, as often happens in campaigns and battles, Sinclair-MacLagan, McCay, and their subordinates had significantly overestimated the strength of Sefik's force and continually called for reinforcements, leading to the diversion of battalions and companies destined for Baby 700.

The lone gun of the 4th Australian Field Artillery Battery being hauled up a path cut by Australian engineers very late on the afternoon of 25 April. The gun came into action at around 6.00 pm, providing the first artillery support to the Anzacs since the mountain gunners of the 26th (Jacob's) Battery were forced out of action at around 2.30 pm. Major General Bridges stopped the remainder of the field guns coming ashore on 25 April, some sent back to their transports on reaching Anzac Cove (AWM G00918).

This overestimation became starkly evident when McCay rang Bridges at 4.40 pm urging him to send more reinforcements to fill a gap at the northern end of Bolton's Ridge. By now Bridges had only Lieutenant Colonel Astley Onslow Thompson's 4th Battalion in reserve. The Otago Battalion was ashore, but these were Walker's men and were needed to protect the 1st Division's left flank. Questioning McCay's plea, Bridges asked whether the reinforcements were absolutely necessary. McCay replied that they were; yet, at the time, a battalion and a half of Turks were attacking almost seven Australian battalions, and few of them were opposite McCay. Relying on McCay's judgement, Bridges acquiesced and, at 4.55 pm, sent the 4th Battalion to Bolton's Ridge, unaware that Baby 700 had just been lost. Eight of the 13 ANZAC battalions committed to the firing line were now on the right flank, while the ground of tactical importance on the left flank was being lost, and few troops remained to defend a thrust down First Ridge into the heart of the ANZAC position.

Stretcher-bearers from an Australian field ambulance carrying a wounded man late on the afternoon of 25 April. The reinforcements coming ashore are probably men of the Otago Battalion (AWM A05784).

THE LOSS OF BABY 700

At around 3.30 pm, Kemal launched the *1/57th* and *3/57th* in another attack down the main range. They came on 'in quick time and absolute silence as trained soldiers should, well extended and searching the scrub', recalled Westmacott. The rapid fire from his platoon 'ripped along the ridge and the whole of that leading section went down in the scrub; but more were to follow.' As the main attack hit the ANZAC line, '[t]he fire from the ridge behind and to the left was so steady and rapid that the Turks went down like ninepins ... The foremost ones got no nearer than sixty yards from us.' Following a lull, the Turks came on again, their artillery lashing the defenders with shrapnel. Casualties mounted as the grim reaper took his toll, and the officers and senior NCOs

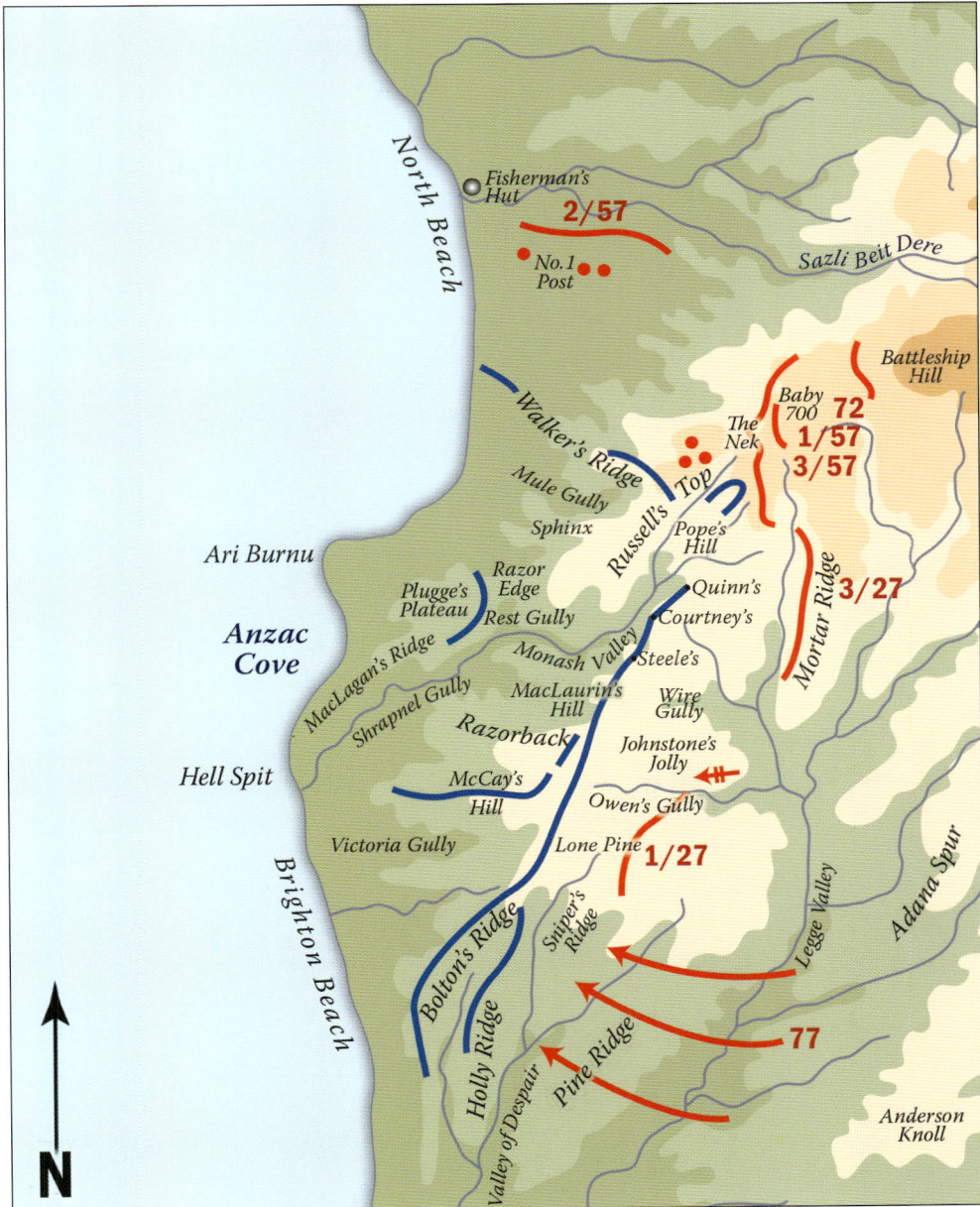

The situation on the evening of 25 April. Reinforced by the *3/57th*, the *1/57th* has driven the Australians and New Zealanders off Baby 700 and reached The Nek. The *1/72nd* reinforces them. Outflanked, Leer's group has withdrawn from Mortar Ridge, and the *3/27th* has occupied the upper reaches of Second Ridge. After bitter fighting, the *1/27th* has reached the main Australian line on Lone Pine. Reinforcing Sefik, the *1/77th* and *2/77th* attack across Pine Ridge and south of Lone Pine. The Australian and New Zealand line runs up Walker's Ridge to Russell's Top, with small parties near The Nek. There is a gap in the line to Quinn's Post, from where the main firing line runs down Second Ridge, along the seaward edge of the 400 Plateau and down Bolton's and Holly ridges.

lost heavily. Among the Aucklanders, Major Stuckey and Lieutenants Baddeley, Harold Allen, Frederick Dodson and William Flower were killed, while Major Alderman and Lieutenants Westmacott and Herbert Richardson were wounded, the latter so seriously he died of his wounds. Sergeant Major James Hobbs was killed, as were three of the four Waikato platoon sergeants. On the left flank Lieutenant Patterson of the 12th Battalion died leading his men in a counter-attack, while Major Gordon of the 2nd Battalion had been killed earlier leading his men forward.

Weakened by heavy losses, outnumbered, and with the Turks working around their flanks on either side of Baby 700, the Australians and New Zealanders finally fell back over the crest in sections, taking what wounded they could. Westmacott saw one Aucklander 'with his foot blown to pulp [come] hopping out of the scrub ... and cried out "For God's sake, don't leave me!" [A] young Australian went back saying "Come on mate, get on my back" and the man held on to him.' Once over the crest the survivors retreated through a staggered line of defence that had been established on the seaward slopes by a mixed group of New Zealanders and Australians.

Further back on Russell's Top the Auckland Battalion's machine-gun section fired over their heads and ripped into the Turks as they came over the crest of Baby 700. High on Mortar Ridge, men of the *10th* and *12th companies* of the *3/27th* saw the *57th* crest the hill to their right and linked up with them. Two platoons of the 2nd (South Canterbury) Company under Grant and stragglers from other units stormed across The Nek and reinforced the Australian and New Zealand line on Baby 700. Grant led a counter-attack and, although it gained an old Turkish trench, heavy fire drove his men back and Grant was seriously wounded, dying of his wounds later that evening. At around 4.30 pm, the *3/72nd* reinforced the *57th* and together they mounted a new attack that swarmed down the slope. Weakened from heavy casualties, with many of their officers killed or wounded, and faced with overwhelming odds, the ANZAC line broke, and the surviving Australians and New Zealanders raced back across The Nek. Others dropped into the gullies on either side; those to the north made their way down Malone's Gully and back to the beach, or ran into and were killed by elements of the *2/57th*. On the upper end of Mortar Ridge, Captain Harold Jacobs, with a group of the 1st Battalion, fell back to the upper end of Second Ridge. Enfiladed on their left, they dropped into Monash Valley, as did the survivors of Leer's company of the 3rd Battalion. The remnants of the *1/57th*, together with *3/57th*, *3/72nd* and two companies of the *3/27th* now held Baby 700 and Mortar Ridge, and enfiladed the Australians and New Zealanders at Quinn's Post.

How many Anzacs had been left on Baby 700 dead or severely wounded is unknown, but the losses had been heavy, and their officers had led from the front. Major Scobie had been hit in the face, and dazed, bareheaded and caked in blood, stumbled down Second Ridge before fainting and being dragged into the Australian line near Wire Gully. Of the ten company commanders who had fought on Baby 700, six had died and three were wounded, while 12 platoon commanders had been killed and at least another seven wounded. At least two men were captured. After bandaging a severely wounded New Zealander, young Bugler Ashton of the 11th Battalion set out to find a stretcher party to bring him in, became disoriented, bumped into a party of Turks in a ravine east of Mortar Ridge, and was taken prisoner. Private Thomas Burgess of the Auckland Battalion lay wounded for three days before the Turks picked him up, only to die of his wounds in a Turkish hospital.

Corporal Hedley Howe of the 11th Battalion and a New Zealand corporal were two of the last men across The Nek. There they stumbled into the pits held by the Auckland Battalion's machine-gun section and one Maxim of the Canterbury Battalion. Some 50 New Zealanders and Australians under a New Zealand sergeant established a defensive line there and held off any further Ottoman attempts to cross the narrow ridge at The Nek. Behind them were two Canterbury platoons under Stewart, and in the ensuing firefight he was killed after leading forward a party of reinforcements. One of his men observed: '[the] poor Colonel … died a noble death . He was directing the boys' fire with his walking stick when he was suddenly hit in the head …' Further back, Braund's two companies were engaged with Turks on the spur opposite Walker's Ridge.

Anzac Cove late afternoon 25 April, showing the congestion of wounded, medical staff, stragglers, troops landing and stores. Described by Private Edward Baigent of the Canterbury Battalion as 'one wild seen [sic] of confusion' (AWM PS1659).

THE ATTACKS PETER OUT

At around 5.00 pm the remaining two companies of the Canterbury Battalion, the 12th (Nelson) and 13th (North Canterbury and Westland), finally landed, well after the rest of the battalion had moved into the firing line. They were followed at 5.30 pm by the leading companies of Lieutenant Colonel Harold Pope's 16th Battalion and two platoons of the 15th Battalion. Godley told Pope to take all available troops up to the firing line. With A and B companies and the machine-gun section of his own battalion, the two platoons of the 15th and a half-company of New Zealanders, Pope set off. As they filed into Shrapnel Gully, the 21st (Kohat) Battery crossed their track and split the column in two. Amid the roar of rifle fire from the heights above, the leading portion reached the fork at the head of Monash Valley in darkness. After reconnoitring the spur that would later bear his name and narrowly avoiding capture, Pope occupied the position with A Company, the machine-gun section and the New Zealanders. The tail of the column eventually entered the line between Courtney's and Steele's Posts. Malone, with two companies of the Wellington Battalion, the 11th (Taranaki) and the 17th (Ruahine), was ashore by 7.00 pm and two platoons of the 11th Company were despatched to support Pope. The remainder of Malone's battalion would not arrive until dawn the following day.

On the extreme ANZAC left, many of the *2/57th* had passed down the seaward ridges of the Sari Bair Range and pushed towards the sea between the Fisherman's Hut and Walker's Ridge, but were stopped by Critchley-Salmonson's small group. To avoid being cut off, Captain Fahy withdrew the survivors of Jackson's company of the 7th Battalion from the Fisherman's Hut and crept south along the beach under fire, eventually reaching the ANZAC perimeter.

On the ANZAC right, Sefik had been reinforced by the two battalions of Saip's *77th Regiment* at around 5.00 pm and, as evening approached, a field battery arrived to relieve his hard-worked mountain gunners. By dusk the *1/27th* had taken three-quarters of Lone Pine and was in contact with the main Australian defensive line along the seaward edge of the 400 Plateau. Sefik now felt that he was strong enough to 'throw the Australians into the sea' and ordered a night attack. It failed under withering fire from the defenders. The *1/27th* was repelled, while the *77th's* attack on the left of the *1/27th* lacked punch. Some of the troops failed to participate and Sefik found numbers of the *77th* hiding in the scrub on Third Ridge. Nonetheless, those who did attack swept across Pine Ridge, overrunning the Australians still there, and hitting the defensive line on the spurs running off Lone Pine and along Bolton's Ridge. There they were stopped short by a hurricane of rifle and machine-gun fire. The parties of Australians still on Pine Ridge were never heard of again. In 1919 Charles Bean and the Australian Historical Mission found their skeletons, still clad in the tattered remnants of their uniforms, lying in the small groups in which they had fought to the end, and in the gully behind the ridge where the wounded had crawled to die.

As darkness fell over the battlefield the fighting raged on. At around 8.00 pm, the mixed party at The Nek discovered that the Canterbury platoons behind them had retired. Carrying the three machine-guns and their wounded, Howe's group fell back along Russell's Top with the Turks in pursuit. Braund's mixed force of Australians and New Zealanders halted the Turks 300 yards further on. The situation was critical but the line held. Braund 'set a fine example of tirelessness' as he consolidated his critical position, deploying reinforcements, organising water parties and ammunition resupply, and keeping the beach informed with several carefully worded and precise messages that reflected a cool commander in control of the situation. All across the battlefield an incessant firing continued as the Ottomans sought to throw the Anzacs back. In the confusion of the night, and against a stout defence, they failed.

FIELD GUN, ORDNANCE QF
18-POUNDER MK 1 AND MK II

Calibre:	3.3-inch (83.8mm)
Barrel Length:	96.96 inches (2.46m)
Gun Weight:	2825 pounds (1281kg)
Action:	Single motion screw breech mechanism with hydro-spring recoil system
Range:	Shrapnel 6000m
Ammunition:	18.5lbs (8.4kg) shrapnel shell with 375 balls @ 41 balls/pound
Battery first line:	176 rounds per gun
Fuze:	Time
Rate of Fire	20 rounds per minute (maximum), 4 rounds per minute (sustained)
Crew:	6 men with 4 reserves at the wagon line

The Ordnance quick-firing 18-pounder field gun was one of two British field guns and was used by the Royal Field Artillery batteries in support of the infantry (the other was the 13-pounder gun of the Royal Horse Artillery attached to the cavalry divisions). The 18-pounder was the gun used by Australian and New Zealand field batteries at Gallipoli. The Mk I was adopted in 1904 and the Mk II in 1906. Drawn by a six-horse team, the gun and accompanying ammunition limber could be galloped into the firing line and brought into action quickly. It was easily manhandled by its crew and could be quickly repositioned. Firing shrapnel shells on a relatively flat trajectory, the gun was used in the direct fire role and in the indirect role from behind low folds in the ground.

Each Australian and New Zealand field battery was equipped with four guns (as opposed to six in a British battery) giving a total of 40 in ANZAC. There was considerable confusion in landing the field guns on 25 April. Some guns came to the beach but were turned back as General Bridges initially directed that they not be landed. The first field gun eventually came ashore late in the afternoon and was brought into action at around 6.00 pm on 25 April. By the evening of 26 April, 14 field guns were ashore.

DIG, DIG, DIG

Despite Braund's calm and positive messages, by now Bridges and Godley had realised the ground of tactical importance had been lost and their line along Second Ridge was in danger of being rolled up from the left. Since late afternoon they had also witnessed an increasing number of men straggling back to the beach from the firing line. At 5.20 pm McCay had sent a message: 'Regret say considerable numbers unwounded men leaving firing line [sic].' Private Edward Baigent of the Canterbury Battalion described Anzac Cove as 'one wild seen [sic] of confusion'. At 8.00 pm, faced with a dire tactical situation, few reserves, stragglers falling back from the firing line and the shambles on the beach, they requested Birdwood to come ashore. Arriving at Bridges' headquarters, he was shocked to learn that both of his divisional commanders recommended the immediate evacuation of the force, the time-honoured acceptance of defeat. Withdrawal from a battlefield in contact with the enemy is a difficult task, and it requires a semblance of control and order among the retiring troops if the retreat is not to become a rout. Withdrawing from a beachhead while pressed by the enemy is a significantly more risky venture, with the certainty that the portion of the force acting as the rearguard and defending the final perimeter will be lost. It requires a sufficiently large perimeter to ensure that the enemy is kept far enough away from the embarkation beaches so as not to unduly interfere with the evacuation. Undertaking an evacuation in the situation facing ANZAC would have seen some troops away safely, but the disorganisation and inexperience of the force, the shallow, narrow beachhead, a pressing enemy and insufficient boats to carry enough men away in the time available would have resulted in chaos and disaster, with the loss of the vast majority of the force ashore. That both Bridges and Godley urged immediate evacuation under these circumstances illustrates the extent of their concern and reflects the prevailing mood of defeat.

Initially Birdwood protested. During the long conference that ensued, only Walker argued against the proposal, but in the end Birdwood acquiesced. Rather than making the decision himself, as Bridges urged, Birdwood put the case to Hamilton aboard HMS *Queen Elizabeth*, which had just arrived at anchorage: 'Both my divisional commanders and brigadiers have represented to me that they fear their men are thoroughly demoralised by shrapnel fire to which they have been subjected all day after exhausting and gallant work in the morning ... If troops are subjected to shell-fire again to-morrow morning there is likely to be a fiasco, as I have no fresh troops available with which to replace those in the firing line. I know my representation is most serious, but if we are to re-embark it must be done at once.'

The message was intercepted by Admiral Sir Cecil Thursby, commanding the 2nd Naval Squadron on board HMS *Queen* at around 11.00 pm. Taking Brigadier Generals R.A. Carruthers and Charles Cunliffe-Owen from the ANZAC staff across to *Queen Elizabeth*, he apprised Hamilton of the request. On being asked, Thursby told Hamilton that he did not believe the troops could be re-embarked either before dawn or in the morning, and that it would take two days to get all of them off. Carruthers considered it impossible to re-embark the force within the necessary time. Hamilton replied to Birdwood: 'Your news is indeed serious. But there is nothing for it but to dig yourselves right in and stick it out ... Make a personal appeal to your men and Godley's to make a supreme effort to hold their ground ... P.S. You have got through the difficult business, now you have only to dig, dig, dig, until you are safe. Ian H.'

The ANZAC position was serious. With the ground of tactical importance lost, the Turks had pushed along Russell's Top to a point close to the junction with Walker's Ridge, enabling them to fire into the rear of the ANZAC line along Second Ridge. The ANZAC left flank was dangerously undermanned. The party under Critchley-Salmonson held the lower end of Walker's Ridge, and there was a gap between him and Braund's mixed group along the upper reaches of Walker's Ridge to Russell's Top. Other than the group on Pope's Hill, a large gap existed between the Top and the Bloody Angle, where Jacob's and Leer's survivors clung to the side of Second Ridge just north of Quinn's Post. Conversely, less the losses of the day's fighting, three and a half Ottoman battalions held the dominating ground on the flank of the ANZAC line, which clung along the seaward edge of Second Ridge. A thrust from Baby 700 down Second Ridge had the potential to roll up the ANZAC centre and right. An attack along Russell's Top could take the Ottomans to the Razor Edge overlooking the length of Monash Valley and enable them to fire into the rear of the whole ANZAC line from Walker's Ridge to McCay's Hill. The only defensible support line for ANZAC to fall back on was Plugge's Plateau and MacLagan's Ridge, currently held by the Otagos and Leane's company of the 11th Battalion, and too small to hold a large body of men. Behind them was the sea.

Looking up Monash Valley towards Baby 700 from Braund's Hill. Russell's Top is on the left and The Nek is marked by the right-hand stand of trees. Pope's Hill projects into the valley to the right of The Nek. The monument projecting above the skyline on Baby 700 is to the *57th Regiment*. Further right Quinn's Post is marked by the small white square in the distance below the crest line. From that point, approaching the forefront are Courtney's Post, Steele's Post and the seaward slope of MacLaurin's Hill. The left of the 3rd Brigade's line along Second Ridge rested on Quinn's Post, while Pope's 16th Battalion and a half company of the Canterbury Battalion occupied Pope's Hill after dark on 25 April. Braund's 2nd Battalion and the New Zealanders held the Top on the left of the photo during the night 25/26 April. This photograph shows how the Turks who occupied the upper end of Russell's Top could fire into the rear of the ANZAC line on Second Ridge (Glenn Wahlert image).

BRIGADIER-GENERAL HAROLD 'HOOKY' WALKER, DSO

Chief of Staff, Australian and New Zealand Army Corps

Walker was a no-nonsense British regular born in England in 1862 who spent a year at Cambridge University before being commissioned into the Duke of Cornwall's Light Infantry in 1884. He served in the Sudan Campaign in 1885–86, was then posted to India and later fought in the South African War. He was a brigadier general on the general staff in India when the Great War erupted, and was appointed Birdwood's Chief of Staff in December 1914.

A man of strong opinions and sound common sense, Walker opposed the Gallipoli landing on the grounds that it had no chance of success. He went ashore at Anzac shortly before 8.00 am to maintain personal contact with the fighting and, in the absence of Colonel Francis Johnston, who had been taken ill, he assumed command of the New Zealand Brigade at around 11.00 am. His determination to avoid unnecessary casualties led to his decision to recall the Auckland Battalion from Walker's Ridge and send it over Plugge's Plateau and up Monash Valley to Baby 700, costing time and resulting in only two companies reaching the ground of tactical importance. On 26 April he took control of the left flank and, during the fighting along Russell's Top on 27 April, he actively supported Lieutenant Colonel George Braund's defence of the position.

Walker took command of the 1st Australian Brigade after the death of Colonel Henry MacLaurin. Promoted major general in July 1915, he assumed command of the 1st Australian Division until he was severely wounded in September. He returned to the division in March 1916 and commanded it throughout the Western Front until July 1918. An astute, trusted and humane leader who was scrupulous in the care of his division, Walker was highly respected, regarded as one of the best divisional commanders in the AIF, and much loved by his men. He commanded the British 48th Division in Italy for the remainder of the war. Promoted lieutenant general in 1923, Walker was appointed Commander-in-Chief Southern Command in India, and retired from the Army in 1928. He died in England in 1934.

CHAPTER 11
STALEMATE

CONSOLIDATION

As light rain descended on the darkened and battered landscape, the firing petered out sometime after midnight and a calm settled over the battlefield. On Baby 700 the remnants of the *57th* and *3/72nd regiments* consolidated their gains. In the south the disorganised *77th Regiment* was pulled back behind Third Ridge. In the confusion the *1/27th* gave up Lone Pine, falling back across Legge Valley to the western slopes of Third Ridge, taking the three mountain guns with them, but leaving a machine-gun platoon, which had been pushed forward earlier that evening, on Johnston's Jolly. All along the firing line, surviving Anzacs and Turks continued digging under the cloak of darkness. All around lay the misery of shattered bodies. Wounded crowded the aid posts behind the lines, while those left behind on Baby 700, in the gully behind Pine Ridge, or simply hidden by the scrub that clothed the outlying spurs died a lonely, agonising death.

A gun of the 4th New Zealand Howitzer Battery in action on Gallipoli later in the campaign. One section (two guns) of the battery landed at dawn on 26 April and came into action on North Beach shortly afterwards, providing a boost for weary infantrymen on the firing line. The other section arrived later in the morning (Alexander Turnbull Library).

During the night the disembarkation of the NZ&A Division continued. The 13th Battalion and the remainder of the 15th were ferried ashore and, close to dawn, Malone eagerly greeted his last two companies as they arrived on the beach. Completing the disembarkation of the infantry, Lieutenant Colonel Richard Courtney's 14th Battalion, together with Monash and the 4th Brigade headquarters, came ashore later that morning.

The 400 Plateau from the south-western edge of Chunuk Bair showing the observation the Turks had over it during the battle, and for the remainder of the campaign. Bean describe the plateau as 'a Greek amphitheater.' Ince Bair is the near ridge with the cutting , along which the right of Tulloch's line fought on 25 April (auhtor's image).

However, there were difficulties getting the artillery into action. So narrow and shallow was the beachhead, and so bad the terrain, that suitable positions for the field guns were difficult to find. One gun from the 1st AFA Battery arrived at 3.00 am, and one section of the New Zealand Howitzer Battery came into action on the beach near Ari Burnu at 6.00 am, considerably heartening the infantry on the firing line. It was joined by the other section around noon. Two guns each from the 4th and 5th AFA batteries, and the whole of the 7th AFA and 2nd NZFA batteries came ashore later in the day, bringing the total to 12 mountain guns, four howitzers and 14 field guns, redressing the imbalance of the day before. For the most part the 1st, 2nd, 3rd and 6th AFA and the 3rd NZFA batteries were sent to support the British at Cape Helles; there was simply no room for them at Anzac.

Twenty ANZAC battalions now faced ten and a half Ottoman — but few were fresh. Of the Ottoman units, only two battalions of the *72nd* were fresh. The *57th* had lost heavily taking Baby 700, and the remains of two and a half battalions of the *27th* were strung out between Baby 700 and Gaba Tepe, while one company of the *2/27th* remained covering the beaches south of Gaba Tepe. Although three companies of the *2/27th* were largely intact, the other battalions had been shredded. Between them, the *27th* and *57th* had lost over 2000 men, 40% of the troops engaged during the day. After their less than impressive performance of the night before, the *77th*'s two battalions were regrouping behind the protection of Third Ridge.

ANZAC was in no better shape. Nowhere did a single brigade remain as a fighting entity. In the 1st Australian Division, only the 4th, 7th and 10th battalions were largely intact. The rest of the infantry were intermingled in company and platoon groups across the whole front from Walker's Ridge to Bolton's Ridge. The reasons were varied: a lack of situational awareness, committing units piecemeal, vague orders, poor control at battalion level, and companies and platoons peeling off to join the firing line in response to calls for reinforcements as they moved up Monash Valley. While the terrain contributed to the chaos, it was not the major factor as is so commonly argued. The situation was better in the NZ&A Division. Intermingled with the 1st Division battalions were the Aucklanders, the Cantabrians and the 16th Battalion spread along Walker's Ridge to the 400 Plateau. However the Otago and Wellington battalions of the New Zealand Brigade were fresh and largely intact, as were the 13th, 14th and 15th battalions of the 4th Australian Brigade. The fragmentation and intermingling of units, however, was to continue during the coming days.

Australians on the seaward slope of Second Ridge on 26 April. Probably taken from Quinn's Post looking across to the rear of Pope's Hill, with Russell's Top on the left background, it shows the rudimentary nature of the trenches on the second day, and how Turks occupying Russell's Top could fire into the rear of the ANZAC line on Second Ridge. The colour patch on the man in the foreground suggests he is from the 11th Battalion (AWM P05382_005).

While ANZAC was completing its disembarkation, the *Fifth Army* was arranging reinforcements for the southern half of the peninsula with two regiments earmarked for the Ari Burnu front. The *64th* of the *3rd Division* and the *33rd* of the *11th*, both from *XV Corps* on the Asiatic shore, were directed to march to Chanakkle where they would be ferried across the Narrows. The *64th* had only two battalions and lacked a machine-gun company. The *3rd Battalion, 7th Artillery Regiment (3/7th Arty)*, was released from the *7th Division* at Bulair, and passed to under command of the *19th Division*, bringing another eight guns onto Third Ridge. However, none of these units would arrive until late afternoon on 26 April at the earliest.

As the sun crept over the Sari Bair Range on Monday 26 April, its rays slowly lit Second Ridge to reveal Second Lieutenant Saadet's machine-gun platoon (two guns) and its protective rifle platoon isolated on the western edge of Johnston's Jolly. The Australians and New Zealanders saw them and opened fire, seriously wounding Saadet and forcing the guns and infantrymen back to the southern end of Mortar Ridge. This triggered a resumption of hostilities, and firing broke out across the battlefield. On Baby 700 the *57th* and *3/72nd* were dribbling batches of men down the slope to consolidate their forward positions at The Nek and on the upper reaches of Second Ridge. Others crept forward to join those on Russell's Top, taking up positions to fire into the rear of Pope's Hill and Quinn's, Courtney's and Steele's Posts, inflicting a rising toll of casualties on their occupants. Peering into the growing light, the 16th Battalion's machine-gun section, with the redoubtable Lance Corporal Percy Black and Private Harry Murray on one of the guns, swung about and, throughout the day, suppressed snipers with bursts of fire. Further along the Top some Turks launched a feeble attack against Braund's line, but were easily repulsed.

At dawn Lieutenant Colonel Granville Burnage's 13th Battalion was despatched up Monash Valley to bridge the gap between Russell's Top and Pope's Hill. Two companies joined the 16th on Pope's Hill and one climbed to Quinn's Post. Reaching the foot of Pope's Hill, Major Sydney Herring's D Company scaled the steep slopes of Russell's Top to effect a junction with the New Zealanders believed to be forward of Braund's position. Reaching the crest they found no-one — New Zealander or Turk — and settled in under fire from the Turks on the slopes of Baby 700. Unable to sustain his position, Herring pulled his men back until they reached Braund's line, where remnants of the Australians, Aucklanders and Cantabrians from the previous day's fighting, and two recently arrived companies of the Canterbury Battalion held the upper reaches of Walker's Ridge and the junction with Russell's Top. After a couple of sorties to regain the lost ground, fire from Baby 700 drove Herring's company back into Monash Valley. During the morning an attempt by a portion of the *57th* to rush Pope's Hill from Baby 700 was repulsed with rifle and machine-gun fire, and naval gunfire from the battleships *Queen* and *Queen Elizabeth*. Meanwhile, the overcrowded centre and right flank continued to attract troops like a magnet: at 9.00 am the bulk of the 15th Battalion was despatched to the 400 Plateau, and Major George Mitchell's 10th (North Otago) Company was sent from Plugge's Plateau to reinforce Steele's Post. All along the line Anzac and Turk spluttered away at each other and sought to consolidate the ground they held.

In the early afternoon Turkish troops worried the Australians and New Zealanders on Russell's Top with incessant sniping. Braund sent Captain George Concannon forward to clear them and attempted to close the gap that existed between his position and Pope's. At 4.50 pm he advised: 'Situation altered. Have report from top of ridge that our troops have gone in with the bayonet. Will advise full position when reported. Are on ridge section 237 BlockW5 to 224 Block C5.' There the line dug in for the night.

LIEUTENANT COLONEL GEORGE BRAUND

Commanding Officer, 2nd Australian Battalion

Born in England in 1866, George Braund emigrated to New South Wales with his parents at the age of 15. A businessman and talented sportsman, he was commissioned into the Armidale Company of the 4th Infantry Regiment of the New South Wales militia in 1893. Braund was a prominent citizen of the town, serving as a magistrate, President of the Armidale Chamber of Commerce and on several public and business boards, while maintaining an active interest in the militia. In 1913 he was elected to the Legislative Assembly of New South Wales, and in July 1914 took command of the 13th Infantry Regiment of the Citizen Military Forces. When the AIF was raised, Colonel Henry MacLaurin approached Braund and asked him to raise and train the 2nd Battalion, which he did with thoroughness, exacting a high standard of discipline and fitness from his men largely through personal example.

Early on 25 April, two of his companies were sent forward to support the 3rd Brigade and, at 1.30 pm, he took the remaining two to the junction of Walker's Ridge and Russell's Top. From the evening of the 25th to the morning of 28 April he conducted a tenacious defence of the Top against several Turkish attacks and, with New Zealand reinforcements, led a bayonet charge clearing the ridge almost to The Nek. When his men were driven back he rallied them and held this vital position against further attack. His written messages to Bridges throughout the action reflect a cool leader who was in control of the situation and determined to hold his position. It was largely through his firm leadership that the Turks were denied possession of Russell's Top with its potentially serious consequences for the entire force.

Lieutenant Colonel William Malone of the Wellington Battalion was highly critical of Braund. However, Malone did not enter the battle until the afternoon of 27 April, when Braund had been in action continuously for 48 hours, and was further down Walker's Ridge. His comments were unjustified, churlish and based on ignorance of the situation; the men who fought with Braund paid tribute to his courage and leadership. Indeed one of Malone's soldiers, Private Oswald Meenkin of the Wellington Battalion, recorded in his diary that 'Colonel Braund … walked around giving orders as if nothing worried him, and the bullets were so many flies', while the men of the 2nd Battalion who fought alongside him throughout the action considered him 'the embodiment of bravery and as cool as though carrying out a field exercise.' On the night of 3/4 May he was moving through the scrub to brigade headquarters when he failed to hear the challenge of a sentry and was killed.

Reputedly a photo taken during the 4th Battalion's disastrous advance across Lone Pine at around 4.50 pm on 26 April. Figures of men can be seen faintly on the skyline to the right of the leg and boot in the foreground. The angle of the photograph suggests it was taken from the top of the Razorback looking south-east towards Lone Pine with McCay's Hill dropping off the plateau to the right (AWM G00919A).

THE 4TH BATTALION ADVANCES

On the firing line, the trenches were little more than shallow, disconnected rifle pits dug wherever the troops had gone to ground. Mid-afternoon Bridges ascended the summit of McCay's Hill through the debris of the previous day's fighting. Angered at finding men sheltering below the crest and finding trenches dug on the reverse slope of Lone Pine, he flew into men and officers alike in an ugly scene, cursing the troops and criticising the arrangements with a torrent of invective. In his first foray to ascertain the situation since the previous morning, he decided to straighten the line between the 10th Battalion on Johnston's Jolly and the 4th on Bolton's Ridge. Bypassing McCay and taking McNicoll of the 6th with him, Bridges strode to the skyline of the blood-soaked plateau and, with his characteristic gruffness, pointed out the alignment he required. Remnants of the 5th, 6th and 7th battalions, together with a company of the 15th, were told to move forward 200 metres to the Daisy Patch at the head of Owen's Gully. Returning to McCay's headquarters he sent a strongly worded note to Wanliss who commanded the troops to be moved, and then stormed off for the cove. This hurried and terse intervention led to a misunderstanding that would have tragic consequences.

Concerned that the orders be correctly interpreted, Major Duncan Glasfurd, a British regular on Bridges' staff, personally led two groups forward and placed them in position before leaving with Bridges. Receiving an order, probably from Wanliss, Major Saker led some 200 men from various battalions forward. Fifty metres on, he fell dead. Without any clear understanding of the objective, the men pushed on, doubling as far as the Daisy Patch when the order 'left form' was given and the line swung due north advancing across the front of the Australian firing line. More confusion followed.

Some thought a general advance had been ordered. Lieutenant Shannon Grills of the 7th Battalion, conducting a burial party at the head of Victoria Gully, saw Saker's line move and was determined not to be left behind. Lieutenant Rafferty of the 12th was told to 'keep straight on as you are going' and believed a general advance was underway. A messenger burst into the 4th Battalion headquarters at 4.30 pm erroneously telling Lieutenant Colonel Onslow Thompson that the battalion was to make a general advance. Accepting the message on face value, his second-in-command, Major Charles Macnaghten, quickly suggested that he take the right and the colonel take the left. Impulsively, both hurried up to the firing line. Without issuing orders to his company commanders, and with no idea as to his objective,

The 4th Battalion's ill-conceived and ill-fated advance north over the 400 Plateau.

Onslow Thompson led the 4th Battalion forward, swung left, climbed blindly onto Lone Pine, and headed north across the lobe, passing east of the Daisy Patch, with the Australian firing line on his left, and the Ottomans on his right. Alarmed that an attack was being launched, the Turks on Third Ridge fired into the 4th's right flank with a hail of small arms fire and shrapnel. Men fell quickly. The remainder reached Owen's Gully where some sank into cover.

Seeking to prevent needless deaths, Major James Heane ordered his group to stay put; however, the bulk of the 4th and the party that had been under Saker climbed out of the gully and onto Johnston's Jolly. Only now did Macnaghten ask about the objective. No-one knew. They pushed on, but the heavy fire drove them to ground. Then came the order to retire. Falling back in disorder and confusion, some dropped into Owen's Gully while others fled back to Bolton's Ridge. There Glasfurd, on an errand from Bridges, found numbers of men returning. Taking charge, he led them forward to the line Bridges originally intended, and set them digging a line to connect the Daisy Patch with the 8th Battalion on Bolton's and Holly ridges.

In Owen's Gully, officers rallied some of the retiring men and tried to lead them forward again, but were driven back under a hail of fire. Onslow Thompson then decided to retire, but was killed leading some of his men across Johnston's Jolly to the ANZAC lines. Others stayed on and clung to the edge of the Jolly until well after dark, when McNicoll recalled them. Through vague orders, impetuosity and a lack of adequate coordination, a simple adjustment of the line had gone badly astray, with unnecessary additions to an already heavy casualty list. The lack of hard training under realistic conditions to practise and test battalion commanders in the art of manoeuvring their units effectively had come home to roost.

During the day Birdwood began establishing more formal control of the ANZAC line. Godley was given responsibility for the left, while Bridges retained control of the right. The front was divided nominally into four brigade sectors. Within the NZ&A Division, Walker's New Zealanders would be responsible for Walker's Ridge and Russell's Top, and Monash's 4th Brigade for the head of Monash Valley and Second Ridge to Courtney's Post. The 1st Australian Division would retain the line from there to the sea along Bolton's Ridge. At 6.00 pm MacLaurin and his 1st Brigade headquarters moved up and relieved Sinclair-MacLagan, taking control of the intermixed ANZAC centre along Second Ridge and the 400 Plateau. McCay retained control of the right flank along Holly and Bolton's ridges.

That evening furious rifle fire thudded into the 8th Battalion's line on Holly Ridge behind the Wheatfield, heralding a local attack by the Turks opposite. By now three 18-pounders of the 7th AFA Battery had been emplaced within a few metres of the firing line. As the Turks charged across the small flat, one gun covering this ground, with its shells timed to burst as they left the muzzle, shredded the attack with continuous bursts of shrapnel like a large shotgun clearing a field of quail. Thus ended Monday's sporadic fighting.

Looking from Johnston's Jolly across Monash Valley to Russell's Top. Plugge's Plateau and the Razor Edge are on the left of the photo, The Sphinx is peeping over the Top in the centre of the photo, and The Nek is at the far right. The fighting on 27 April between the Turks and the Australians and New Zealanders under Lieutenant Colonel Braund took place between The Nek and the area of the two trees to the right of The Sphinx and to the left of the bare-faced spur, and shows how critical the position would have been had the Turks taken Russell's Top (Glenn Wahlert image).

27 APRIL

Tuesday 27 April dawned another clear day, and Kemal was determined to throw the Anzacs back into the sea with a concerted effort all along the line using his freshest troops to lead the assault. By now 16 Ottoman battalions were concentrated against 20 Anzac. While they were still outnumbered in infantry, they had an advantage in artillery, nine batteries against six ANZAC. In the renewed offensive, Major Servet's *64th Regiment*, supported by the *57th* and the *3/72nd*, would drive across The Nek and along Russell's Top, while Lieutenant Colonel Ahmet Sevki's *33rd*, which was still arriving from the Narrows, would strike the centre of the ANZAC line on Second Ridge. Simultaneously the *1/72nd* and *2/72nd*, supported by the survivors of the *1/27th* and *3/27th*, and the reorganised *1/77th* and *2/77th*, would attack the ANZAC right flank from the south-east. However, friction afflicted the Ottoman forces this day. Fighting broke out on Russell's Top early that morning drawing in the *57th* and *3/72nd* prematurely, and coordinating six regiments from four different divisions proved too difficult for Kemal's divisional staff.

At daybreak the ANZAC centre was shelled and a party of Turks, believed to be two squadrons of dismounted cavalry, attacked MacLaurin's Hill and Steele's Post, but were driven off with considerable losses. At the same time, on Russell's Top, Braund's men noticed that a new trench had been dug in front of their position during the night. To deny the Turks use of the trench Captain Concannon's company of the 2nd Battalion occupied it. It was the beginning of a hard day's fighting. Shortly after, his men were driven out, but a counter-attack at the point of the bayonet retook the contested trench. Finding themselves under fire from Turks further along the Top, Concannon mounted another bayonet attack that advanced the line a further 120 metres. Furious fighting ensued. Encouraging their men, he and Captain Alfred Shout of the 1st Battalion moved up and down the line. Warned 'You'll be killed', Concannon replied: 'That's what I came here for.' A minute later he fell dead. Braund went forward and decided to reinforce the advanced position, providing some depth along Russell's Top. With only some 150 exhausted Australians and New Zealanders who had been fighting for two days and holding the most critical point of the line, he sought assistance from the New Zealand Brigade.

New Zealanders dug in along Walker's Ridge around 28 April. The cap badge of the man facing the camera on the left suggests that they are probably men of the 17th (Ruahine) Company of the Wellington Battalion (Alexander Turnbull Library).

Walker joined Braund's headquarters on Walker's Ridge at around 10.30 am where he assumed control of the ANZAC left flank. Of his four battalions, the Canterbury was now strung out along Walker's Ridge, with the right fighting alongside Braund's men; the Otago, less Mitchell's company, was on Plugge's Plateau; the Auckland was split up and intermixed with the Australians on Russell's Top and along Second Ridge; and the Wellington was in reserve on North Beach. Much to Malone's annoyance, at around midday Walker ordered him to despatch two companies to support Braund. Up went the 7th (Wellington West Coast) and 9th (Hawkes Bay), together with the machine-gun section under Major Herbert Hart, the battalion's second-in-command. While the New Zealanders proved a welcome addition, the narrowness of Russell's Top now saw the firing line become congested and casualties immediately incurred. At 1.30 pm Braund decided to clear Russell's Top of Turks. With fixed bayonets the New Zealanders and Australians rose and steadily advanced along the ridge clearing out pockets of Turks as they went. Resistance stiffened, and heavy fire from Baby 700 finally drove them to ground short of The Nek. The dangerous gap that had existed between Walker's Ridge and Pope's Hill was now closed. At the same time, the 14th Battalion was sent in to bolster Monash's right flank at Courtney's and Quinn's Posts.

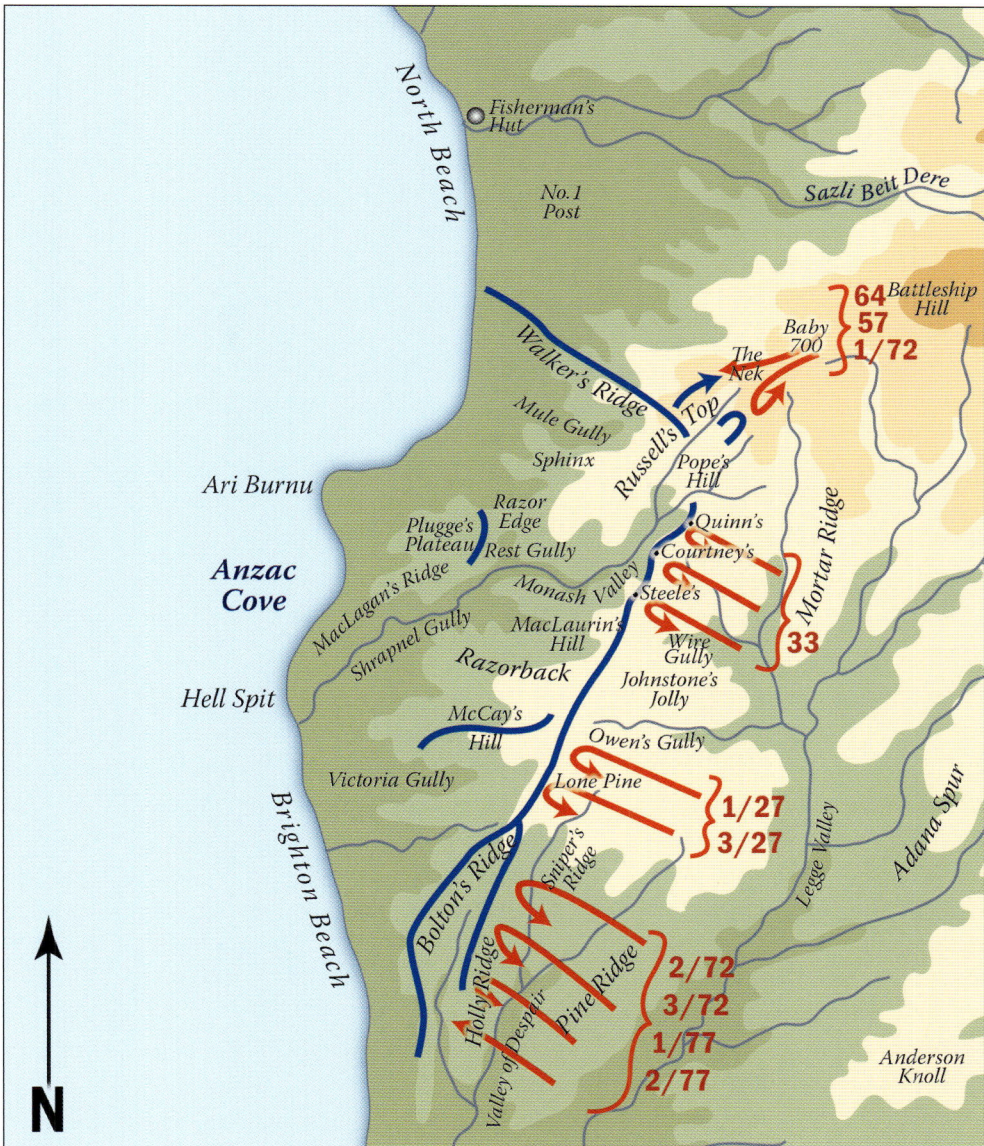

Turkish counter-attacks 27 April. Attacking piecemeal throughout the day the Ottomans are repulsed with heavy casualties. The *57th* and the *1/27th* are drawn into the fight early with Braund's Australians and New Zealanders. At 2.30 pm the *64th Regiment* attacks from Baby 700 and eventually pushes onto Russell's Top where it is halted by Braund's men and repulsed by Anzacs on Pope's Hill. Later the *33rd Regiment* attacks the centre of Second Ridge and is bloodly repulsed. On Lone Pine the *1/27th* and *3/27th* retake much the southern lobe of the 400 Plateau. The *2/72nd*, *3/72nd*, *1/77th* and *2/77th* attack south of Lone Pine but are repulsed by the Australian line along Holly and Bolton's ridges.

With reinforcements arriving late and unable to effectively synchronise their offensive, the Ottomans launched their attacks piecemeal. The power of the magazine-fed, breech-loading rifle and the machine-gun shattered each assault as it was delivered. Sometime between 10.00 and 11.00 am the *1/72nd* and *2/72nd*, supported by the *77th Regiment*'s two battalions, made their assault against the ANZAC right from the south-east, but were repulsed with heavy losses. Despite this, by noon they had established themselves among the spurs running off Lone Pine and on the southern portion of Holly Ridge.

Behind Baby 700 Servet's two battalions of the *64th Regiment* were ready by 2.30 pm. So was the Royal Navy. As his infantry moved forward some six lines deep, the battleships *Queen Elizabeth* and *Queen* plastered them with huge 15 and 12-inch shells, throwing the attack into disarray. 'For a few minutes scarcely anything of the hill could be seen except a low lying curtain of green smoke.' Gallantly the Turks regrouped and moved forward as Anzac rifle and machine-gun fire from Walker's Ridge, Russell's Top and Pope's Hill contributed to the slaughter. Initially the New Zealanders and Australians on Russell's Top held, and Braund's 'high pitched voice could be heard above the continuous din of rifle and machine-gun fire: Steady men! steady!' But as the Turks renewed their attacks the line eventually broke, falling back in disorder. Rallying the retreating men, Braund and Hart took them forward again, establishing the line beyond the junction with Walker's Ridge and averting disaster. There they were joined by the Wellingtons' 17th (Ruahine) Company. By now the *64th*'s attack was broken, and any attempt to move along Russell's Top from Baby 700 was cut down by the crossfire of the Wellingtons' machine-guns on Walker's Ridge, and the 16th's on Pope's Hill. Late that afternoon the Otagos moved up Monash Valley to effect a link between Russell's Top and Pope's Hill.

Moving off after the *64th* had launched its attack, Sevki's *33rd Regiment*, with one battalion leading and two in support, advanced in good order against the ANZAC centre. The distance was short and the ground was open. Men of the 1st, 3rd, 10th, 11th and Auckland battalions, and the 14th Battalion's recently arrived machine-gun section, mowed them down in a relentless hail of fire. As successive waves sought to reach the ANZAC line, they were swept away in a devastating hurricane of rifle and machine-gun fire. Exposing themselves unnecessarily, MacLaurin and his brigade major, Francis Irvine, were both killed within ten minutes of each other, and command of the centre devolved to Owen of the 3rd Battalion. Accepting failure, Kemal called off the attacks at around 5.00 pm and prepared to mount them again under cover of darkness. At around 9.00 pm, heralded by bugle calls and much shouting, the Ottomans flung themselves against the ANZAC line in an all-out effort to breach it: the *57th, 64th* and *3/72nd* attacked Russell's Top, Pope's Hill and Quinn's Post; the *33rd, 1/27th* and *3/27th* stormed the centre and the 400 Plateau; and the *1/72nd, 2/72nd, 1/77th* and *2/77th* flung themselves against the Australian right flank from Lone Pine to Bolton's Ridge. Against a furious fusillade of small arms and machine-gun fire, each was unable to make the desired breakthrough and was repulsed with heavy losses. By midnight it was all over. The Ottomans could not drive the Anzacs into the sea, and the Anzacs were in no position to advance. Stalemate reigned supreme. Despite attempts on both sides to gain more ground over the coming week, the front remained virtually unchanged for the next three months.

Members of the Canterbury Battalion in an early trench possibly on Walker's Ridge after the fighting on 27 or 28 April (Alexander Turnbull Library).

RESULTS AND COST

The Anzacs clung to the line they had held since the night of 25 April, running from the foot of Walker's Ridge on North Beach to Russell's Top, followed by a gap to the isolated post on Pope's Hill. From there, another gap existed where the right fork of Monash Valley sliced through the line. It began again at Quinn's Post, clinging desperately to the seaward edge of Second Ridge all the way to Lone Pine, and then along Bolton's and Holly ridges for 1300 metres before bending back to Brighton Beach. It was roughly 400 acres of no tactical value whatsoever. The Ottomans held the Fisherman's Hut and the ridge running up to Baby 700. From there they dominated much of the ANZAC position, holding the upper section of

Second Ridge down to Quinn's Post, and then closed up on the ANZAC line along Second Ridge, holding most of the 400 Plateau. Further south they held the spurs running off the plateau, including the southern portion of Holly Ridge, around to their original trenches on Bolton's Ridge at what became known as the Balkan Gun Pits. The ANZAC position was precarious, with the sea immediately behind their left and right, while in the centre only Plugge's Plateau and MacLagan's Ridge provided a defensible second line. The only tangible result had been to draw the *19th Division* away from the main landing at Cape Helles, although that hardly mattered as the *25th* and *26th regiments* had easily contained the 29th Division's landing.

It had been a disappointing result all round although, like many commanders, Hamilton, Birdwood, Bridges and Godley put the best light on the situation in their post-operation reports, focusing on the strength of the enemy, the difficulty of the terrain and the gallantry of their own troops, and masking the failure as an heroic achievement. No mention was made of Sinclair-MacLagan's decisions or the request for evacuation on the night of the 25th. That they had not even taken their initial objectives seemed not to matter. Spin is far from a late twentieth-century phenomenon, and the reputations of the senior officers had to be preserved.

Wednesday 28 April was a quiet day. The Turks continued to move reinforcements into the southern peninsula, and the Anzacs began sorting out their jumbled units. Braund's 2nd Battalion and the Aucklanders and Cantabrians with them, were relieved by the Wellington Battalion that morning. Under Braund's firm hand they had held the critical point of the line since the evening of 25 April with little rest and much hard fighting. At 4.00 pm the RMLI Portsmouth and Chatham Battalions of the RND arrived, and a relief in place of the intermingled units on the 400 Plateau was effected that night. On Thursday two more battalions, Deal (RMLI) and Nelson (RNR), came ashore and continued the relief. Some semblance of order was restored as the intermingled ANZAC units sorted themselves out over the next few days and counted the cost.

Casualty figures do not indicate who won or lost or, as has become the fashion, demonstrate the incompetence of commanders. They are simply a reminder that war is a very bloody business, win or lose. Accurate casualty figures in large battles are difficult to ascertain and rarely agree, and the landing at Anzac is no exception. Bean provides figures for the 1st, 2nd and 3rd Australian brigades over the period 25–30 April when the first roll calls were made. He lists 4931 killed, wounded and missing, a staggering 41.6% of the 12,000 infantry who landed with those brigades. Of these, 498 were recorded as killed and 2468 wounded, while the 1976 missing included unrecorded wounded sent off in transports and men who later returned to their units. The NZ&A Division's losses are not recorded, but they were considerably less than those of the 1st Australian Division. The Commonwealth War Graves Commission (CWGC) lists 613 Australians and 147 New Zealanders killed on 25 April. Alternatively, the Australian Light Horse Studies Centre website lists 748 Australians killed, and Richard Stowers (*Bloody Gallipoli: the New Zealanders' Story*) names 153 New Zealanders killed, of whom 100 were Aucklanders. These figures do not include those who died of their wounds over the next few weeks. In the three days' fighting covered in this book, the CWGC website names 843 Australians and 169 New Zealanders who died during 25–27 April, while Stowers lists 213 New Zealand dead.

The Ottoman losses are sketchy. On 25 April Sefik recorded that his *27th Regiment* lost 950 men, 35% of those engaged, and it has been estimated that the *57th* lost some 1000 men, 33% of the regiment. Ed Erickson writes that, during the attacks on 27 April, the losses in the *27th*, *57th* and *72nd regiments* reached 30 to 40%. Those of the *33rd*, *64th* and *77th* are unknown, but are likely to be comparable. Accurate losses for both sides will never be known, but whatever they were, they were terrible and unimaginable in today's society. They are a reminder that war and campaigns should not be entered into lightly.

For the rest of the campaign, the battle lines of the evening of 27 April barely changed. The Anzacs clawed their way back along Russell's Top to The Nek during the next week; on 3 May an attempt to regain the head of Second Ridge failed in a bloody repulse; and in August the Australians gained 100 yards at Lone Pine for the cost of 2000 men. On the left flank, the great August Offensive saw Malone's Wellington Battalion and some British and Gurkha units briefly hold Chunuk Bair before being driven off, and Monash's 4th Australian Brigade capture an insignificant ridge in the tangled mass on the northern slopes of Sari Bair, but nothing worthwhile was achieved, only an enlarged area to defend between Anzac and Suvla Bay. In reality Anzac and Suvla resembled a self-sustaining prisoner-of-war camp that kept the Anzacs and the British IX Corps defending terrain of no tactical or strategic value whatsoever.

The remnants of D Company, 1st Battalion on the beach at Anzac Cove after being relieved on 29th April. This was Major Blair Swannell's company which fought on Baby 700 during the afternoon of 25th April. It had landed with about 227 officers, NCOs and other ranks, and lost heavily during the fighting (AWM A040540).

HOWITZER, ORDNANCE, QF 4.5-INCH

Calibre:	4.5-inch (114mm)
Barrel Length:	71 inches (1.78m)
Gun Weight:	3010 pounds (1365kg)
Action:	Horizontal sliding block breech with hydro-spring recoil system
Range:	7330 yds (6700m)
Ammunition:	Separate charge and shell; 35lb (15.875kg) high explosive shell; 35lb shrapnel shell with 481–492 balls @ 35 balls/pound
Battery first line:	108 rounds per gun
Fuze:	Time and percussion
Rate of Fire:	4 rounds per minute
Crew:	6 men

The Ordnance 4.5-inch howitzer was the standard British field howitzer during the Great War. Unlike the field gun, the howitzer had a high trajectory allowing it to fire onto targets close behind ridges and into dead ground. Introduced in 1909, there were six guns to a battery, although the New Zealand battery had only four guns. Hauled by a six-horse team, the gun and its ammunition limber could be quickly brought into action on the firing line.

ANZAC was equipped with only one battery (New Zealand) of 4.5-inch howitzers, with the first section of two guns coming into action on the beach at about 6.00 am on 26 April. The second section arrived at around noon.

FIELD GUN, QF, KRUPP 75MM MODELS 1903, 1910 AND 1911

Calibre:	75mm
Barrel Length:	2.25m
Gun Weight:	1079kg
Action:	Horizontal sliding block breech mechanism with hydraulic buffer and spring recoil system
Range:	Shrapnel 5400m, HE 5900m
Ammunition:	6.35kg shrapnel shell with 270 x 11g balls or 295 x 10g balls; 6kg high explosive shell
Battery first line:	188 rounds per gun
Fuze:	Time and percussion
Rate of Fire:	8 rounds per minute
Crew:	7 men

The Krupp 75mm quick-firing field gun was the export model of the German Army's 77mm Krupp QF field gun which was sold to a number of European armies and was the standard field gun in the Ottoman Army. Drawn by a six-horse team, the gun and accompanying ammunition limber could be galloped into the firing line and brought into action quickly. It was easily manhandled by its crew and could be quickly repositioned. Although it had a relatively flat trajectory, it was used in both the direct and indirect fire roles.

The *9th Division* had four batteries of Krupp 75mm but they were not deployed against ANZAC. The *19th Division* only had two batteries of this gun, while the other two field batteries were equipped with the older Krupp 87mm Model 1886 field gun. Contrary to some views, these guns did not engage the Anzacs on 25 April; the *19th Division*'s field guns arrived on the battlefield around dusk and during the night of 25/26 April.

CONCLUSION

Neither side could claim victory. The Anzacs quickly broke through the Ottoman beach defences, but failed to exploit their success. They did not achieve their initial objectives, let alone the intention of cutting the Ottoman lines of communication at Mal Tepe. By nightfall they had come close to defeat, a situation the senior commanders accepted that evening when they recommended an immediate evacuation. It was only the inability to re-embark much of the force in the time available, and Hamilton's message to stay and dig, that averted catastrophe and abandoning the battlefield to the enemy. However, they held the line they had chosen to defend, although with the loss of Baby 700 it was a precarious position.

The Ottomans were far more successful. Badly outnumbered and at an initial disadvantage, they recovered quickly. Although they failed to drive the Anzacs into the sea, their aggressive reaction secured them the vital ground and took the ground of tactical importance in the ANZAC defensive line. Importantly, they contained the incursion to a shallow, narrow beachhead of no tactical value and stymied the ANZAC operation in its infancy. In this they were assisted by the two fateful decisions made by Sinclair-MacLagan, and Bridges' inaction. It was a points decision to the Turks by a fair margin.

Jay Winter writes that 'The reasons one side wins a war are not always the same as the reasons the other side loses.' The same applies to campaigns and battles. Eliot Cohen and John Gooch (*Military Misfortunes: The Anatomy of Failure in War*) point to the complexity and systemic nature of failure in battle. The reasons for failure and victory often have deep roots, not all of which originate on the battlefield. Battles are difficult, bloody and chaotic events influenced by conflicting inputs, not the least of which are the actions of the enemy. At the core of the fighting are human beings with varying capabilities, temperaments and frailties. Innate psychological factors, stress and mistakes under pressure, poor or inaccurate information, a lack of situational awareness, the inevitable effect of Clausewitz's friction and luck all contribute to the results, as does differing technology and the capabilities and doctrine of the opposing forces.

The landings at Gallipoli were born of fanciful strategic aims that evolved through the muddled thinking of the British War Council, many of whom had little understanding of naval and military operations. Nor were they well served by the professional head of the Royal Navy. Fisher's ill-judged and grandiose proposal of 3 January simply fanned Churchill's determination to pursue a Dardanelles campaign when more measured and pragmatic advice was required. Kitchener, while Secretary of State for War, was also Britain's leading soldier, and he failed to provide sound advice. His opposition to committing military forces was undermined when he agreed to release the 29th Division for the equally suspect Salonika venture. While Fisher tried to apply the brakes to the naval operation without military support, he eventually succumbed to an operation in which he had no faith, as did Kitchener. Neither presented a sound case on the merits or otherwise of the campaign, nor the resources required to prosecute it to a successful conclusion, although in the circumstances success was highly unlikely. Despite being technically competent officers within their own services, both Fisher and Kitchener failed in their responsibility to provide sound and pragmatic professional advice to facilitate informed decisions. Instead they eventually acquiesced within an ill-considered political agenda, echoing Julian Corbett's pre-war concern: 'How often have officers dumbly acquiesced in ill-advised operations simply for lack of mental power and verbal apparatus to convince an impatient Minister where the errors of his plan lay?' (*Some Principles of Maritime Strategy*) Succumbing to Churchill's enthusiasm, it was a case of the loudest voice carrying the day in the Council. This represented a critical failure in collective strategic direction.

Consequently, Hamilton was despatched to support a poorly conceived naval operation that was floundering, with instructions that there could be no suggestion of abandoning the project, and was given an ad hoc, inadequate and partially trained force to undertake the task. Opposing him were superior numbers and a well-organised, better trained and more experienced force, including the best corps in the Ottoman Army. Arriving in theatre Hamilton believed that the only option to help the Navy was an amphibious assault to secure the southern portion of the peninsula. This was flawed operational thinking, as the Ottoman batteries and defences on the Asiatic shore of the Dardanelles would not be taken, leaving them to continue interfering with any subsequent naval assault. There was no reconsideration of the resources needed, and he chose, or felt compelled, to commit his forces early without adequate preparation or rehearsal. It is unlikely, however, that he had a choice. There was no prospect of further resources, he had been told that the project could not be abandoned, the government wanted early results, and a delay would have given the Ottomans more time to strengthen their defences. Dealt a less than promising hand, he made do with the cards he held. Thus the MEF was committed to an operation for which it was under-resourced and inadequately prepared. Despite Churchill's self-serving 'ifs' after the war, Hamilton had been given an impossible task. It is highly unlikely that the campaign would have achieved any of its objectives even if events had unfolded as planned on 25 April. The lessons from this are twofold: first, before embarking on a campaign, a pragmatic assessment of its value, success and outcomes needs to be undertaken. Second, having decided to embark on a campaign, governments and strategic-level commanders must ensure that sufficient resources are provided to ensure a strong chance of success. Fighting campaigns on a shoestring ultimately leads to failure and the unnecessary loss of life. If one goes to war, it must be with the object of winning, and to win the campaign it must be resourced properly, or indeed over-resourced.

Whether the Anzacs should have been landed at Gaba Tepe is outside the scope of this study. Of the writers who have criticised Hamilton's plan, only one has offered an alternative: landing the whole force south of Gaba Tepe and striking east to secure the Kilid Bahr Plateau, a plan that Hamilton originally mooted, but abandoned due to insufficient landing boats to carry a force large enough to complete the task in the initial assault, the cramped beaches, and what he believed were strong defences. Given its objective, the ANZAC plan was logical. Any force with the task of cutting the Ottoman land communications and sealing off the Kilid Bahr Plateau first had to secure the Sari Bair Range, and the easiest routes to the vital ground were along the southern ridges. The quickest access to them was from Brighton Beach; a landing south of Gaba Tepe would have entailed a lengthy approach and a vulnerable flank. The only option to secure a suitable covering position and beachhead was to take Third Ridge and seize the adjacent high ground on the main range quickly. Anything less would mean occupying inferior ground, severely restricting the landing of the main body, handing the Ottomans an easier means of sealing off the incursion and providing insufficient room to enable a successful breakout.

From a soldier's perspective, and noting that these were force or army-level orders to a corps commander, Hamilton's orders to Birdwood were quite clear on what was expected. In many ways they were prescriptive and gave Birdwood little room to determine how he would effect the landing. Once the beachhead had been secured, however, he had sufficient latitude on how he might take Mal Tepe and cut the Ottoman land communications. This was sensible, as any action beyond the beachhead depended very much on the prevailing situation and the reactions of the enemy. Bridges' and MacLagan's orders, likewise, provided clear direction as to the initial and final objectives to be achieved by the 1st Division and 3rd Brigade respectively.

While ANZAC had good intelligence of the Ottoman dispositions and a logical plan to achieve its objectives, the force never undertook full operational rehearsals at Lemnos. The troops simply practised disembarking into boats and rowing to shore under battalion arrangements. The one occasion a practice included acting as a covering force was cursory in the extreme, involving only the leading companies who simply occupied the ground immediately above the beach, with the troops back on board their transport by 3.00 am. In Birdwood's and Bridges' defence, the haste with which the operation was mounted, the time constraints imposed on them, the crowded harbour and the inclement weather may have precluded useful rehearsals, but the above practice suggests there was no attempt to replicate the advance inland, or land the follow-on waves of the 3rd Brigade. The lack of realistic rehearsals to practise the operation on the ground was a significant omission in the preparation of the force and its commanders. Conversely the Ottoman defenders not only regularly rehearsed their defensive arrangements, they did so over the ground on which the battle would be fought, giving them a tremendous advantage in terrain knowledge and practical experience that the Anzacs could not hope to replicate. Furthermore, at Anzac the disparity in training and levels of experience between the opposing forces was marked. While the Anzacs achieved an overwhelming superiority of 50:1 at the point of landing and outnumbered the defenders during the first four days, these differences had a significant effect on the battle.

Despite the best preparations, most plans do not survive first contact with the enemy, particularly if they are poorly executed, while friction and the fog of war add their disruptive contributions to the chaos of battle. Friction emerged as the tows cast off from the battleships and teenage midshipmen struggled to maintain alignment in the pitch dark unsure of exactly where the landing beach lay ahead of them. They naturally strove to maintain contact with their neighbours, thus narrowing the frontage which, together with well-intentioned course adjustments, threw the leading wave ashore slightly north of the intended site. Despite this the misplaced landing was not a major cause of the ANZAC failure, nor did it significantly disorganise the force or tear 'the plan to shreds'. Once ashore the covering force quickly secured the heights above Anzac Cove and drove the weak Turkish garrison inland, punching a huge gap in the Ottoman defences. While the Australians may have been initially disoriented, once on top of Plugge's Plateau they realised where they were and where their objectives lay. Following a brief respite, Weir and Salisbury immediately set off for theirs, and Drake-Brockman was in the process of linking up with the bulk of his battalion in Rest Gully before heading along Russell's Top when Sinclair-MacLagan intervened. Some disorganisation among units occurred, but not nearly as much as has been claimed. Only the 12th Battalion was so scattered that it ceased to operate as an entity, but this had more to do with loading the battalion across seven destroyers, Clarke's decision not to wait for his remaining companies to land, Sinclair-MacLagan's decision to throw Whitham's and Smith's companies into the line, and that of the right-hand company to join the rush up McCay's Hill. Nor did the misplaced landing deposit the 3rd Brigade out of reach of its objectives; the vital ground was closer, and the centre of Third Ridge was about the same distance away. Only the lower reaches of Third Ridge and Gaba Tepe were further than anticipated. The misplaced landing may have resulted in fewer casualties than had it proceeded as planned — certainly several of the participants believed so. If the misplaced landing did have an impact on the battle, however, it was evident in its effect on Sinclair-MacLagan. Originally pessimistic about the operation, his misgivings could have only increased once he realised that they had landed further north, albeit only slightly, of where they had intended.

The ANZAC plan was poorly executed. War is a business of taking calculated risks, and he who waits for certainty in battle will wait forever. History is replete with examples of commanders in advantageous positions losing through caution or inaction, while the boldness and aggression of others have turned dire situations into victory. In the end Australian caution and Ottoman boldness decided the fate of the landing. Sinclair-MacLagan's decisions to halt on Second Ridge and divert the 2nd Brigade curtailed exploitation of the initial success, wrecked the plan, and condemned the Anzacs to a purely defensive battle almost from the outset. In making them he acted hastily without acquiring an even adequate battle picture and he went well beyond the bounds of his responsibilities with the information available to him. Why he acted as he did we will never know. Perhaps he took counsel of his fears for his brigade's survival, perhaps his misgivings about the operation were compounded by the misplaced landing, perhaps he lacked confidence in himself, or perhaps he recognised the inadequate level of training and experience of his brigade and felt they lacked the ability to undertake the difficult task they had been given. What is apparent, however, is that he had been catapulted into a situation that was well beyond his level of expertise. Command of a brigade was an enormous step from his previous command of a rifle company. Nor had he an opportunity to gain that experience. Plucked out of Egypt after two months and sent to Lemnos, neither he nor his battalion commanders had undertaken any realistic field exercises that would have given them a sufficient feel for the difficulties of higher command in battle. This lack of command and operational preparation, together with his misgivings, profoundly influenced the battle, and it is little wonder that, when faced with the unexpected, he opted for a cautious approach and fell back on what he felt comfortable with — a defensive posture that avoided the risks and complexities of the offensive, and which better suited the level of training of his brigade. In reality he was a product of a system and the circumstances that threw inadequately trained and inexperienced commanders prematurely into battle.

Napoleon's maxim of the moral as to the physical being three as to one was founded on command confidence, a belief in one's own ability, and a capacity to anticipate and overcome difficulties and the unexpected. Judging from his comments prior to the landing, Sinclair-MacLagan appears to have lacked these attributes although, given his serious misgivings over the entire operation, his overriding thought may have been that his inexperienced and inadequately trained brigade was not equal to the task of a covering force. However, this does not excuse his failure to even attempt to complete the task allocated to him. In the event the majority of his officers and men performed well. In direct contrast was the battle-tested Sefik, confident in his own ability, overcoming a considerable disadvantage to reach Third Ridge first, taking the time to position his force on superior ground and gain a reasonably accurate battle picture before committing it to a course of action. Correctly assessing the situation and despite being outnumbered, Sefik resolved to attack to prevent ANZAC regaining the initiative, and acted as a covering force to buy time for reinforcements to arrive — the very task Sinclair-MacLagan had been given. Fundamental to his success was his willingness to accept risks. He was also better trained, more experienced and had rehearsed his battle plans over the ground on which he fought.

Sinclair-MacLagan's decisions were compounded by Bridges' inaction. A generous assessment would rate Bridges' performance as mediocre at best. By any measure it was uninspiring. As the divisional commander responsible for securing Sari Bair, he failed to rectify the situation. Early in the morning, despite believing there was nothing to stop the advance continuing, he did nothing to regain the momentum. He never took control of the battle, never sought to gain an even adequate battle picture, and never sought to impose his will or influence on the battle — the very actions expected of a commander. He simply accepted the situation presented to him and, rather than moving to a position where he could assess the evolving situation himself, he remained at Anzac Cove at the end of telephone lines responding to calls for reinforcements. Yet Bridges' background was not dissimilar to that of Sinclair-MacLagan. With a singular lack of field command experience, his reputation was made as a competent administrator and policy adviser in peacetime, very different attributes to the psychological and technical demands of commanding a division in battle. He had not acquired the requisite experience in handling his formation during the training in Egypt, and it was unlikely that he ever intended to do so. As early as January 1915 he was keen to get the 1st Division into action. Nor did his temperament suit him for high command. Bridges' expertise lay in his administrative and organisational capabilities, and his greatest achievements were the founding of the Royal Military College and the raising of the AIF. When saddled with the heavy responsibilities of commanding a division in battle, committed to operations without any requisite training, and confronted with an unexpected situation, it is little wonder that Australia's 'best soldier' in peacetime was found wanting.

Inexperience percolated down the chain of command. While he made little contribution to the battle, McCay performed satisfactorily although, like Sinclair-MacLagan, he significantly overestimated enemy numbers, and together their calls for reinforcements muddied the picture for Bridges. MacLaurin and Johnston never got into the battle, and we will never know how they would have performed. Johnston's later efforts at Gallipoli indicate he would have been no better than his contemporaries, while MacLaurin died before he could demonstrate his worth. At battalion level the performance was patchy. The shock of battle was too much for Lee, and Onslow Thompson's impetuosity and poorly organised advance cost him his life and the 4th Battalion dearly. Wanliss, Bolton and McNicoll lost control of their units but performed satisfactorily with the forces they had; Plugge also lost control of his battalion, but played little part in the battle thereafter, drawing a certain amount of opprobrium from some of his officers. Weir and Elliot retained a firm grip of their units, with Weir showing a readiness to reach his objective despite the misplaced landing, while Stewart showed promise before he was killed. Braund's cool and strong leadership under trying conditions ensured that the critical position on Russell's Top was held.

At company and platoon level, where the training had been focused, the performance was generally good. Using their initiative, Tulloch and Plant reached their objectives, and Loutit came close to reaching his before a lack of support forced them to retire. In defence the company and platoon commanders led from the front, fighting tenaciously. Those who fought on the front line made the Turks pay dearly for their gains, and many of them made the supreme sacrifice in doing so. Courage on either side was not an issue. That junior officers and soldiers performed so well was a credit to the individuals, yet once the heavy losses in officers was felt, the numbers of troops straggling back to the beach reflected the raw, inexperienced force they were.

In most instances Ottoman leadership and command capabilities were strong at all levels, demonstrated in their ability to undertake the more difficult offensive operation in challenging terrain. Starting at a disadvantage, Sefik and Kemal quickly deployed to the threatened point, identified the vital ground and seized a superior position. Rather than acting hastily once contact was made, they rapidly acquired good situational awareness before committing their forces to the attack, something the ANZAC commanders failed to do when adopting the defensive. Their orders were clear and they did not break up their units and commit them to battle piecemeal. Fighting a holding battle in the centre and concentrating their strength on the high ground, they struck at both ANZAC flanks limiting Bridges' ability to shift forces to meet the main attack on the ground of tactical importance. At battalion and company level the performance was generally good. Captain Halis fought aggressively and bravely on Mortar Ridge, continuing to direct the *3/27th* and refusing pleas to move to the rear after being wounded. Major Malatyali Ibrahim also led the *1/27th* aggressively during the bloody fight for Lone Pine, while Captain Zeki competently led the *1/57th*'s counter-attack on the Sari Bair Range until forced to retire wounded. Captain Ata, however, was later criticised by Sefik for losing control of the *2/57th* and allowing it to slip off towards the Fisherman's Hut during the attack against Baby 700.

In contrast, the Australian command made hasty decisions based on poor situational awareness and was drawn to the low ground, reinforcing a preconceived notion of a counter-attack from Gaba Tepe that never came. Although the terrain contributed, vague orders, hastily committing formations and units to the action piecemeal, and a lack of firm control at battalion level disorganised the force more than anything else. While Bridges sought to reinforce Baby 700, the route up Monash Valley added to the disorganisation as impetuous responses to premature and unnecessary calls for reinforcements siphoned off companies destined for the ground of tactical importance. Sinclair-MacLagan recognised the importance of Baby 700, but neglected to ensure that sufficient troops were sent there. While these elements of friction frustrated his intention, Bridges failed to impose his will and make sure that it was followed through. This was primarily due to poor battlefield awareness, largely because Bridges did not place himself in a position where he could exercise reasonable control of events; nor did he establish effective command arrangements to control the left flank despite having MacLaurin and his headquarters sitting idly by throughout the day. Sinclair-MacLagan and McCay muddied the situation with urgent calls for reinforcements and Bridges failed to go forward and take a grip on the battle. Birdwood effectively remained on the sideline and made no effort to take control when he came ashore on the afternoon of 25 April. Instead he returned to his ship leaving Bridges in charge of a deteriorating situation.

The lesson for commanders arising from the actions of those at the Anzac landing is best summarised by Major General E.K.G. Sixsmith (*British Generalship in the Twentieth Century*):

> The lessons of war that are ageless are those that come from a study of the mind and will of the commander. Not what he asked a unit to do at a particular time, nor even the brilliant plans which he thought out in the quiet before battle, but how he imposed his will upon the enemy and upon his own men, how he recognised the possible without rejecting the difficult. Above all it is necessary to recognise through the commander's mind the meaning of the initiative in battle and to see how one on the point of defeat might yet retain or regain that initiative.

A further lesson to be learned from the landing at Anzac is that thorough, realistic and testing training of the whole force is a major component of success in battle. This is particularly true for commanders at all levels. It is not good enough that senior commanders excuse themselves from the rigorous training they expect of their subordinates. If they are to lead in battle they must be exercised and tested under realistic and tough conditions into which the grit of friction, the fog of war and the unexpected must be injected. Those who lack the mental toughness, judgement, ability to quickly adapt to changing circumstances, sense of acquiring a realistic battle picture, and the resolve to achieve the objective must be weeded out. Command in battle is not something for which everyone is suited, and it is too late to wait until the furnace of war identifies those who are not up to the task.

Nonetheless, had Sinclair-MacLagan not taken the decisions he did, and had Bridges taken control of the battle, the subsequent fate of the landing can only be speculated. Battles are notoriously fluid affairs that can turn on an incident. The enemy does not simply allow a force to execute an intention; he strives to thwart, confuse and defeat in a hard, brutal confrontation. In this the Ottoman defenders were adept. Superior training, preparation, battlefield leadership and boldness enabled them to quickly contain the incursion. They were, however, assisted by poor Australian command decisions.

While the 1st Division might have secured the covering position had Sinclair-MacLagan not altered the plan so drastically, it is highly unlikely that the Anzacs would have achieved their object of securing the Mal Tepe Ridge. Not only did they lack the expertise for such a difficult offensive task, they had insufficient resources to undertake it given the enormous size of the final objective to be defended and the opposition confronting them. They would have had to fight hard for the Mal Tepe feature against the *27th Regiment* and the *19th Division* and the subsequent Ottoman reinforcements, and their right flank would have been particularly vulnerable to Ottoman forces reaching Maidos and the Kilid Bahr Plateau. The Anzacs lacked the training and battle experience to conduct what would have been a complicated and difficult advance and attack to secure the ridge. Furthermore, the power of modern weapons in the hands of such a well-trained enemy would have decimated them just as they shredded the Ottoman attacks against them on Second Ridge. Noel Loutit probably summarised this best in 1934 when he wrote in *Reveille* that the Anzacs were 'boys sent to do a man's job'.

POSTSCRIPT

Since the increased interest in the battle from the late 1990s and the desire of thousands of Australians and New Zealanders to visit the battlefield each year, Anzac Cove has been drastically altered, and some would say destroyed. The need to widen the old narrow coastal road to cater for the increased tourist traffic has seen the resulting spoil cover much of the beach, and a stone wall has been erected to preserve the last narrow ribbon of pebbles. It bears little resemblance to its appearance in 1915 or even 1990, and one can no longer take the walk from the northern tip of the cove up along the Ari Burnu spur, over the knoll held by the Turkish rifle squad and up onto Plugge's Plateau. Ironically, its destruction is the result of the verve with which Antipodeans have flocked to see what they regard as sacred ground.

Elsewhere, while the terrain has not altered, the vegetation has. Accounts written and photographs taken during the first few days of fighting describe and show the scrub from knee to waist high with patches of clear ground scattered across the hills. Sefik described Johnston's Jolly as flat and bare, as it was when I visited in 1988 and, from its eastern edge, gazed over a wide and grassy Legge Valley free of any shrubs. In 1988 the scrub along the ridges was much like it was on 25 April 1915, providing easy access and allowing panoramic photographs to be taken over most of the area. Now a National Park with grazing prohibited, the shrubs now dominate the landscape, over head height in most places, including on Johnston's Jolly and down Legge Valley. Where in 1988 one could stand on the crest of Battleship Hill (Dus Tepe) and look along the line Tulloch's men held to Ince Bair, from the road the view is now obscured by thick vegetation.

In 1988 Anzac was a lonely spot, rarely visited, with a quiet calm about it — a silence befitting the remembrance of an heroic tragedy and senseless loss of life. Interspersed across this tranquil landscape were the neat, well-kept Commonwealth War Graves cemeteries, some hidden down tracks, bearing testimony to the enormous sacrifice of the Australian, New Zealand, British, Indian, and Gurkha soldiers who fought so gallantly in this tortuous terrain. The imposing but simple Australian National Memorial at Lone Pine had replaced the tangle of trenches on that tiny bloody field, while the equally impressive but simple New Zealand National Memorial stood among pines on Chunuk Bair. Oddly there was no sign of the gallant sacrifice of the Ottoman soldiers who were defending their homeland, other than a single grave of a Turkish officer hidden on the inland slope of Second Ridge. When asked why there were no Turkish cemeteries, the young Turkish officer with me poignantly replied, 'The whole battlefield is a Turkish graveyard.' The only other intrusions on this melancholy battlefield were the coastal road and a narrow strip of bitumen snaking along Pine Ridge, up past Lone Pine and between the former no man's land on Second Ridge to Baby 700, then crawling up the main range and over Hill 971. Three structures were dotted along Sari Bair, standing like enormous white television screens of rock on which were hewn Turkish inscriptions. There was a sense of quiet reflection and sadness about the area. This is no longer the case.

Today, Anzac is well and truly on the tourist route, transforming the earlier tranquility. On North Beach, where the 11th Battalion came ashore, is a ceremonial area where the annual Anzac Day services are conducted. The roads are wider with large, intrusive parking bays either side of Anzac Cove. These are also more extensive, carrying the daily tourist buses packed with Antipodeans and other tour groups wanting to tick a visit to Gallipoli off their 'bucket list'. Initially stopping at what is left of Anzac Cove, they then do the circuit, winding their way up Second Ridge and the main range to Chunuk Bair, briefly dropping off at a couple of prearranged stops — the buses parked nose to tail — before trundling down Third Ridge and back to their accommodation. Others are more reflective, paying homage to the sacrifice in the pilgrimage made by thousands each Anzac Day. The consequence of such renewed interest has changed the ambience and character of the battlefield. This Commonwealth fascination has spawned an increased Turkish interest in the campaign. A fine museum sits behind Gaba Tepe and is the starting point for the tours across the Anzac battlefield, while on the Chessboard — across from Pope's Hill — stands the cemetery and huge memorial to the Ottoman *57th Regiment*. Atop Chunuk Bair a large memorial to Ataturk, the former Lieutenant Colonel Kemal, sits beyond the New Zealand National Memorial. Other areas however, are not so accessible, such as the tangled hills to the north of the main range, the scene of much tragedy during the August Offensive.

This is the price paid for the remarkable renewed interest in this battlefield; remarkable because so many of the Australians and New Zealanders who visit have such little knowledge of what actually occurred there in 1915. Hopefully this book will provide some of those visiting this hallowed ground a sense of what transpired there during the first four days of the campaign, when the inexperienced and partially trained young men from Australia and New Zealand entered the catastrophe of the Great War and paid so dearly with their blood in a wasteful campaign that was never destined to succeed. And when they visit, they might also pay tribute to the gallant Ottoman foe who defended his homeland against the invaders and acknowledge the graciousness of the Turkish people who allow the commemoration of the Allied forces who attacked their country through memorials, cemeteries and the ceremonies on North Beach, at Lone Pine and on Chunuk Bair each Anzac Day. This grace is reflected in the words of Ataturk carved in stone atop Plugge's Plateau:

> Those heroes that shed their blood and lost their lives ... you are now lying in the soil of a friendly country. Therefore rest in peace. There is no difference between the Johnnies and the Mehmets to us where they lie side by side here in this country of ours ... You, the mothers, who sent their sons from faraway countries wipe away your tears; your sons are now lying in our bosom and are in peace, after having lost their lives on this land they have become our sons as well.

APPENDIX 1

WHAT WAS THE INTENDED LANDING SITE?

Both the Australian and British official histories place the intended landing site at the northern end of Brighton Beach (Map 7 and Sketch map 6 respectively), although Bean also shows the intended landing of the 7th Battalion in Anzac Cove. The British history shows the actual landing as occurring further north, centred around Ari Burnu, adding to the impression that the 3rd Brigade came ashore well off target, a view reinforced by the oft-quoted Commander Dix that the landing occurred a mile north of where it should have been. But the intended location has been questioned in recent times.

In 1994 Denis Winter (*25 April 1915: The Inevitable Tragedy*) argued that the 3rd Brigade came ashore exactly where the landing was intended; that is, the brigade was supposed to land astride Anzac Cove. He dismisses both Waterlow's and Dix's accounts that suggest they landed north of the intended beach, despite both being responsible for navigating the tows, preferring instead to accept the comment of Lance Corporal Howe of the 11th Battalion that the naval officers were able to navigate accurately. Winter claims that three plans evolved during the planning process, each successive one shifting the landing further north. He writes that, 'The orders themselves cannot be produced since issue for both the second and third plans were secret and strictly limited, and no copies are available in the public domain even to this day.' This begs the question of how, if no copies were in the public domain in 1994, and none have been found since, Winter was able to discuss the second and third plans and where they placed the landing. Contradicting himself, he then alleges that Birdwood secretly decided to land at Anzac Cove and that Birdwood's, Dix's and Waterlow's accounts, plus those of others, were all falsifications concocted to shore up an agreed cover story. He presents no evidence to support this allegation, nor does he explain why they would wish to concoct a cover-up to mask the fact that they had landed exactly as planned. His argument is unconvincing, largely based on conjecture, incorrect assertions, and a lack of familiarity with the difficulty of navigating in darkness.

Robin Prior suggests that the landing was in the correct location, within the parameters of the covering position to be attained — from the Fisherman's Hut to Gaba Tepe — and in this sense he is correct. But in a scathing assessment of the planning and imprecise location for the landing (*Gallipoli: The end of the myth*), Prior writes, 'It appears the main priority of the military and naval commanders was to land the Anzac force somewhere between Gaba Tepe and the Fisherman's Hut. Not one instruction given by any authority for the landing place is much more precise than this.' Yet he notes earlier that the only precision came from Admiral Thursby who 'fixed the right flank of the landing *about* one mile north of Gaba Tepe' (Prior's emphasis) and stated that the landings would extend from that point for '8 cables', which suggests the landing was intended along the northern stretch of Brighton Beach, as indicated in the Australian and British official histories. Prior is correct that Hamilton's 'Instructions

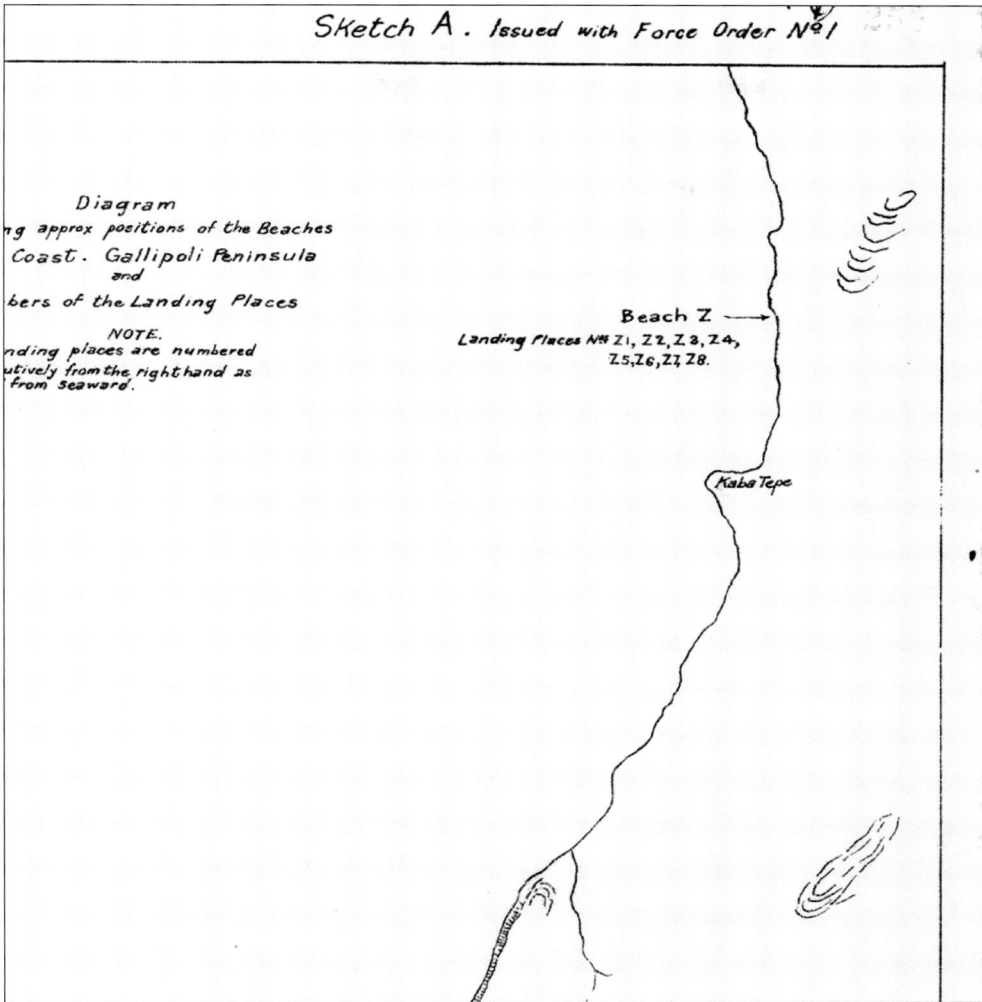

Sketch A of MEF Order No. 1 showing the intended location of Z Beach.

To GOC A&NZ Army Corps' dated 13 April 1915 (AWM4/1/25/1 Part 5) simply state that the landing was to be made 'on the beach between KAPA TEPE and FISHERMAN's HUT.' While this might seem vague, such instructions fell well within the parameters of *Field Service Regulations* regarding orders that 'The general principle is that the object to be attained, with such information as affects its attainment, should be briefly but clearly stated; while the method of attaining the object should be left to the utmost extant possible to the recipient.' From an army-level commander to a corps commander given the task of conducting the operation, this was not unusual, and was generally in line with the much-vaunted German directive control or *auftragstaktik*.

However, other evidence indicates that Hamilton was much more precise. In the weeks prior to the landing, the senior commanders and their staffs held a series of conferences to

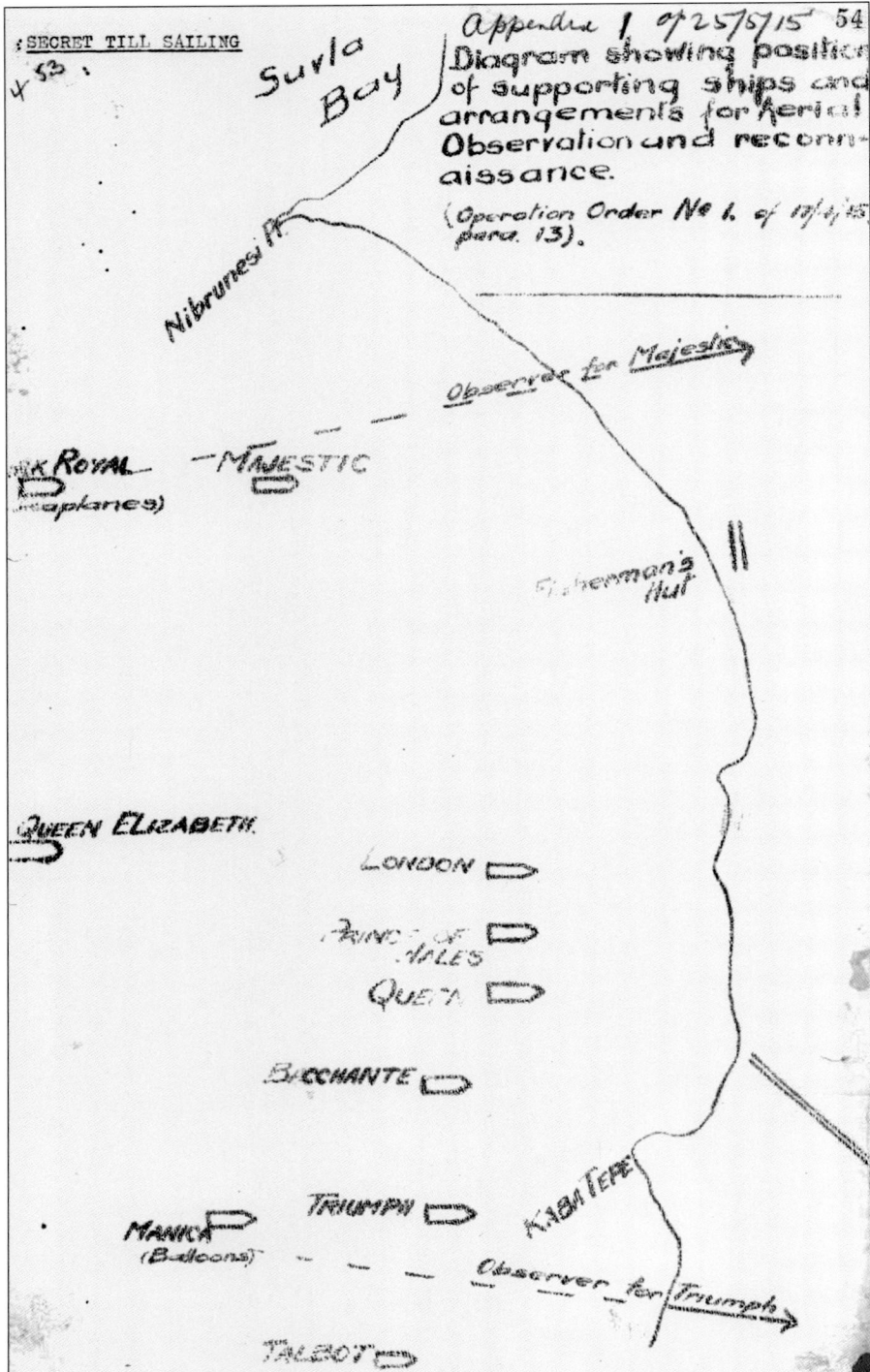

Sketch map in 1st Australian Division War Diary showing the intended positions of the battleships *Queen, Prince of Wales* and *London*, carrying the first wave of the 3rd Brigade, off the northern half of Brighton Beach.

plan the details of the operation, and these are reflected in other instructions and orders that make it quite clear where the forces would land. Sketch A to MEF Order No. 1 dated 13 April 1915 (AWM4/1/25/1 Part 5) shows Z Beach marked with an arrow at the northern end of Brighton Beach, just below Hell Spit, with the note 'the landing places (Z1, Z2, Z3, Z4, Z5, Z6, Z7, Z8) are numbered consecutively from the right hand as viewed from seaward.' This places the intended site running south from below Hell Spit, occupying the northern half of Brighton Beach. As mentioned by Prior, Appendix IV to the Naval Orders for the Second Squadron dated 18 April 1915 (AWM4/1/25/1 Part 6) directs HMS *Queen*'s 'boats will land on the beach about 1 mile north of Kapa Tepe. *Prince of Wales*'s boats four cables north of *Queen*. *London*'s boats four cables north of *Prince of Wales*', which places them on the northern half of Brighton Beach on a frontage of 8 cables or 1600 yards. A sketch map in the 1st Australian Division War Diary (AWM4/1/42/3 Part 2) places the three battleships in the same locations off the beach. The 3rd Australian Brigade's Operation Order No. 1 dated 21 April 1915 (AWM4/23/3/1 Part1) lists the initial objectives immediately above the beach for the first wave companies: the 9th Battalion's is Sq 212a6–224w7 (the central portion of Bolton's Ridge); the 10th's is Sq 224w1 and Sq 224r4 (the northern end of Bolton's Ridge); and the 11th Battalion's is the SW edge of spur 400 Sq 224 M and N (McCay's Hill, immediately south of Hell Spit). These same objectives are listed in the battalions' orders. For example, the 10th Battalion's Operation Order No. 1 dated 23 April 1915 (AWM25/367/17 Part1) describes the initial objectives as 'trenches and gun at Sq 224w1 and Sq 224r4'; and the 11th Battalion's Operation Order No. 1 dated 24 April 1915 (AWM4/23/28/1) lists its first objective as 'SOUTHWESTERN edge of spur 400 in Sq 224 M and N'. Clearly the Navy, Sinclair-MacLagan, and his battalion commanders had no doubt where the landing was to occur.

The various orders and instructions at division, brigade and battalion level show the intended site as immediately south of Anzac Cove along the northern stretches of Brighton Beach, as indicated in the Australian and British official histories. The actual landing was slightly north of this, astride Anzac Cove, with the right flank of the second and third waves of the 3rd Brigade overlapping the left flank of the intended landing. Thus, rather than missing the whole of the landing site by a mile, as inferred in the British *Official History* and Dix's comment, the actual landing was offset to the north, with a company each of the 9th and 12th battalions landing where the 11th Battalion was originally intended to go ashore, and taking the 11th's initial objective on McCay's Hill. Thus, as Prior suggests, the landing occurred roughly where it was supposed to, although in considerably more difficult terrain.

APPENDIX 2

WHY THE MISPLACED LANDING?

Various reasons have been proffered for the misplaced landing. Much credence has been given to a strong current pushing the tows north, but it would need a strong current indeed to push the steamboats 2000 metres off course over the 3000 metres they travelled to shore, and there is no evidence of such a strong current running up the peninsula. Midshipman Bush averred that the current was negligible, and modern fishermen who operate in the area confirm this. In 1990 Lieutenant Commander Tom Frame also confirmed it and, after researching the relevant data, wrote that, if a current had existed that day it would have been to the north-east at a maximum of 0.25 to 0.5 knots, calculating that this would have displaced the boats by 400 yards (366 metres) at most. A Turkish anecdote claims that the defenders noticed a buoy well offshore, and a member of the garrison swam out, resetting it off Anzac Cove. This story founders on the fact that the Royal Navy never set a buoy off Brighton Beach.

Navigation errors are far more credible. Navigating in the pitch dark is difficult enough on land. There one can relate to physical features as checkpoints on the route, while paces and compass bearings taken assist with determining distance travelled and location. At sea it is a much more difficult proposition unless accurate fixes can be taken. Departing Imbros, HMS *Triumph*, the marker ship, had to steer on a set course at a set speed for a set time, with only a magnetic compass to guide her, which was less reliable than the gyroscopic compasses used today. While the engine revolutions indicated the speed of the ship, the actual speed could be slightly faster or slower, and speed could be different because of tidal set and current; thus accurate fixes needed to be taken to confirm a location. Sitting offshore in a boat on 25 April 1990, with moonset seven minutes later than on 25 April 1915, Frame found there were no clearly distinguishable landmarks from which to fix a ship's position. With the principal features of the coastline too indistinct to allow taking an accurate fix, Frame averred that there was always the possibility of a margin of error as to where *Triumph* would drop anchor, and considered that it was 'largely a matter of good fortune if *Triumph* did manage to get within 500 yards (457 metres) of the rendezvous [Latitude 40 degrees 13 minutes North Longitude 26 degrees 10 minutes East] in any direction.' Further, the charts available in 1915 put Gaba Tepe 460 yards (420 metres) north of its actual location. That the destroyer tows landed the second wave astride of Anzac Cove suggests that the margin of error, plus the incorrect position of Gaba Tepe on the charts, also placed HMS *Triumph* north of its intended position. But by how far?

Taking the estimated flanks of the intended landing (212a6 on the southern flank and 224q2 on the northern flank) and those where the destroyer tows placed the second wave (estimated as 224q5 on the southern flank and 224a3 on the northern flank), the displacement of the southern flank is 1150 metres, and for the northern flank is 1800 metres, with an overlap of 300 to 400 metres between the left flank of the intended landing and the right flank of the actual landing. However these are based on estimates of the intended and actual flanks, coordinates that lack precision, and the maps used at the time, which themselves are not precise and contain errors.

In an unpublished paper Bill Refshauge, working from the ship's perspectives, naval charts and the rendezvous coordinates given to *Triumph*, records a detailed analysis of a range of factors to arrive at credible estimations of the displacement of the first wave, and those from the destroyer tows. Taking into account the chart error, the difference between statute and nautical miles, the positions of the destroyers when landing the troops, and the fact that they took station from the position of the battleships, which in turn took their position from *Triumph*, he has calculated that the southern flank of the second wave landed 1000 yards (914 metres) north of its intended site.

Compare these two sets of calculations with events 29 years later. After months of preparation, rehearsals and better navigation aids, the US 4th Infantry Division managed to miss Utah Beach by 2000 yards (1830 metres) on D Day in 1944 in broad daylight.

While *Triumph* and the battleships were not on their intended positions, the error appears to be partly due to the misplacement of Gaba Tepe on the charts, magnetic compasses that lacked the accuracy of today's gyroscopic compasses, and an indistinguishable coastline from which to gain an accurate fix. Taking into account the chart error, the position they navigated to in darkness was within the limits of an acceptable misplacement. As Refshauge writes, 'the Navy's navigation appears to have been outstandingly good, perhaps by a mix of luck and design. By achieving very closely what their orders required, the battleships were out of position for the landing — but they were within very small limits of where their orders indicated they were to be. It was not their performance that led the Navy's ships to fail the military.'

But the error was greater for the first wave than it was for the destroyer tows which had moved in directly for shore from their close-in stations taken from the positions of the battleships. Once the battleship tows carrying the first wave were despatched, further errors could and did occur and, as Bush commented, the steamboat compasses they relied on to guide them to the shore were 'notoriously unreliable'. Commander Dix, the Senior Naval Officer in charge in No. 12 tow from *London* on the far left, and Lieutenant Commander Waterlow, in charge of No. 1 tow from *Queen* on the far right, tasked with guiding the tows to the correct position on the beach, both stated that the tows shifted north. But was this due to the effect of a current?

Bush and Metcalf both admit that they altered course to port (left or north) and Metcalf has taken responsibility for doing so. In charge of No. 2 tow, he had departed *Queen* when prompted to get moving, leaving Waterlow's No. 1 tow behind him and 50 metres to starboard (right or south), and soon lost sight of him in the darkness. Fearing he was heading too close to Gaba Tepe, Metcalf recalled that 'it was very dark ... About a quarter of an hour later I realised we were heading very close to the northern side of Gaba Tepe. ... Without any delay I altered course two points to port. After a quarter of an hour, finding the tows to port of me had conformed, I again altered course a point and a half to port.' This had the effect of pushing the battleships' tows north and of bunching them closer together. While in hindsight it is easy to be critical of Metcalf's decisions, it is worth remembering that he was a teenage midshipman navigating in pitch darkness with a huge weight of responsibility on his young shoulders. The map shows his calculations of his two alterations in course, the subsequent course taken by the battleship tows, and where they landed. This placed the first wave north of Brighton Beach, and bunched closer than intended as the men struck the beach at Anzac Cove and on the southern extremity of North Beach, leading to a far greater discrepancy than that experienced by the remainder of the 3rd Brigade.

Thus, considering both the destroyer tows and Metcalf's testimony, there seems to be little doubt that navigation errors, certainly with the swing of the tows to the north, are the most likely cause of the misplaced landing and the bunching of the first wave. The whole brigade, however, did not land a mile north of the intended site as has so often been claimed, rather its right flank overlapped the intended site by around 300 to 400 metres.

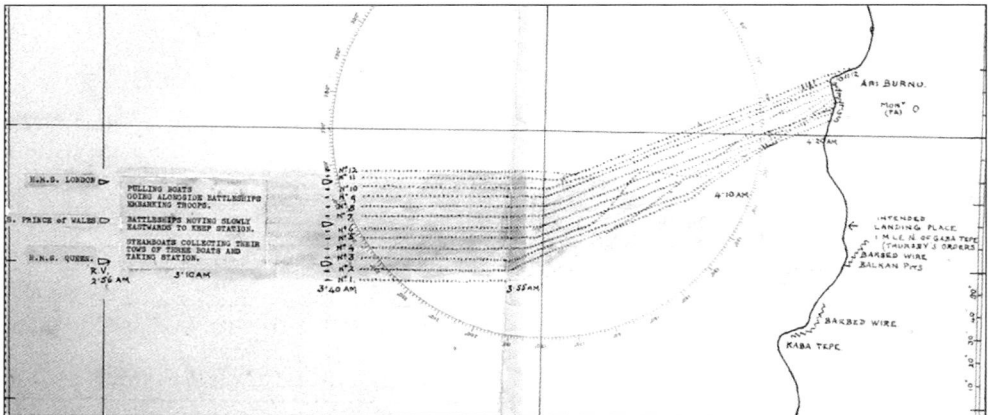

The sketch map drawn by Metcalf showing his estimation of the diversion of the battleship tows resulting from his changes in course.

APPENDIX 3

TURKISH MACHINE-GUNS AT THE LANDING

With the exception of Peter Hart's *Gallipoli* and Ed Erickson's *Gallipoli: The Ottoman Campaign*, both the English language books and popular opinion describe the Australians coming ashore under machine-gun fire. The Turks, however, assert that there were no machine-guns on the beaches, but rather a single rifle platoon of 85 men at Anzac Cove and a nine-man rifle squad from Ibrahim's platoon on the southern end of North Beach. An examination of Australian participants' accounts reveals contradictions, with some participants describing landing under Turkish machine-gun fire, others mentioning only rifle fire, and several simply saying they landed under fire. The war diaries of the 10th, 11th and 12th battalions record landing under heavy rifle and machine-gun fire, while that of the 9th records heavy rifle fire. The clearest example of these contradictions refers to the landing on North Beach. Landing in the first wave, Sergeant Thomas Newson of the 1st Field Company writes that 'the beach was ablaze with rifle fire' (letter published in the *Queanbeyan Observer* and the *Queanbeyan Age* 13 August 1915), while Sapper John Moore wrote 'CRACK, every man's heart gave a jump. ... Then crack, crack, a few seconds, then a continuous volley. This was in turn added to by the vicious spilling cracking of machine guns, with the zip-zip-zip as the bullets hit the water like a shower of red-hot coals, ... ' (*Anzac Jack*). Moore's sequence of shots accords with others who mention the scattered Turkish rifle volley, followed by the machine-guns in the steam pinnaces opening fire, but the words immediately following clearly show he meant Turkish machine-guns. Lance Corporal Bert Dixon (letter dated 4 May 1915 printed in *The Albany Advertiser* on 9 June 1915) and Bugler Fred Ashton (memoir printed in *The West Australian* on 26 April 1990), both of the 11th Battalion, mention landing under rifle fire, while Lieutenant Arthur Selby, a Duntroon graduate, and also of the 11th Battalion, told Charles Bean that there was a 'pretty hot fire' on the plateau, but that he did not see any machine-guns and did not think there were any (AWM 38 3DRL 8042 Part 7). On the other hand, Albert Facey, in his acclaimed memoir, *A Fortunate Life*, writes that 'the Turks had machine-guns sweeping the strip of beach where we landed — there were many dead already when we got there. Bodies of men ahead of us were lying all along the beach ... the Turkish fire was terrible and mowing into us ... Men were falling all around me.'

Neither Dixon, Ashton nor Selby, nor several other accounts of 11th Battalion and 1st Field Company men who landed on North Beach, mention such heavy casualties. Indeed they speak of light casualties. While Selby was with B Company of the 11th Battalion, Dixon, Ashton, and Facey were in D Company and would have landed with the second wave in the same place, at around the same time — so why such a significant discrepancy? A search of their respective service records reveals the answer. Ashton was at the landing and was captured by the Turks that afternoon forward of Second Ridge. Dixon was also present and was wounded on 29 April. However Facey, who enlisted in January 1915 with the Third

Reinforcements, did not arrive at Gallipoli until 7 May, 12 days after the landing, thus his account is clearly fabricated as he was never at the landing. Two other members of the 11th who landed that morning also record machine-guns. Lieutenant Aubrey Darnell wrote: 'we went clear over a machine-gun' — yet there is no official record of a machine-gun being captured either by the 11th Battalion or any other unit that day, nor does Bean mention any captured machine-guns. In a post-war unpublished memoir, Corporal Thomas Louch recorded a gun on Ari Burnu: 'two turks in the machine-gun nest … got their gun into action … then the picket boat came in and silenced them. The two men were knocked over backwards, taking their gun with them.' Given that it was pitch dark, Ari Burnu would have been well to Louch's right and, unlike Plugge's Plateau, the knoll was not silhouetted against the skyline in the emerging dawn. He must have had remarkable eyesight or, as a colleague commented, 'x-ray vision'.

Sergeant John Swain from D Company of the 12th Battalion, who landed in same area, also mentions machine-guns. In a letter to his mother dated 1 May 1915 (printed in *The Albany Advertiser* on 5 June 1915), he wrote: 'There were about 700 Turks on the beach, with machine-guns, and as I was among the first to land, we got it, "hot as mustard" but you should have seen them when we got ashore, I never had such a time in my life. It was Ho! for the bayonet, and jab, jab, jab … It didn't take long to clear the trenches on the beach, and it was then a scramble up the cliffs.' Swain's company landed north of Ari Burnu, but sometime after the 11th Battalion had come ashore, as the tows had to return to the destroyers to pick up his company, which came ashore in the third wave some 20 minutes later. Not only was the number of Turks grossly exaggerated, the only Turks in that area of North Beach comprised a nine-man rifle squad who had long since headed inland. By the time Swain's company arrived, the first wave was already on Plugge's Plateau and the Turkish defenders were decamping inland. Exaggeration of the forces and weapons opposing them is not uncommon among soldiers, in fact most accounts overstate the opposition they faced. It would seem that Facey and Swain were reluctant to allow the truth to interfere with a good story.

The Fisherman's Hut, where four boatloads of the 7th Battalion suffered heavy casualties — 80 killed and wounded of 140 men — provides the strongest case for the Australians facing machine-gun fire. Jackson wrote that 'there appeared to be two machine-guns' and his use of the word 'appeared' indicates that this was speculation rather than a definite sighting. Ibrahim wrote of his amazement at the destruction his '90 riflemen' inflicted on Jackson at the Fisherman's Hut. However, two squads had been detached well to each flank, so these could be discounted, leaving seven squads totalling 63 riflemen, plus those with platoon headquarters. Four boats each packed with 35 men made a very concentrated target during the three to four minutes required to cover the last 200 metres to shore. Using conservative figures, perhaps 50 riflemen firing 15 to 20 rounds a minute for three minutes would have delivered between 2250 and 3000 rounds. With a 10% hit rate, and using the lower figure, 250 rounds would have found a human target, or more than one round per man in the boats, although several of the men would have been hit two or more times. Had two machine-guns also been present, another 500 to 600 rounds a minute, or an additional 1500 to 1800 rounds over three minutes, in a much more concentrated and deadly cone of fire would have torn into the boats. Using the lower figure and a 30% hit rate would have seen an extra 450 rounds rip into Jackson's men, or a total of 700 rounds — a neat five rounds per man. Under this maelstrom few of Jackson's men would have remained unhurt. According to Sefik, the *1st Platoon* exhausted its ammunition firing on the initial landing further south and in engaging Jackson's boats. Recent information from Turkish sources reveals that the platoon expended both its first and second line ammunition holdings, amounting to over 7000 rounds for those around the Fisherman's Hut, which would explain the heavy fire, if not the level of Turkish marksmanship.

It has been suggested that, with many Australian 'first-hand' accounts mentioning landing under machine-gun fire, they cannot all be mistaken. Quantity of accounts, however, is not necessarily a measure of accuracy. Moreover, it is equally possible that all the accounts mentioning Turkish machine-gun fire could be incorrect, since they landed in darkness and the machine-guns on the steam pinnaces opened fire just after the initial shots rang out from the heights above. There is a well-known tendency for troops under fire, particularly raw and inexperienced troops, to exaggerate the numbers of enemy and weapons opposing them, and to claim fire from weapons that are later revealed not to be there. It is important to consider where these men were when the steam pinnace machine-guns opened fire. Some accounts are from those in the initial two waves who landed within ten minutes of each other, and others are from men who were still on the destroyers and transports offshore. The machine-guns on the naval pinnaces opened fire several minutes before the second wave reached the shore, and the pinnaces were between the shore and the men who were on the destroyers or transports. Thus those in the second wave and on the ships further offshore who record machine-gun fire would certainly have heard the Maxims on the steam pinnaces ahead of them, and these would have been indistinguishable from any the Turks were reputed to possess. It is highly probable that these men would have mistaken the guns firing from the pinnaces for Turkish machine-guns.

What of those in the first wave? My own experience under fire in combat and that of other veterans I have interviewed, suggests that, while different weapons may be distinguishable under light fire, they are indistinguishable as the fire ramps up and the soldier is surrounded by an overwhelming cacophony of noise. Under such circumstances it is difficult to determine the source of the fire, let alone pick out specific weapons from the incessant din. With the sound of the pinnaces' Maxims reverberating from the heights in front of and above them adding to the crescendo, it is not inconceivable that those in the first wave also mistook these for Turkish machine-guns. Thus while several genuinely believed they landed under Turkish machine-gun fire, it is not impossible that they could have been mistaken, and hence all 'first-hand' accounts of landing under Turkish machine-gun could well be wrong.

Furthermore, there is a contradiction in the Australian accounts. While several from the first wave mention machine-guns, other accounts either make no mention of them, or simply refer to rifle fire, while at least one openly disputes the later stories and newspaper accounts of landing against heavy opposition. Indeed, some veterans spoke of landing against light opposition. A good number of accounts that mention landing under machine-gun fire are clearly anecdotal, written well after the event by men who were not in the initial wave, or even at the landing, and relying on hearsay. Rumours run rife among troops, and a comment or opinion by one soldier is often taken as fact by others and repeated with a verve of authenticity. Accounts of the 2nd Brigade landing in Anzac Cove under machine-gun fire are problematic; the 3rd Brigade had captured the heights above the cove, and the *2nd Platoon* had departed before the first units of the 2nd Brigade (7th Battalion) arrived at around 5.30 am. 'Pompey' Elliot, who led them, makes no mention of machine-guns as they came ashore, just of the presence of shrapnel.

Yet the accounts that mention hearing machine-gun fire clearly influenced Bean when he wrote Volume I of the *Official History*. On the morning of 25 April Charles Bean, watching from a transport offshore, described the initial firing in his diary, writing that he could hear the 'sound of continuous rifle fire' (AWM 38 3DRL 606-4-1). In Volume I of the *Official History* he writes: 'From the top of Ari Burnu a rifle flashed. A bullet whizzed overhead and plunged into the sea. A second or two of silence ... [sic] four or five shots as if from a sentry group. Another pause, then a scattered, irregular fire growing fast ... Each steamboat carried a machine-gun in her bows, not to be used except by order of the senior officer of the troops in the tow. The picket boat, with Major Salisbury's tow of the 9th Battalion, immediately backed out and began to fire, her small gun pointing up towards the flashes on the edge of the plateau above.' (Volume I, pp. 252–53) Other primary sources agree that the machine-guns on the steamboats opened fire immediately after the initial Turkish rifle shots. Later (page 254), Bean introduces the first of several Turkish machine-guns: 'a machine-gun was barking from some fold in the dark slopes north of the knoll; another was on the knoll itself or on the edge of the plateau above and behind it' while, a page later, he writes: 'A fierce rifle fire swept over the men.' On page 256 another gun is identified 'north of the point where the 11th landed, a machine-gun in the foothills 500 yards to their left was shooting into the men ...' while, on page 257: 'From the left hand edge of the plateau above could be seen the flash of a machine-gun.' On page 270 Lieutenant Colonel Clarke directs Lieutenant Rafferty to silence a machine-gun on the beach north of Ari Burnu, but in describing Rafferty's advance to the Fisherman's Hut there is no mention of finding it or being fired on by a machine-gun, nor did Rafferty mention encountering one. On page 271 Bean writes that, as Tulloch came ashore, 'A machine-gun on some height beyond Walker's Ridge was playing on them.' When Jackson's boats approached the Fisherman's Hut after dawn he writes: 'When about 200 yards from the shore the enemy, who were entrenched on a knoll behind the Fisherman's Hut and a knoll about 500 yards south-east, opened fire on the boats with machine-guns and rifles', conveniently ignoring Jackson's account that there '*appeared to be* two machine-guns' (7th Battalion War Diary April 1915) (my emphasis). In Bean's account the Turkish machine-guns add up to twice the number held in the *27th Regiment*'s machine-gun company, and in two locations where the Turkish *Official History* maps show they had no troops.

It is noteworthy that Bean's history and credible first-hand accounts speak only of 'hearing' machine-guns, 'seeing flashes in the dark' or, in the case of Jackson, simply speculate. Nor did any unit war diary or official report mention capturing a machine-gun on 25 April, as would be expected given that they, like artillery pieces, were prized trophies and were always recorded, even in 1918 when they were far more commonplace. Had a machine-gun been on Ari Burnu, as Bean and Louch suggest, it would have been extremely unlikely that the Turks could have manhandled the 62-kilogram monster, together with the water cooling apparatus and ammunition boxes up the steep slope of Plugge's Plateau ahead of the Australians who, according to Bean's account, swiftly scaled the height and captured one of the Turkish riflemen from that squad. Not only is the spur a steep climb, it ends in a sheer three to four foot 'cliff' where it meets the plateau. Yet there is no mention of finding any machine-gun or its ancillaries at Ari Burnu, just a claim by Bean that a pit for machine-guns was found on the knoll.

The only first-hand account of a machine-gun being captured in the cove is an article written by 'No 94' published in *The School Paper* of the Queensland Education Department in April 1916 and reprinted in C.M. Wrench's *Campaigning with the Fighting 9th*. It is written in the same dramatic style as Swain's letter and there are discrepancies in the article. Approaching the beach in the first wave, the author writes that suddenly 'machine-gun and shrapnel broke upon us' and of 'boat after boat' being broken up. Yet the leading waves were not subjected to shrapnel as the single Turkish field gun at Gaba Tepe did not fire until 4.45am, after the 9th Battalion had landed. Since only the one gun at the promontory fired on the landing, it could hardly have broken up 'boat after boat'. He also describes smashing the gun, a remarkable feat given the sturdiness of a Maxim. Neither Bean nor the 9th Battalion's war diary mentions this capture. The article has the distinct tone of the heroic written for public consumption and morale. While Oliver Hogue's *Trooper Bluegum at the Dardanelles* describes the capture of a machine-gun and the killing of the German officer with it, this was based on hearsay from a 'witness' who was not at the landing, and Hogue did not arrive at Gallipoli until mid-May. Nor were there any German officers with Faik's company.

Not only do some Australian primary sources mention only rifle fire, the Ottoman sources dispute the siting of any machine-guns covering the beaches. In Bean's account there are at least six separate guns firing on the Australians as they landed, plus another two at the Fisherman's Hut, yet the *27th Regiment* only had four, which Sefik says were not deployed with the *2/27th*, but held in reserve near Maidos, and were only brought forward after 6.00 am. The *57th*'s machine-gun company departed Boghali after 8.00 am. So, given the significant shortage of these weapons in the Ottoman Army, where did this plethora of machine-guns come from? Certainly not from the *27th* or *57th regiments*. This question has never been answered by those arguing that the Turks had machine-guns covering the beaches.

Considering the issue tactically, while Bean's history only mentions single Turkish machine-guns firing from different locations at the initial landing, in the doctrine under which the Ottomans operated, the machine-gun company deployed the four-gun company in line as a single fire unit, much the same as an artillery battery, or if circumstances demanded, the company could be divided into two platoons with the two guns in each platoon deployed side by side. Indeed contemporary photographs taken of Turkish machine-guns in the field show this to be the case. Deploying the guns singly was actively discouraged. Thus Bean's account does not reflect the tactical employment of machine-guns by the Ottomans. Moreover, the doctrine directed that the guns not be placed up front in a static defence, but be held in reserve under regimental control until the point of greatest threat was determined, and then deployed to counter that threat, which is eminently sensible given the scarcity of the weapons and their weight and hence relative lack of mobility once battle was joined. Sefik states that he held his guns in reserve under regimental control with the rest of his battalions, which reflects Liman von Sanders' defensive plan and the prevailing doctrine of the day. More pertinently, if the Turks were not expecting a landing at Anzac Cove or along North Beach, why would they deploy every gun Sefik had on the extreme left flank, rather than covering the more likely landing beaches either side of Gaba Tepe where they believed any landing in the area would be made? Similarly, if the defensive posture was to hold the coast lightly with powerful reserves held centrally so as to respond quickly to the point of assault, why would Sefik deploy these valuable and scarce assets on the coast, and at the least likely point of assault? Nor is Plugge's Plateau a suitable place to site a machine-gun. It offers no fields of fire except at long range out to sea or well along North Beach, and such fire would be plunging, the poorest use of machine-gun fire. No soldier worth his salt would deploy a machine-gun there, and the Ottomans were well-trained troops. The only known 'machine-guns' deployed on the beaches were the two mechanical Nordenfelts at Gaba Tepe, 3000 metres from Hell Spit which was at the extreme range of the weapon.

Nor does the photographic evidence showing Anzac Cove very early in the morning support the view that the Australians landed under machine-gun fire and suffered heavy casualties, as depicted in film and television. The eight photographs of Anzac Cove taken between an hour and three hours of the initial landing, including the recently discovered image covering almost the whole of the cove except for the extreme southern end, show the beach remarkably free of corpses, with only two probable but indistinct corpses evident. Only one photograph, taken at around 8.00 am, clearly shows a body lying near the water's edge. If machine-guns had opened up on Anzac Cove, the photographic evidence shows they were clearly ineffectual.

Considering the wide range of evidence, and other factors, not just from the very narrow focus of some of the Australian 'first-hand' accounts, it is highly likely that many of those who claim to have landed under machine-gun fire were genuinely mistaken, believing that the noise of the Maxims on the pinnaces came from Turkish guns. Other accounts have been found to be false and exaggerated, and many are clearly anecdotal and based on hearsay. Furthermore, several of the Australian accounts support the Turkish claim that there were only riflemen covering the beach. While most Australians would like to believe that their forefathers could not be mistaken or fabricate what occurred, and that the landing was an heroic effort against heavy machine-gun fire, after hours of sifting and evaluating a range of evidence, both Australian and Ottoman, the results suggest that there were no Turkish machine-guns covering the Anzac beaches on 25 April 1915.

APPENDIX 4

TULLOCH'S FORCE ON BATTLESHIP HILL

The size of Tulloch's force on Battleship Hill has often been given as 60 men. The figure is first mentioned by Bean: 'Tulloch's party crossed the Nek. [He] had about 60 men with him.' On the next page, however, Bean adds that 'Lieutenants Reid and Buttle [who], with about thirty men, had been sent on across the Nek by Lalor.' This raises the number to 90.

On 1 June 1920 Buttle wrote to Bean. He had commanded 16 Platoon and Reid 15 Platoon, both of D Company. Both platoons were in Rest Gully when Drake-Brockman directed Reid to take his platoon, and Buttle to take a portion of his to support the 12th Battalion. One can only assume that Buttle took at least half his platoon, as he would not have simply taken a section and left the majority behind. Assuming he took two sections — 24 men — he and Reid would have had close to 75 men with them, perhaps more. Having been sent across The Nek by Lalor, they met Lieutenant Jackson and his platoon 'coming from the right' and afterwards met Captain Tulloch and joined forces (AWM38 3DRL 8042 Part 7). This would bring Tulloch's force closer to 180 men, possibly more, or the best part of a company. Confronting them were the *1st* and *3rd platoons* of Faik's *8th Company, 2/27th*, plus some men of the *2nd Platoon*, perhaps 150 to 180 men given losses suffered during the retreat up the range, and noting that Ibrahim had left a rifle squad at the Aghyl Dere.

APPENDIX 5

TIMING OF THE *27TH REGIMENT'S* ARRIVAL

Both Bean and the Turkish *Official History* record that the *27th Regiment* departed Maidos at 7.30 am. Bean also writes that Captain Dougall first saw the Turks arriving at the southern end of Third Ridge at around 9.30 am. Sefik disputes this, arguing that he left just after 6.00 am. He recalls arriving near Hill 165 at 7.40 am, although in another paragraph he states that it took him two hours to reach that location, which would have been just after 8.00 am given the time he departed. The Turkish *Official History* also records that it took the *27th* two hours to complete the journey. A time and space calculation, noting the delays along the route, particularly as the last portion of his route was through scrub and thus slower than on the tracks across the plain, would support a two-hour time-frame for the head of the column to reach Hill 165. Sefik recounts that it was another hour before the tail of his column arrived behind Hill 165. Thus, based on Sefik's timings, the first troops of the *27th* would have reached Hill 165 not long after 8.00 am while the tail of the column would have arrived around 9.00 am.

APPENDIX 6

TIMING OF KEMAL'S COUNTER-ATTACK

Largely influenced by Bean's and Kemal's accounts, Australian and British histories describe Kemal's counter-attack as commencing variously from 10.00 to 10.30 am, although the British *Official History* states that the leading elements of the *57th Regiment* trickled into action against Tulloch, and the mountain battery supporting the *57th Regiment*'s attack did not open fire until 1.00 pm. Kemal wrote that it began at 10.00 am, yet this is not supported by other Turkish sources. While Kemal suggests an early departure from Boghali, Harvey Broadbent, using Turkish primary sources, argues that the documents 'confirm that far from moving out instantly, Mustafa Kemal seemed to be slow in moving ... and reveal his initial reluctance to move without orders and the prevarication of his superiors' (*Wartime* Issue 46). In his account (*The Dardanelles. The Ari Burnu Battles and the 27th Regiment*), Sefik reproduced the note he received from Halil Sami between 10.00 and 10.30 am on which is marked the time it was sent (8.25 am). This document reports that Kemal departed Boghali at 8.10 am, and Sefik stated that the *57th Regiment* began arriving on the battlefield after 10.00 am. This is consistent with the time it would have taken the head of the *57th*'s column to move across the grain of the country with a departure from Boghali at 8.10 am.

There are also contradictions between descriptions of the route taken by the *57th*. Kemal claims they moved directly to Hill 971 and then came down the main range to Chunuk Bair. In February 1919, Lieutenant Colonel Ahmet Zeki Bey, who had commanded the *1/57th* as a captain, accompanied Bean around the battlefield. He recalled that they had been ordered to Ari Burnu and, having only a rough idea of where their destination lay, struck out in the general direction of Ari Burnu, not Hill 971. Moving with Kemal at the head of the column, Zeki stated that they moved south of Hill 971 towards Chunuk Bair with the intention of intercepting 'the English' before they reached the heights of the main range. He showed Bean where he and Kemal first arrived on the battlefield — on Third Ridge north of Scrubby Knoll. Bean drew a sketch from that point, 'just north of Scrubby Knoll', showing the main range, including Baby 700, Battleship Hill, Chunuk Bair and Hill 971 in the distance (*Gallipoli Mission*, p. 136). A detailed Turkish map made in 1916 and held by the Australian War Memorial shows the route of the *57th* crossing Third Ridge north of Scrubby Knoll, but whether the route was drawn by Bean or the Turks is unknown. While Kemal claims that he steadied the retreating troops on Chunuk Bair, Zeki told Bean that this actually occurred in the valley east of Third Ridge — the Kuru Dere. Zeki further stated that the *57th*'s column was badly strung out, which is consistent with a force moving as rapidly as possible across broken, scrub-covered country, and that initially it was only possible to get a portion of his battalion, the leading company, into action. They then moved over Third Ridge and Dik Dere where they engaged the Australians in a lengthy fight on the south-eastern slopes of Battleship Hill. It was only later that the *1/57th* and *2/57th* drove Tulloch's group from that feature (*Gallipoli Mission* and AWM 3DRL 8042, Item 56).

At 11.30 am, Sefik received Kemal's reply to the message he had sent at 10.30 am, telling Sefik to hold his attack until the *57th Regiment* was ready, and that the *57th* would attack once Sefik's assault had commenced. There is also a message, marked 11.30 am, from Kemal to the *57th Regiment*'s commander, Major Avni, discussing the tactics to be employed in the attack. Sefik recalls that he issued his orders at midday and launched his attack at 12.30 pm. Using Turkish primary sources, Ed Erickson (*Gallipoli: The Ottoman Campaign*) writes that the attack was launched sometime between 12.30 and 1.00 pm. Interestingly, Lieutenant Colonel Weir of the 10th Battalion told Bean that 'the enemy didn't seem to get beyond Gun [Third] Ridge till midday, abt [sic] midday we saw a gt [sic] number of troops moving to our N over Gun Ridge' (AWM Extract Book 3DRL 1722 Item 2).

Bean never mentions the timing. In Chapter XX (Volume I: *The Story of Anzac*), he describes Kemal's move to the battlefield and the counter-attack, but there is no mention of when this occurred. Using Bean's account, historians appear to have based the time of the attack on three incidents in Chapter XIII. First, Bean records that Tulloch reached the inland slopes of Battleship Hill at around 9.00 am and fought there for about half an hour, suggesting that Tulloch withdrew at around 9.30 am. Yet in a 1918 interview with Bean, Tulloch mentions an incident that occurred while he was on Battleship Hill, adding that it was 'during a lull, about noon probably' and before he was forced to retire. Bean's claim that Tulloch fought on Battleship Hill for about half an hour comes from Tulloch's interview — but it must be read in context. Tulloch spoke of the incident 'about noon' then goes on to mention the enemy fire increasing, followed by Reid being wounded — *then* he mentions that they fought on for half an hour, and that he commenced his withdrawal half an hour after Reid crawled to the rear (Notebook 1918, AWM 3DRL 606, Item 226). Thus Tulloch himself states that he was still on the feature around midday and, taken in context, the 'half an hour' occurred sometime after the incident which occurred 'about noon'. This accords with the Turkish view that the counter-attacks occurred after midday. Coe's letter also supports Tulloch's view, and that of the Turks, when he wrote that they 'got it heavy at 2 pm', and that 'six battalions' attacked at 2.30 pm.

Of the second incident Bean writes that, at 9.15 am, Lieutenant Margetts noticed Turks entering a trench on the seaward side of Battleship Hill and, a few pages later, describes Margetts withdrawing, leaving the crest and slopes of Baby 700 open to the Turks. Yet, in his account, Margetts mentions only the left flank on the seaward slope of Baby 700 withdrawing, while Lance Corporal Laing describes only Margetts' group withdrawing, asserting that his party on the far left flank advanced and withdrew five times, but not recording how far (AWM 38 3DRL 8042 Part 7). In the *Official History* Bean refers to this as Baby 700 'lost and retaken five times'. Neither Margetts nor Laing mentions the rest of Lalor's, Robertson's or Drake-Brockman's men (the best part of two and a half rifle companies) being driven off the hill and, curiously, nor does Bean.

In the third incident Bean writes that Swannell's company, arriving at 11.00 am, swept up Baby 700 under Kindon, driving the Turks off the feature. Yet, when writing to Bean after the war, Kindon does not mention driving the Turks off Baby 700, only that he encountered rifle fire after cresting the hill (AWM 3DRL 606 25-1).

The troops Margetts saw at 9.15 am were members of Faik's *8th Company, 2/27th* and possibly the *1st Platoon*. Captain Fahy mentions that the Turkish firing at the Fisherman's Hut ceased shortly after his party took shelter behind the sand hummocks. Thus it must have been around 6.00 am, or earlier, when Ibrahim withdrew the *1st Platoon* up the Sazli Beit Dere, which brought him out onto the main range near Battleship Hill and Chunuk Bair, a distance of 3000 metres with a hard climb towards the end. This would put him on the heights before 9.00 am. The *3rd Platoon* withdrew up the main range opposing the Australian advance until Tulloch stopped on Battleship Hill. Sefik mentions that these two platoons confronted the Australians on Battleship Hill in a lengthy firefight, holding them until Kemal arrived. In total the two platoons, with elements of *2nd Platoon,* would have numbered around 150 to 180 men, confronting the 180 men under Tulloch on Battleship Hill and the 500-odd Australians on Baby 700. Given the relative strengths it is unlikely that they drove Tulloch off the first feature and contested Baby 700 five times. It is more likely that Margetts' group sparred with some Turks on the far left of the line on the seaward slopes of Baby 700, while the inland slopes were still held by Robertson, Drake-Brockman and others, and Tulloch still held the crest and the inland shoulder of Battleship Hill.

Given that the head of the *57th* departed Boghali around 8.10 am, initially arrived on the battlefield after 10.00 am, and that it was badly strung out due to the broken terrain over which it had travelled, it would have been physically impossible for the *1/57th* and *2/57th* to have mounted a regimental counter-attack between 10.00 and 10.30 am down the main range from Chunuk Bair. It may be that the *2/57th* moved parallel to the *1/57th*, rather than behind it, and was further north closer to the main range. But even then it would take some time to move into position and coordinate a properly organised counter-attack.

What probably occurred, and what makes military sense and accords with Tulloch's and the Turkish accounts, was that Kemal ordered the head of the column to attack Tulloch's men on Battleship Hill as a holding action to counter the perceived Australian advance towards Chunuk Bair, hence Kemal's recollection of the attack occurring just after 10.00 am. He then began organising a regimental counter-attack to drive them back down the range. Even without the column badly strung out, mounting the counter-attack would have taken time. At best the column had a time past a point (the time taken for a column or convoy to pass a given point) of at least an hour or longer before the battalions, the machine-gun company and the mountain battery could concentrate and move into their allotted positions. Once the *2/57th* arrived on Third Ridge it then had another 1000 metres to travel north to its position astride the range on Chunuk Bair. Orders had to be issued through the chain of command and time taken for the troops to deploy to their assault formations. All this would have taken at least an hour and a half — probably longer — which means that the *57th* could not have mounted its counter-attack before midday and probably did so later. This accords with the accounts of Tulloch, Weir, Zeki, Sefik and Erickson.

TABLE ONE. TIMELINE

Build-up of Opposing Forces on the Anzac Battlefield 25–27 April 1915

The Anzac battlefield is defined as the area from Gaba Tepe along Third Ridge to Chunuk Bair and thence to the Fisherman's Hut on North Beach. The *6th Company* of the *2nd Battalion, 27th Regiment*, did not participate in the battle but remained in the coastal defences south of Gaba Tepe.

The timeline shows the periods when the ANZAC and Ottoman units arrived in the Anzac area.

DATE/ TIME	ANZAC	OTTOMAN
25 APRIL		
0430 - 0510	9th Battalion. 10th Battalion. 11th Battalion. Headquarters 3rd Brigade. 12th Battalion.	5th, 7th, 8th Companies, 2nd Battalion, 27th Regiment. One Mountain Battery, 3rd Battalion, 9th Artillery Regiment. Gaba Tepe battery (one working gun).
0530 - 0700	7th Battalion. 6th Battalion. 8th Battalion. Headquarters 2nd Brigade.	
0700 - 0800	Tactical Headquarters 1st Australian Division. 5th Battalion. Headquarters 1st Brigade. 1st Battalion. 3rd Battalion. Two companies 2nd Battalion. Two companies 4th Battalion.	
0800 - 0900	One company 2nd Battalion.	Headquarters 27th Regiment. 1st Battalion, 27th Regiment. 3rd Battalion, 27th Regiment. Machine-gun Company, 27th Regiment.
0900 - 0930	One company 2nd Battalion.	----
1000 - 1200	Headquarters New Zealand Brigade. Auckland Battalion. Remainder Headquarters 1st Australian Division. 26th (Jacob's) Mountain Battery. Two companies Canterbury Battalion.	Headquarters 57th Regiment. 1st Battalion, 57th Regiment. 2nd Battalion, 57th Regiment. 3rd Battalion, 57th Regiment. Machine-gun Company, 57th Regiment. One Mountain Battery, 9th Artillery Regiment. One Mountain Battery, 39th Artillery Regiment.

Table 1

DATE/ TIME	ANZAC	OTTOMAN
1200 - 1300	One company Canterbury Battalion. Two companies 4th Battalion.	
1400 - 1500	Headquarters New Zealand and Australian Division.	
1500 - 1600	Otago Battalion. One field gun 4th AFA Battery.	Headquarters 19th Division.
1600 - 1700		Headquarters 72nd Regiment. 1st Battalion, 72nd Regiment. 2nd Battalion, 72nd Regiment. 3rd Battalion, 72nd Regiment. Machine-gun Company, 72nd Regiment. One Mountain Battery, 39th Artillery Regiment.
1700 - 1800	Two companies Canterbury Battalion. 21st (Kohat) Mountain Battery. Two platoons 15th Battalion. 16th Battalion.	Headquarters 77th Regiment. 1st Battalion, 77th Regiment. 2nd Battalion, 77th Regiment. One Field Battery 39th Artillery Regiment.
Total	Sixteen battalions, two mountain batteries and one field gun.	Ten and a half battalions, three machine-gun companies, three mountain batteries and one field battery.
Night 25/26 APRIL	Two companies Wellington Battalion. Remainder 15th Battalion. 13th Battalion. One field gun 1st AFA Battery. One section NZ Howitzer Battery.	Three field batteries, 39th Artillery Regiment.
26 APRIL		
0500 - 0600	Two companies Wellington Battalion.	
AM	14th Battalion. One section NZ Howitzer Battery.	
PM	Two guns 4th AFA Battery. Two guns 5th AFA Battery. 7th AFA Battery. 2nd NZFA Field Battery. One field gun 1st AFA Battery withdrawn and re-embarked.	3rd Battalion, 7th Artillery Regiment.
Total	Twenty battalions, two mountain batteries, one howitzer battery, three field batteries.	Ten and a half battalions, three machine-gun companies, three mountain batteries and six field batteries.

DATE/ TIME	ANZAC	OTTOMAN
27 APRIL	1st NZFA Battery.	Headquarters 64th Regiment.
		1st Battalion, 64th Regiment.
		2nd Battalion, 64th Regiment.
		Headquarters 33rd Regiment.
		1st Battalion, 33rd Regiment.
		2nd Battalion, 33rd Regiment.
		3rd Battalion, 33rd Regiment.
		Machine-gun Company, 33rd Regiment.
Total	Twenty battalions, two mountain batteries, one howitzer battery, and four field batteries.	Sixteen and a half battalions, four machine-gun companies, three mountain batteries and six field batteries.

ORDER OF BATTLE AT ANZAC 25–27 APRIL 1915

AUSTRALIAN AND NEW ZEALAND ARMY CORPS (ANZAC)

Headquarters Australian and New Zealand Army Corps

1st Australian Division
Headquarters 1st Australian Division

1st Australian Infantry Brigade (New South Wales)
Headquarters 1st Australian Infantry Brigade
1st Battalion
2nd Battalion
3rd Battalion
4th Battalion

2nd Australian Infantry Brigade (Victoria)
Headquarters 2nd Australian Infantry Brigade
5th Battalion
6th Battalion
7th Battalion
8th Battalion

3rd Australian Infantry Brigade
Headquarters 3rd Australian Infantry Brigade
9th Battalion (Queensland)
10th Battalion (South Australia)
11th Battalion (Western Australia)
12th Battalion (Tasmania, South Australia and Western Australia)

1st Australian Field Artillery Brigade (New South Wales)
Headquarters 1st Australian Field Artillery Brigade
1st Australian Field Artillery Battery
2nd Australian Field Artillery Battery
3rd Australian Field Artillery Battery

2nd Australian Field Artillery Brigade (Victoria)
Headquarters 2nd Australian Field Artillery Brigade
4th Australian Field Artillery Battery
5th Australian Field Artillery Battery
6th Australian Field Artillery Battery

3rd Australian Field Artillery Brigade
Headquarters 3rd Australian Field Artillery Brigade
7th Australian Field Artillery Battery (Queensland)
8th Australian Field Artillery Battery (Western Australia)
9th Australian Field Artillery Battery (Tasmania)

Engineers
    1st Australian Field Company (New South Wales)
    2nd Australian Field Company (Victoria)
    3rd Australian Field Company (Queensland, New South Wales, South Australia, Western Australia and Tasmania

1st Australian Divisional Signal Company

Army Medical Corps
    1st Australian Field Ambulance (New South Wales)
    2nd Australian Field Ambulance (Victoria)
    3rd Australian Field Ambulance (Queensland, South Australia, Western Australia and Tasmania)

1st Australian Divisional Train

1st Australian Divisional Ammunition Column

New Zealand and Australian Division
Headquarters New Zealand and Australian Division

New Zealand Infantry Brigade
    Headquarters New Zealand Infantry Brigade
    Auckland Battalion
    Wellington Battalion
    Canterbury Battalion
    Otago Battalion

4th Australian Infantry Brigade
    Headquarters 4th Australian Infantry Brigade
    13th Battalion (New South Wales)
    14th Battalion (Victoria)
    15th Battalion (Queensland and Tasmania)
    16th Battalion (Western Australia and South Australia)

New Zealand Field Artillery Brigade
    Headquarters New Zealand Field Artillery Brigade
    1st New Zealand Field Artillery Battery
    2nd New Zealand Field Artillery Battery
    3rd New Zealand Field Artillery Battery
    1st New Zealand Howitzer Battery

Engineers
    New Zealand Field Company

New Zealand and Australian Division Signals Company

Army Medical Corps
    New Zealand Field Ambulance

New Zealand and Australian Divisional Train

New Zealand and Australian Divisional Ammunition Column

Corps Troops
7th Indian Army Mountain Brigade
    21st (Jacob's) Battery
    26th (Kohat) Battery

Ceylon Planters' Rifles

OTTOMAN ARMY

III CORPS

9th Division
    Headquarters 9th Division (Until pm 25 April)

    Cavalry Detachment

    27th Infantry Regiment
        Headquarters 27th Infantry Regiment
        1st Battalion
        2nd Battalion (less 6th Company)
        3rd Battalion
        Machine-gun Company

    3rd Battalion, 9th Artillery Regiment

19th Division
    Headquarters 19th Division

    Cavalry Squadron

    57th Infantry Regiment
        Headquarters 57th Infantry Regiment
        1st Battalion
        2nd Battalion
        3rd Battalion
        Machine-gun Company

    72nd Infantry Regiment
        Headquarters 72nd Infantry Regiment
        1st Battalion
        2nd Battalion
        3rd Battalion
        Machine-gun Company

    77th Infantry Regiment
        Headquarters 77th Infantry Regiment
        1st Battalion
        2nd Battalion

    39th Artillery Regiment
        Headquarters 39th Artillery Regiment
        1st Battalion

2nd Battalion
3rd Battalion

Engineer Company

Medical Company

Divisional Train

Divisional Ammunition Column

Detached from 7th Infantry Division 26 April
3rd Battalion, 7th Artillery Regiment

XV CORPS (from 27 April)

Detached from 3rd Division
64th Infantry Regiment
    Headquarters 64th Infantry Regiment
    1st Battalion
    3rd Battalion

Detached from 11th Infantry Division
33rd Infantry Regiment
    Headquarters 33rd Infantry Regiment
    1st Battalion
    2nd Battalion
    3rd Battalion
    Machine-gun Company

FURTHER READING

BOOKS

Aspinall-Oglander, Brigadier General C.F.
History of the Great War, Military Operations, Gallipoli, vols 1 and 2, Heinemann, London, 1929–32.

Bean, C.E.W.
The Official History of Australia in the War of 1914–1918, Vol. I, *The Story of Anzac,* Angus & Robertson, Sydney, 1941.

Broadbent, Harvey
Gallipoli: The Fatal Shore, Penguin, Melbourne, 2009.

——
Gallipoli: The Turkish Defence, Allen & Unwin, Sydney, 2015.

Bush, Eric
Gallipoli, Allen & Unwin, Sydney, 1975.

Cameron, David
25 April 1915: The Day the Anzac Legend was Born, Allen & Unwin, Sydney, 2007.

Carlyon, Les
Gallipoli, Pan MacMillan, Sydney, 2010.

Erickson, Ed
Gallipoli: The Ottoman Campaign, Pen & Sword Military, UK, to be published in 2015.

——
Ottoman Army Effectiveness in World War I: A Comparative Study, Routledge, London, 2014.

——
Ordered to Die: A History of The Ottoman Army in the First World War, Greenwood Press, Westport, US, 2001.

Hart, Peter
Gallipoli, Oxford University Press, US, 2011.

Pedersen, Peter
The Anzacs: Gallipoli to the Western Front, Penguin, Sydney, 2010.

Pugsley, Chris
Gallipoli: the New Zealand Story, Reed, Auckland, 1984.

Rhodes James, Robert
Gallipoli, Batsford, London, 1965.

Sefik Aker
The Dardanelles. The Ari Burnu Battles and the 27th Regiment, AWM MSS 1886.

Stowers Richard
Bloody Gallipoli: the New Zealand Story, Bateman, Auckland, 2005.

Wait, Fred
The New Zealanders at Gallipoli, New Zealand Government, Auckland, 1919.

Williams, Peter
The Battle for Anzac Ridge: An Anzac Victory. 25 April 1915, Australian Military History Publishers, Loftus, Sydney, 2007.

ARTICLES

Broadbent, Harvey   'Gallipoli's First Day: Turkish documents separating myth and reality', *Wartime*, Issue 46, April 2009.

Roberts, Chris   'The landing at Anzac: a reassessment', *Journal of the Australian War Memorial*, No. 22, April 1993.

——   'Turkish Machine Guns at the Landing', *Wartime*, Issue 50, April 2010.

INDEX

A

Achi Baba 58, 76, 80

Adana Spur 109, 120, 124–5, 127, 136

Adil, Private Sahin 95, 120, *120*

Ahmed, Sergeant 93

Aitken, Private Murray 92

Alderman, Major Walter 149, 156, 163

Allen, Lieutenant Harold 163

American Civil War 14

amphibious landing 71–2

Anafarta Valley 60, 83

Anderson Knoll 98, 109, 113, 120–1, 129, 148, 151

Annear, Captain William 93, 96

Antwerp 25

Anzac Cove 50, 58, *62*, 65–6, *67–8*, 70, 82–4, 87–8, *90*, 90–2, 94–5, 100, *101*, *102*, 103, *104*, 108, *108*, *111*, 114, *115*, 117, *118*, *119*, *129*, *130*, 133–4, 139, *143*, *147*, *148*, *154*, 160, *164*, *167*, *184*, 190–1, 195–7, 200–1, 203–4, 207–9

ANZAC forces 218–20 *see also* Australian Imperial Force (AIF), New Zealand Expeditionary Force (NZEF)

Anzac legend 4–5

Ari Burnu *64*, 65, *66*, 67, *90*, 90–1, *92*, 94, 96, *102*, *104*, *108*, *111*, 119, 125, *132*, 133, *144*, *149*, 149–50, *151*, *154*, 157, 159, 171–2, 195, 197, 205, 207–8, 212

artillery 17–20
   airburst 17
   ground burst 17

Ashmead-Bartlett, Ellis 4

Ashton, Bugler Fred 96, 163, 204

Australia and New Zealand Army Corps (ANZAC) 5–6, 10, 28, 36–44, 73, 75–8, 171–2, 189–92, 218–21

Australian Army 9–10
   artillery brigades *19*, 39
   battalions 10, 13
   field guns 19
   infantry 10, 13, *13*, 39, *40*, *42*
   militia 36–7, 40, 51
   platoons 13
   rifle companies 10, 13
   structure 8–9
   training 36–8, *40*, 41–4, *42*
   volunteers 26, 35–8, 40–1, 51

Australian Imperial Force (AIF) 10, 38–9, 41, 50–1, 81, 90, 107, 134, 169, 174, 191
   1st Australian Division 20, 39–44, 49, 73, 78, 80–2, 83–4, 117, *129*, *130*, *132*, 133–4, 142, 144, *144*, 154, 161, 169, 172, 177, 183, 189, 191, 194, 199–200, 215
   1st Battalion *102*, 123, 137, 139, 142–4, 153–4, 163, 179, *184*, 215

1st Brigade 51, 83–5, *101*, *110*, *118*, *119*, 123, 133, 137, 139–40, 169, 177, 183, 215

1st Field Artillery Brigade (New South Wales) 83, 87, 90, 92–3, 204

1st Field Battery (1st AFA Battery) 171, 216

1st Light Horse Brigade 39, 42–3

2nd Battalion 51, 123, 139–40, 142, *143*, 144, 151, 154, 156, 163, 168, 174, 178, 183, 215

2nd Brigade 15, 51, 83–5, *93*, *101*, *102*, *104*, 106–7, *111*, 114–17, *115*, 122, 124–5, 128, 131, 133, 140, 150, 183, 190, 207, 215

2nd Field Artillery Brigade (Victoria) *108*

2nd Field Battery (2nd AFA Battery) 171

2nd Light Horse Brigade 39, 44

3rd Battalion 41, 43, *102*, 123, *135*, *137*, 137–9, 142, 144, 153, 163, 181, 215

3rd Brigade 31, 39, 44, 49, 73, 78, 82–5, 87, *92*, 94–5, 98–104, 107, 109, 112–14, 116–18, 122–5, 128–9, 131–3, 137, 139–40, 145, 150, 168, 174, 183, 189–90, 197, 199–200, 203, 207

3rd Field Artillery Brigade

3rd Field Ambulance 87, 108

3rd Field Battery (3rd AFA Battery) 171

4th Battalion *114*, *119*, 123, 134, 139–40, 161, 172, *175*, 175–7, 192, 215–16

4th Brigade 39, 41, 43, 51, 171–2, 177, 184

4th Field Battery (4th AFA Battery) 158, *160*, 171, 216

5th Battalion 15, 41, 51, 83–4, 85, 93, *102*, 115–16, 133, 136–7, 140, 143–4, 175, 215

5th Field Battery (5th AFA Battery) 171, 216

6th Battalion 15, 51, 83–4, *93*, *104*, *105*, 106, 114–15, 116, 131–2, 143–4, 175, 215

6th Field Battery (6th AFA Battery) 171

7th Battalion 15, 51, 83–5, *93*, *101*, *104*, *105*, 106, 114–16, 131, 140, 143–4, 165, 172, 175, 197, 205, 207, 215

7th Field Battery (7th AFA Battery) 171, 177, 216

8th Battalion 15, 41, 83–5, 93, 103, *114*, 115–16, 131–2, 143–4, 177, 215

9th Battalion 41, 44, 51, 83–7, 89–91, 94–8, 100, 104–5, 109, 111–14, 117, 120–2, 124–5, 128–9, 131–2, 140, 142–4, 153, 200, 207–8, 215

10th Battalion 44, 51, 83–5, 87, *89*, 89–91, 94–8, 100, 104–5, 109, 111–13, 117, 120–1, 128–9, 140, 143, 172, 175, 200, 204, 213, 215

11th Battalion 5–6, 44, 66, 83–4, 86–7, *87*, *88*, 89, *89*, 91–7, 99–100, 105–6, 109–10, 113, 117, 122, 124–5, 128–30, 137–8, 142, 144, 153, 163–4, 168, *172*, 181, 196–7, 200, 204–5, 207, 215

12th Battalion 51, 66, 83–6, 92–3, 95–6, 98–101, 104–5, 108–10, 113, 117, 122, 124–5, 129, 131–2, 140, 142–4, 153, 163, 176, 190, 200, 204–5, 210, 215

13th Battalion 171–3, 216

14th Battalion 171–2, 180–1, 216

15th Battalion 41, 164–5, 171–3, 175, 216

16th Battalion 164, 168, 172–3, 181, 216

fire support 144–5, *160*, 171–3, 181

Avni, Major Huseyin 53, 147, 213

B

Baby 700 62–5, *63–4*, *65*, 67, 82–3, 96–7, 99, *99*, 105, 109–10, 112–13, 122–5, 133, 137, 139–45, 149–50, 152–7, *153*, 160–3, *168*, 168–71, 173, 180–2, 184, 187, 193, 195, 212–14

Bacon, Admiral Sir Roger 25

Baddeley, Second Lieutenant Herman 156, 163

Baden-Powell, Colonel 49, 52

Baigent, Private Edward 164, 167

Balkan Gun Pits 183

Balkan Wars (1912-1913) 10, 45–7, 53–4, 127, 159

Barnes, Captain Charles 113

battalions 10, 13

Battleship Hill 62–3, *63*, 65, 82–4, 100–1, 106, 109, 122–3, 125–6, 129–30, 136, 140–2, 148, 152–3, *153*, 155, 195, 210, 212–14

Bean, Charles 4–5, 40–1, 96–7, 103, 119–20, 125, 128, 149, 151, 165, 183, 197, 204–5, 207–13

Official History of Australia in the War of 1914-1918 5

Bennett, Major Henry 132, 150–1

Birdwood, Lieutenant General Sir William 43–4, 46, 49–50, *50*, 52, 73, 76–8, 81–3, 101, 134, 149, 157, 160, 167, 169, 177, 183, 189, 193, 197

Biyuk Anafarta 58, 60

Black, Lance Corporal Percy 173

Blackburn, Private Arthur 121, 129–30

Boghali 24, 57–60, 112, 121, 125, 129, 159, 208, 212, 214

Bolton's Ridge 64–5, 67, 78, *78*, 83, *83–4*, 97–8, 100, 113, 116–17, 121–2, 125, 132–3, 143, 150, 161–2, 165, 172, 175, 177, 180–3, 192, 200

Bouvet 30, *32*, 33

Braithwaite, Colonel William 145

Brand, Major Charles 105, 111, 113

Braund, Lieutenant Colonel George 51, 140, 144, 151, 156–7, 164–5, 167–9, 173–4, *174*, 178–81, 183, 192

Brennan, Captain Edward 92–3

Bridges, Major General William 43–4, 49–50, 52, 73, 80–5, 96, 105, 107, 133–4, *134*, 136–7, 140, 144–145, 157–8, 160–1, 166–7, 174–5, 177, 183, 187, 189, 191–4

brigade organisation 8–9

Brighton Beach 58, 64–5, 67–9, 77–8, *77–8*, 82–3, *86*, 89–90, 93, 95, 98, 100, 117, 131, 182, 189, 197, 199–201, 203

British Army 8

command philosophy 22

machine gun deployment 15–17

Staff College 36, 49, 52

standard infantry division *9*

structure 10

British Expeditionary Force (BEF) 9, 26, 31

British Navy 23, 25

Broadbent, Harvey 7

Brown, Major Ernest 138

Brown's Dip *131*

Bulair 24, 54–5, 57–8, 73, 75, 172

Burgess, Private Thomas 164

Burnage, Lieutenant Colonel Granville 173

Bush, Midshipman Eric 89–90, 201–2

Butler, Lieutenant Edward 96

Buttle, Lieutenant Clement 110, 123, 210

C

Camburu 114

Cape Helles 17, 24, 30, 54, 56, 58–60, 73, 75–7, 79, 157, 171, 183

Carden, Admiral Sir Sackville 25, 27–8, 30–3

Carruthers, Brigadier General R.A. 167

Cass, Major Walter 115

casualties 14, 91–2, 103–4, 108, *119*, 154, 161–3, 183–4, 209

cavalry 8

Chapman, Lieutenant Duncan 90

Chunuk Bair 62–3, *63–4*, 77, 81, 83–4, *85*, 100–1, 106, 122–3, 125, 129–30, *130*, 184, 195–6, 212, 214

Churchill, Sir Winston 23, 25–8, 31–4, 46, 55, 187–8

Citizen Military Force (CMF) 37–8, 40–1, 51

Clarke, Lieutenant Colonel Lancelot 51, 83, 92, 96, 99–100, 106, 110, 129, 144, 190, 207

Clausewitz's friction 5, 89, 187

Coe, Sergeant Fred 8, 90, 153–4, 213

Combs, Private George 89

command and control 21–2

commanders 49–53, 187–94

communications 6, 8, 20–1, 131, 144, *144*, 188–9

Concannon, Captain George 173, 178–9

Constantinople 23, 25–6, 27–8, 31, 56, 76

Coulter, Captain Charles 140

Courtney, Lieutenant Colonel Richard 171

Courtney's Post 109, 113, 156, 165, *168*, 173, 177, 180

Cowdrey, Private Albert 156

Craven, 'Digger'

Peninsula of Death 4

Critchley-Salmonson, Captain Arthur 157, 165, 168

Cunliffe-Owen, Brigadier General Charles 167

D

Daisy Patch 175–7

Dardenelles 23, *24*, 25–33, *32*, 44, 47, 54–6, 58, 60, 63, 75–6, *86*, 159, 187–8
   defence *29*, 55–70
Darnell, Lieutenant Aubrey 89, 205
Dawkins, Lieutenant William 43
Dawson, Major Ross 137
de Robeck, Admiral Sir John 33–4
Denton, Major James 113
Derham, Lieutenant Alfred 136
Dik Dere 123, 126, *130*, 212
disorganisation 6, 131, 189–90
Dix, Commander 197, 200, 202
Dixon, Charles
   The Landing at Anzac 4, 103
Dixon, Lance Corporal Bert 204
Dobbin, Lieutenant Colonel Leonard 137, 139, 144
Dodson, Lieutenant Frederick 163
Donkin, Private Reginald 154
Dougall, Captain John 95, 98, 113, 211
Drake-Brockman, Major Edward 93, 97, 99, 105, 110, 113, 190, 210, 213–14
E
Egyptian Expeditionary Force (EEF) 31
Elliott, Lieutenant Colonel Harold 'Pompey' 51, 106, 108, 114–15, 131–2, 143–4, 192, 207
Elliott, Major Charles 96
Erickson, Ed 184
   Gallipoli: The Ottoman Campaign 33, 204, 213
Everett, Captain Reginald 113
F
Facey, Albert 5–6, 204–5
   A Fortunate Life 5, 204
Fagan, Private Anthony 156
Fahy, Captain 165, 214
Faik, Captain 67, *69*, 88, 93, 97–8, 100, 110, 112, 115, 208, 210, 214
Fethers, Major Erle 133
field guns 17–20
   Howitzer, QF 4.5-inch 20, 185, *185*
   Krupp QF 75mm 20, 48, 186, *186*
   QF 18-pounder (Mk I) 20, 166, *166*
   QF 18-pounder (Mk II) 166, *166*
First Battle of Ypres 26
First Ridge 63, *64*, 65, *66*, 82, *99*, 100, 161
Fisher, Lord 26–7, 187–8
Fisherman's Hut 62, 67, 70, 76–7, 81, 83, 100, 106, 108, 127, 152, 154–5, 158, 165, 182, 193, 197–8, 205–8, 214–15
Flockart, Captain Roger 133
Flower, Lieutenant William 163
Fortescue, Lieutenant Charles 41, 112

400 Plateau 62, 64, *64*, *66*, 68, 83, 93–4, 96–9, 105, 109, 111–13, 117, 120–2, 125, 131, 133, 136, *140*, 141–2, 144, 146, 148, 150, 158, 162, 165, 172–3, 176–7, 180–1, 183
Fowles, Sergeant Herbert 96
Frame, Lieutenant Commander Tom 201
French Army 9, 14, 23, 28, 79
   Corps Expeditionnaire d'Orient (CEO) 35, 76–7, 80
G
Gaba Tepe 24, 58–60, 62–3, 65–70, 73, 76–9, 81–5, *83–4*, *86*, 87–9, 96–8, 100–1, 107–8, 114, 117, 119, 122, 127, 132, 141, 143, 148, 171, 188–90, 193, 196–7, 201–2, 208–9, 215
Gallipoli 25
   maps 24, 57, 59, 62, 70, 74, 79, 80, 81, 84, 94, 95, 112, 116, 122, 125, 139, 141, 150, 152, 162, 176, 180
   reasons for failure at 6, 187–94
Gartside, Major Robert 132
Gascon 134
George, Lloyd 26
German Army 8
   machine gun deployment 15–17
German Navy 23, 25
Glasfurd, Major Duncan 175, 177
Godley, Major General Sir Alexander 37–8, 43, 49–50, *52*, 52–3, 82, 145, 157, 164, 167–8, 177, 183
Gordon, Major Charles 140, 154, 163
Grant, Major David 156, 163
Greece 25–7
Grills, Lieutenant Shannon 175
Gun Ridge 63, 213
H
Haig, Lieutenant James 109, 111, 120, 124–5, 136
Hakki, Second Lieutenant Ismail 67–8, 98, 112–13, 117, 121, 124–5
Halil Sami, Colonel 53–4, 122, 141, 157, 212
Halis, Captain 53, *69*, 119, 138, *138*, 140, 192
Ham, Private William 43
Hamdi, Senior Captain 119
Hamilton, General Sir Ian 32–4, 37–8, 50–1, 75–81, 167, 183, 187–9, 197–8
Hankey, Maurice 26, 31
Harris, Sergeant 156
Harrison, Corporal Percy 91, 112
Hart, Major Herbert 179, 181
Hart, Peter
   Gallipoli 204
Hayri, Captain 147
Heane, Major James 177
Hearder, Captain Dixon 44
Hell Spit 65, 67, *77*, 82–3, *86*, 94–5, *102*, 104, 114, *118*, 120, 131, *143*, 200, 209

Herbert, Captain Mervyn 121
Herring, Major Sydney 173
Hill, Captain Phillip 137
Hill 165 18, 109, 120–2, 124–5, 127–8, 136, 141, 148, 211
Hill 971 (Koja Chemin Tepe) 60, 62–3, *63*, 77, 80, 83–4, *85*, 98, 125, 195, 212
Hill Q 63, *63*, 80, 82–4, *85*
Hitch, Private Herbert 152
HMAT *Galeka* *93*, 106
HMAT *Lutzon* *145*
HMAT *Novian* *93*, 115
HMS *Ark Royal* 119
HMS *Bacchante* 89, *101*, 144
HMS *Chelmer* 93
HMS *Colne* 93
HMS *Inflexible* 28, 30, 33
HMS *Irresistible* *33*
HMS *London* 87, *87*, 88, *89*, 199–200, 202
HMS *Manica* 119
HMS *Ocean* 28, 33
HMS *Prince of Wales* 44, 87, *89*, 199–200
HMS *Queen* 73, 87, 89, 167, 173, 181, 199–200, 202
HMS *Queen Elizabeth* 30, 167, 173, 181
HMS *Ribble* 100, *129*
HMS *Scourge* 93
HMS *Triumph* 201–2
Hobbs, Sergeant Major James 163
Hobbs, Colonel Talbot 134
Hogue, Oliver
    Trooper Bluegum at the Dardanelles 208
Holly Ridge 64, *83–4*, 132, 162, 177, 180–3
Holmes, Major General William 107
Howe, Corporal Hedley 164–5, 197
Ibrahim, Major Malatyali 119, 192
Ibrahim, Second Lieutenant Ibradili 66–7, 91–3, 96, 100, 103, 105–6, 112, 123, 204–5, 210, 214
Imbros 87–8, 201
Ince Bair 123, 126, *130*, 136, 140, 195
Indian Army 26, 35, 43, 49–50
    7th Mountain Artillery Brigade 20, 82
    21st (Kohat) Battery 146, 158, *158*, 165, 216
    26th (Jacob's) Battery *142*, 144, 146, *147*, 148, 151, 158, *158*, 160, 215

I

inexperience 6, 85, 131, 167, 190–4
infantry 10, 13
intelligence 73–4, 189
    inadequate 6
    preparation for landing 72–5
Irvine, Major Francis 181
Ismet, Major 66–7, 88, 93, 106, 115, 119

J

Jackson, Captain Isaac 94–5
Jackson, Lieutenant Samuel 110, 123, 210
Jackson, Major Alfred 105–6, 108, 165, 205–7
Jacobs, Captain Harold 163
Jellicoe, Admiral Sir John 25
Johnston, Colonel Francis 49, 149, 169, 192
Johnston, Lieutenant Colonel James Lyon 83, 93, 144
Johnston's Jolly *99*, 111–12, 116, 121, 129, 133, 136, 139–40, 142, 148, 151, 170, 173, 175–7, *178*, 195

K

Kanli Sirt 111
Kavak Dere 121
Kemal, Lieutenant Colonel Mustafa 6, 53–4, *69*, 112, 115, 123, 125–7, 129, 141, 147, 157–9, *159*, 161, 178, 181, 192, 196, 212–14
Kilid Bahr Plateau 24, 29, 58–60, 63, 69, 73, 75–7, 80, *86*, 114, 188–9, 194
Kindon, Major Frederick 137, 143, 156, 213–14
Kirkpatrick, Major General 38
Kitchener, Field Marshal Lord 25–8, 31–2, 36–7, 42, 49–50, 75, 187–8
Kojadere village 115, 136
Krupp guns *see* field guns; mountain guns
Kum Kale 76, 79
Kum Tepe 148, 157, *159*
Kuru Dere 125, 212

L

Laing, Corporal Elmer 93, 110, 213
Lalor, Captain Joseph 110, 113, 154, 210, 213
Lamb, Major Malcolm 138
landing at Anzac 187
    amphibious 71–2
    counter-attack 151–4, *152*, 212–14
    intended site 197–200
    misplaced 87–104, 190, 192, 201–3
    objectives 75–6
    plan 76–86
    preparation 72–5
    reasons for failure 6
    timeline 215–17
Layh, Captain Herbert 106
Leane, Captain Raymond 93, 113, 168
Lee, Lieutenant Colonel Harry 51, 96, 144, 192
Lee-Enfield rifle *see* rifles
Leer, Captain Charles 138–42, 155, 162–3, 168
Legge Valley 63, 99, 111, 113, 120, *130*, 132, 136, 151–2, 170, 195
Lemnos Island 31, 44, *72*, 73, 189–90
Liman von Sanders, General Otto 45–6, 54–6, 58–60, 70, 98, 127, 209

Lone Pine 18, *65*, 70, *78*, *83–4*, 111–13, 116, 122, 127, *130*, *131*, 132, 136–7, *140*, 141, 143, 147–8, 150–2, 155, 157, 162, 165, 170, *175*, 175–7, 180–2, 184, 192, 195–6

Louch, Corporal Thomas 205, 208

Loutit, Lieutenant Noel 85, 96, 98, 109, 111–13, 120–1, 124–5, 129, 136, 138, 192, 194

M

McCay, Colonel James 51, 115–16, 131–2, 133, 137, 160–1, 167, 175, 177, 192–3

McCay's Hill 64, *66*, 66–7, 78, 83, *86*, 94–5, 100, 111–13, 116–17, 125, *131*, 132–3, 137–9, *140*, 143, 168, *175*, 175, 190, 200

McDonald, Corporal Alexander 93

McGuire, Major Albert 137

machine guns 8, 10, 14–17, 204–9
    Maxim heavy machine-gun 10, 15–17, *16*, 84, 88, 90, 92, *128*, 206, 208–9
    Nordenfelt 17, 69, 209
    Vickers 15–16

MacLagan's Ridge 65, 82, 95–6, *99*, *104*, *118*, 133, 168, 183

MacLaurin, Colonel Henry 51, 83, 144, 160, 169, 174, 177, 181, 192–3

MacLaurin's Hill 112, 116, *135*, 136–9, 142, *168*, 178

Macnaghten, Major Charles 176–7

McNicoll, Lieutenant Colonel Walter 51, 106, 114–15, 132, 144, 175, 177, 192

Mafeking 49, 52

Maidos 24, 54, 58–60, 63, 67, 69–70, *74*, 76, 86, 98, 114, 119, 122, 127, 129, 133, 157, 159, 194, 208, 211

Mal Tepe 54, 60, 63, 76–7, 80–1, *86*, 126, 157, 171, 187, 189, 194

Malone, Lieutenant Colonel William 43–4, 51, 157, 165, 171, 174, 179, 184

Malone's Gully 163

Mansfield, Sapper Sedgwick 92

Margetts, Lieutenant Ivor 110, 213–14

Masefield, John
    Gallipoli 4

Mauser rifle *see* rifles

Maxim heavy machine gun *see* machine guns

Maxwell, Lieutenant General Sir John 31

Mediterranean Expeditionary Force (MEF) 32, 35, 72, 75, 188, 198, 200
    29th Division 27–8, 32, 35, 76–7, 79–80, 183, 187

Meenkin, Private Oswald 174

Mena, Egypt *35*, 43

Metcalf, Midshipman Savill 89–90, 202–3

Milne, Captain John 94–5, 100, 113

Mitchell, Lance Corporal George 44, 90

Mitchell, Major George 173, 179

Monash, Colonel John 50–1, 171, 177, 180, 184

Monash Valley *64*, 65, *65–6*, 97–100, *99*, 112–13, 137–8, 140, *140*, 149, *150*, 156, 163, 165, *168*, 168–9, 172–3, 177, *178*, 181–2, 193

Moore, Lieutenant Colonel Athelstan 157

Moore, Sapper John 90, 204

Mortar Ridge 63, *130*, 138–42, 148, 153, 155, 162–4, 173, 192

mountain guns 17–20, *18*, *19*
    BL 10-pounder 146, *146*
    Krupp QF 75mm 18, *18*, *19*, 20, 48, 146

Mudros Harbour 72–3, *73*, 78, 87, *87*, 88

Muharrem, Second Lieutenant 67, 88, 91, 93, 103, 112

Mule Gully 149

Munir, Major Mehmet 157

Murray, Private Harry 173

Mustafa, Second Lieutenant 115, 120, 136

N

Narrows 24, 30, 32–3, 55, 58, *59*, 75–6, 120, 172, 178

navigation 201–3

The Nek *63–4*, 65, *99*, 110, 112, 137, 139–40, *142*, 154, 156, 162–5, *168*, 173–4, 178, *178*, 180, 184, 210

New Zealand Army 9–10
    field guns 20
    training 36–8, 41–3

New Zealand Expeditionary Force (NZEF) 10, 38, 39, 41–3, 49–50, 52
    1st (Canterbury) Company 156
    1st New Zealand Field Battery (1st NZFA Battery) 217
    2nd New Zealand Field Battery (2nd NZFA Battery) 171, 216
    2nd (South Canterbury) Company 156, 163
    3rd (Auckland) Company 156
    3rd New Zealand Field Battery (3rd NZFA Battery) 171
    6th (Hauraki) Company 150, 156
    7th (Wellington West Coast) Company 179
    9th (Hawkes Bay) Company 179
    11th (Taranaki) Company 165
    12th (Nelson) Company 164
    13th (North Canterbury and Westland) Company 164
    15th (North Auckland) Company 156
    16th (Waikato) Company 149–50, 156, 163
    17th (Ruahine) Company 165, *179*, 181
    Auckland Battalion 39, 42–3, 51, 140, 142, 145, *145*, *147*, *148*, 149, *149*, 150, *154*, 155–7, 163–4, 169, 172–3, 179, 181, 183, 215
    Auckland Mounted Rifles 39
    Canterbury Battalion 39, 145, 149, *154*, 157, 164, 167–8, 173, 179, *182*, 215–16
    Canterbury Mounted Rifles 39
    Howitzer Battery *170*, 171, 216
    New Zealand Field Artillery Brigade (NZFA Brigade) 20, 38–9, 43, 219

New Zealand Infantry Brigade 38–9, 42–3, 49, 219
New Zealand Mounted Rifles Brigade 39, 43–4
Otago Battalion 39, *154*, 157, 161, *161*, 168, 172, 179, 181, 216
Otago Mounted Rifles 39, 43
structure 39, *39*
Wellington Battalion 39, 42–3, 51, 157, 165, 172, 174, 179, *179*, 181, 183–4, 216
Wellington Mounted Rifles 39
Newson, Sergeant Thomas 92–3, 204
North Beach 58, 60, 65, *66*, 67, 91, *91–2*, 93–5, 99–100, 103, *110*, 149, 170, 179, 182, 196, 203–5, 209, 215
No. 1 Outpost 67, 106

O

Onslow Thompson, Lieutenant Colonel Astley 161, 176–7, 192
Operation Fortitude 71
Operation Overlord 71
order of battle 218–21
Ottoman Army 45–8, 192–3, 220–1
1st Battalion, 9th Artillery Regiment (1/9th Arty) 60
1st Battalion, 26th Regiment (1/26th) 59
1st Battalion, 27th Regiment (1/27th) 67, 70, 98, 106, 119, 122, 125, 140–1, 143, 148, 152, 155, 157, 162, 165, 170, 178, 180–1, 192, 215
1st Battalion, 57th Regiment (1/57th) 48, 122–3, 125, 129–30, 136, 141, 147, 152–3, 155, 161–3, 192, 212 214–15
1st Battalion, 72nd Regiment (1/72nd) 162, 178, 181, 216
1st Battalion, 77th Regiment (1/77th) 162, 178, 180–1, 216
1st Platoon 66–7, 91–2, 96, 100, 105–6, 112, 121, 123–5, 141, 206, 210, 214
2nd Battalion, 9th Artillery Regiment (2/9th Arty) 60
2nd Battalion, 26th Regiment (2/26th) 59
2nd Battalion, 27th Regiment (2/27th) 59, 66, 68, 70, 97, 124–5, 136, 141–2, 148, 171, 208, 210, 214–15
2nd Battalion, 57th Regiment (2/57th) 48, 126, 147, 152–5, 158, 163, 165, 193, 212, 214–15
2nd Battalion, 72nd Regiment (2/72nd) 178, 180–1, 216
2nd Battalion, 77th Regiment (2/77th) 162, 178, 180–1, 216
2nd Company 151
2nd Platoon 66–7, 88, 90–1, 96–7, 111–13, 120, 129, 207, 210, 214
3rd Battalion, 7th Artillery Regiment (3/7th Arty) 172, 216
3rd Battalion, 9th Artillery Regiment (3/9th Arty) 60, 68–70, 215
3rd Battalion, 26th Regiment (3/26th) 59
3rd Battalion, 27th Regiment (3/27th) 53, 67, 70, 98, 106, 119, 122, 125, 136, 138, 140–1, 148, 155, 162–3, 178, 180–1, 192, 215
3rd Battalion, 39th Artillery Regiment (3/39th Arty) 157
3rd Battalion, 57th Regiment (3/57th) 48, 147, 157, 161–3, 215
3rd Battalion, 72nd Regiment (3/72nd) 163, 170, 173, 178, 180–1, 216
3rd Battalion, 77th Regiment (3/77th) 57, 60
3rd Division 14, 57, 79, 172
3rd Platoon 67, 93, 97, 99–100, 110, 112, 121, 123–5, 141, 210, 214
5th Company 67, 70, 97, 100, 115, 120, 136, 142, 215
5th Division 55–7, 75–6
6th Company 67, 69–70, 215
7th Artillery Regiment 172, 216
7th Company 67, 70, 82, 98, 100, 112–13, 121, 124, 141, 148, 215
7th Division 14, 47, 54, 57–8, 76, 172
8th Company 66–7, 69–70, 82, 115, 121, 123–5, 129, 141, 210, 214–15
8th Division 47, 54
9th Artillery Regiment 20, 48, 60, 68–70, 215
9th Division 14, 18, 20, 47–8, 53–4, 57–9, 66–7, 88, 106, 126, 171, 186
10th Company 140, 148, 163
11th Division 14, 57, 79, 148, 172
12th Company 140, 148, 163
19th Division 6, 14, 18, 20, 47–8, 53–4, 57–60, *69*, 98, 112, 115, 126–7, 141, 157, 159, 171–2, 183, 186, 194, 216
19th Regiment 48
24th Division 48
25th Regiment 47, 59–60, 157, 183
26th Division 48
26th Regiment 47–8, 51, 55, 59–60, 157, 183
27th Regiment 5, 18, 47, 53, 55, 59–60, 66–8, *68*, *69*, 70, 87, 97–8, 106, 112, 119, 121–2, 124–5, 127–9, 131, 133, 136, 138, 140–3, 147–8, 152, 155, 157, 159, 162–3, 165, 170–1, 178, 180–1, 184, 192, 194, 207–8, 210–12, 214–15
31st Division 53
33rd Regiment 172, 178, 180–1, 184, 217
39th Artillery Regiment 20, 48, 157–8, 215–16
57th Regiment 18, 48, 53, *68*, 122–7, 128–30, 136, 141, 147, 152–5, 157–9, 161–3, 165, 168, 170–1, 173, 178, 180–1, 184, 192–3, 196, 208, 212–15
64th Regiment 172, 178, 180–1, 184, 217
72nd Regiment 18, 48, 148, 157–9, 162–3, 170–1, 173, 178, 180–1, 184, 216
77th Regiment 48, 57, 60, 127, 148, 157, 159, 162, 165, 170, 172, 178, 180–1, 184, 216
III Corps 14, *47*, 47–8, 53–5, 57–8, 126, 157, 159, 171, 220–1
VI Corps 48
XV Corps 14, 54–5, 57–8, 76, 172, 221

artillery brigade *19*, 20
battalions 10
Channakale Fortified Area Command (CFAC) 29–30, 47, 55
command philosophy 22
fire support 144
Fifth Army 6, 55, 55–60, 98, 115, 172 First Army 46
First Army 46
Fourth Army 46
infantry 10, *10*, *13*, *45*, *68*
machine gunners *15*, 15–17
platoons 13
rifle companies 10
Second Army 46
Sixth Army 46
structure 8–10, 45–8, *48*
Third Army 46
training 45–6
Yanya Corps 53–4
Ottoman Navy 23, 25
Owen, Lieutenant Colonel Robert 137, 139, 144, 181
Owen's Gully 111–12, 175, 177

P

Palamutlu Ridge 67, 69–70
Pasha, Colonel Enver 25, 46
Pasha, Major General Mahmet Esat 47, *47*, 53–4, *54*, *126*, 159, *171*
Pasha, Salih Hulusi 54
Patterson, Lieutenant Penistan 110, 163
Peck, Captain John 99
Petersen, Lance Corporal Jack 156
Pine Ridge 65, 111, 127, 132, 150–1, 162, 165, 170, 195
Plant, Lieutenant Eric 109, 112–13, 120–1, 129, 192
Plugge, Lieutenant Colonel Arthur 51, 53, 149
Plugge's Plateau *64*, 65, *66*, 67, *67–8*, 73, 82, *90*, 91–100, *97*, *99*, 105, *108*, 112–13, *118*, 128, 132–3, 137, *149*, 149–50, *151*, 156, 168–9, 173, *178*, 179, 183, 190, 192, 195–6, 205, 208–9
Plumer, Lieutenant Colonel Herbert 52
Pope, Lieutenant Colonel Harold 164–5, 168, 173
Pope's Hill 65, *65–6*, 139, 168, *168*, *172*, 173, 180–2, 196
Prior, Professor Robin 5
Gallipoli: The end of the myth 197
Prisk, Lieutenant Ralph 132

Q

Quinn's Post 109, 113, 139–40, 142, 156, 162–3, 168, *168*, *172*, 173, 180–3

R

Rafferty, Lieutenant Rupert 96, 106, 176, 207
railways 8
Razor Edge *63–4*, 65, *66*, 73, *97*, 99, *99*, *118*, 168, *178*
Razorback 64, 114, 133, 137, *140*, *175*
Redif units 45–6, 53

Refshauge, Bill 202
Reid, Lieutenant Mordaunt 110, 123, 152, 210, 213
Rest Gully *97*, *99*, 99–100, 105, 129, 190, 210
Richardson, Captain Clifford 140, 154
Richardson, Lieutenant Herbert 163
rifle companies 10, 13
rifles 13
    Lee-Enfield (SMLE) 0.303-inch No 1 MK III 11–14, *12*
    Mauser 7.65mm *Gewehr* 98 Model 1903 11, *11*, 13
Rigby, Lieutenant William 154
Roberts, Major Stephen 113
Robertson, John
    Anzac and Empire 6
Robertson, Major James 91, 213–14
Robertson, Major Sydney 98, 113, 154
Robin, Lance Corporal Phillip 121, 129–30
Row, Major Robert 156
Royal Marine Light Infantry (RMLI) 28, 32, 35, 183
Royal Naval Division (RND) 25, 35, 75, 79, 183
    Chatham Battalion 183
    Deal Battalion 183
    Nelson Battalion 183
    Portsmouth Battalion 183
Royal Naval Reserve (RNR) 35, 183
Russell's Top *63–4*, *64*, 65, *65–6*, 73, 83, *91–2*, 93, 96–7, *97*, 99, *99*, 110, *110*, 113, *118*, 128–9, 137, 139, *140*, 149, 151, 156, 162–3, 165, *168*, 168–9, *172*, 173–4, 177–82, *178*, 184, 190, 192
Russia 23, 25–7, 31
Russo-Japanese War (1904–1918) 8
Ryder, Captain John 121, 125, 136

S

Saadet, Second Lieutenant 173
Sadik, Captain 68, 93, 111–13, 136, 142
Saip, Captain 157, 165
Saker, Major Richard 133, 175, 177
Salisbury, Major Alfred 96, 98, 105, 112–13, 128, 136, 190, 207
Salonika 27–8, 53, 127, 159, 187
Sari Bair Range 52, 54, 58–60, *59*, *61*, *62*, 63, *63–4*, 67, *68*, 73, *74*, 76–8, 80, 81, *81*, *86*, *93*, 116, 122, 141, 148, 157, 159, 165, 173, 184, 189, 191, 193, 195
Sazli Beit Dere 106, 112, 123, 214
Schuler, Philip
    Australia in Arms 4
Scobie, Major Robert 140, 163
Scrubby Knoll 18, 95, 120–1, 125–6, *130*, 147, 157, 159, 212
Second Ridge 62–5, *65–6*, 67, 82–3, 93, 95–7, 99–100, 105, 110–13, 117, 120–4, 128, 133, 139–42, 148, 150, 155, 160, 162–3, 167–8, *168*, *172*, 173, 177–80, 182–4, 190, 194–6, 204

Sefik, Lieutenant Colonel Mehmet 5, 47, 53, 66–9, *69*, 85, 98, 106, 112, 114, 119–22, *127*, 127–9, 136, 141, 143, 147–8, 150–2, 157–8, 160, 162, 165, 184, 191–2, 193, 195, 206, 208–9, 211–14

Selby, Lieutenant Arthur 204

Semerly Tepe 67, 70, 127

Serbia 27

Servet, Major 178, 181

Sevki, Lieutenant Colonel Ahmet 178, 181

Shout, Captain Alfred 179

Shrapnel Gully 64–5, 95–6, 98, *99*, 105, 111–12, 114, 149, 156, 165

Silt Spur 64

Sinclair-MacLagan, Colonel Ewan 49, 78, 81, 83, 85–6, 100, 105, 107, *107*, 112–17, 128–9, 133, 136–7, 143–4, 160, 177, 183, 187, 190–4, 200

Sixsmith, Major-General E.K.G
   British Generalship in the Twentieth Century 193

Skeen, Lieutenant Colonel Andrew 46

Smith, Major Ernest 100, 105, 113, 190

SMS *Breslau* 23

SMS *Goeben* 23, 30

Sniper's Ridge 64, 132, 143

Snoxall, Sergeant Percy 12–13

Souchon, Admiral Wilhelm 23, 25

South Africa 41, 49–52, 107, 134, 146, 169

The Sphinx *63*, 65, *91*, 93, 96–7, *99*, 100, 110, *110*, *178*

Steele's Post 109, 113, 138–9, 165, *168*, 173, 178

Stewart, Lieutenant Colonel Douglas 145, 156–7, 164, 192

Strickland, Lieutenant Fred 106

Stubbings, Private Arthur 106

Stuckey, Major Frederick 156, 163

Suez Canal 25, 43

Suleyman, Sergeant Major 67, 110

Suvla Bay 56–8, 60, 96, 159, 184

Swain, Sergeant John 205, 208

Swannell, Major Blair 137, 154, 184, 213

T

tactics 6
   adaptation 21, 97
   amphibious landing 71–2
   covering force 81–2
   withdrawal 167

Talbot-Smith, Lieutenant Eric 91, 96, 98, 111

Territorial Force (TF) 36–40, 51

Third Ridge 62–3, 65, 77, 80–5, 95, 98–100, 111–13, 115, 117, 119–31, 133, 135–8, 141, 147, 151, 165, 170, 172–3, 177, 189–91, 196, 211–15

Thomas, Lieutenant George 111–12

Thursby, Admiral Sir Cecil 167, 197

Tilley, Private Arthur 110

timeline 215–17

trenches 167–8, 178

Triple Entente 23, 25

Tulloch, Captain Eric 92, 96, 99, 109–10, 113, 122–6, 129–30, 136, 140–3, 152–5, 192, 195, 207, 210, 212–14

Turks *see also* Ottoman Army
   accounts of the landing 5

U

Uyar, Associate Professor Mesut 7

V

Vaughan, Private George 110

Vickers machine gun 15–16

Victoria Gully 83, 100, *131*, 175

von Thauvenay, Lieutenant Colonel Perrinet 55

W

Walden's Point 77

Walker, Brigadier General Harold 'Hooky' 81, 149, 161, 167, 169, *169*, 177, 179

Walker's Ridge 65, *91–2*, 96, 99, 110, *110*, 139, 149–51, 156–8, 162, 164–5, 168–9, 172–4, 177, *179*, 179–82, *182*, 207

Wanliss, Lieutenant Colonel David 51, 115, 133, 144, 175, 192

Waterlow, Lieutenant Commander John 89, 197, 202

weapons 6, 8
   artillery *see* artillery
   field guns *see* field guns
   machine guns *see* machine guns
   mountain guns *see* mountain guns
   rifles *see* rifles

Weir, Lieutenant Colonel Stanley 51, 83, 91, 96–9, 112–13, 142, 144, 190, 192, 213–14

Weir Ridge 64

Wells, Major Richard 132

West, Private Arthur 156

Western Front 26–7, 50, 169

Westmacott, Second Lieutenant Spencer 43, 51, 53, 149, 156, 161, 163

White, Colonel Brudenell 133

White's Valley 137

Whitham, Captain John 93, 100, 132, 143, 150–1, 190

Williams, Private Arthur 93

Wilson, Private Alex 8, 90

Winter, Denis
   25 April 1915: The Inevitable Tragedy 197

Wire Gully *135*, 136, *137*, 138, 163

Worsely, Leading Seaman 90

Z

Zeitoun, Egypt 43

Zeki, Captain Ahmet *123*, 125–6, 130, 136, 147, 192, 212, 214